Woodruff

A Study of
Community Decision Making

by
Albert Schaffer
and
Ruth Connor Schaffer

The University of North Carolina Press
Chapel Hill

Woodruff

A Study of Community Decision Making

For Our Parents

Acknowledgments

The authors wish to express their appreciation to all of the residents, organizations, government employees, and officials of Woodruff, past and present, whose co-operation, friendship, and interest made this study possible. Our greatest debt is to Rupert B. Vance, whose comments on an earlier draft led us to take the "second look" that clarified, for us, the decision-making process in Woodruff.

We wish, in addition to convey our thanks to the University Research Committee of the University of Alabama for its assistance.

Most especially we wish to acknowledge our debt to Mary Ann Wildman, Sally Z. LaBadie, Susie J. Lavender, C. Raymond Rayfield and Jennie Flowers, who labored in our behalf, and our gratitude to Edith Cherry Schaffer, who gave us the time to research and write.

ALBERT SCHAFFER
RUTH CONNOR SCHAFFER

Contents

Tables

Part I
Woodruff
and the
Decision-Making Pattern

1. Theoretical Framework

Introduction

A series of community events in the late nineteen-fifties pointed up certain ecological and social problems in Woodruff which reflected trends in urbanization in twentieth-century America. The city of Woodruff, with little undeveloped residential or industrial land and almost completely surrounded by the township of Woodruff, had had little success annexing territory. Its service area had experienced large-scale population growth of a heterogeneous nature during the industrial developments of World War II and in postwar years. Traditional city-township differences that had existed for years were strengthened in the struggles for area growth. Combined with other area characteristics, they led to the selection of Woodruff as the subject of this research.

The General Problem

One generation of scholars may return to problems and ideas that concerned scholars of an earlier period. Theories that have been in disrepute or discarded for years may be recast in a "modern" form and given wide circulation. Structural-functionalism, which can claim organicism as a prominent ancestor, is a good example.[1] A basic tenet of this societal theory, which receives its fullest expression in the writings of Talcott Parsons,[2] concerns the primacy of the whole over the parts. Parsons expresses this idea in the concept of functional prerequisites, conditions for survival of the system that are to be fulfilled by particular parts.[3] The close articulation between the social system and its parts is evident in the idea that each of four subsystems fulfills a designated prerequisite.[4] The requirements of the whole seem to determine the functions of the components. These particulars illustrate a general principle of Parsons' social system theory and of structural-functionalism: that in the long run a social structure that endures must make some notable contribution to the maintenance or continuity of the system as a whole.[5] A system tends to change in the direction of improved integration of its parts with the whole.

At the same time critics have pointed out that some social systems

1. For a discussion of the antecedents of structural-functionalism see Don Martindale, *The Nature and Types of Sociological Theory* (Boston: Houghton Mifflin Company, 1960), pp. 446–50. For another account of the origins of this school see Walter Buckley, "Structural-Functional Analysis in Modern Sociology," in Howard Becker and Alvin Boskoff, eds., *Modern Sociological Theory* (New York: Holt, Rinehart and Winston, 1957), pp. 236–40.

2. Over the years Parsons has been prolific in the development of social system theory. Among the writings that express his point of view are the following: Talcott Parsons, *The Social System* (Glencoe, Ill.: The Free Press, 1951); Talcott Parsons, Robert F. Bales, and Edward A. Shils, *Working Papers in the Theory of Action* (Glencoe, Ill.: The Free Press, 1953); Talcott Parsons, "Pattern Variables Revisited," *American Sociological Review,* 25 (August, 1960), 467–83; Talcott Parsons, "The Point of View of the Author," in Max Black, ed., *The Social Theories of Talcott Parsons: A Critical Examination* (Englewood Cliffs, N. J.: Prentice-Hall, Inc., 1961), pp. 311–63; Talcott Parsons and Edward A. Shils, eds., *Toward a General Theory of Action* (New York: Harper and Row, 1962). For a recent statement of social system theory which emphasizes communication and decision making see Charles Ackerman and Talcott Parsons, "The Concept of 'Social System' As a Theoretical Device," in Gordon J. DiRenzo, ed., *Concepts, Theory, and Explanation in the Behavioral Sciences* (New York: Random House, 1966), pp. 24–40. Parsons applies social system theory to a variety of problems in Talcott Parsons, *Sociological Theory and Modern Society* (New York: The Free Press, 1967).

3. Parsons, Bales, and Shils, *Theory of Action,* pp. 85–103.

4. Talcott Parsons and Neil J. Smelser, *Economy and Society: A Study in the Integration of Economic and Social Theory* (Glencoe, Ill.: The Free Press of Glencoe, 1956), pp. 16–38.

5. Parsons, Bales, and Shils, *Theory of Action,* pp. 102–3.

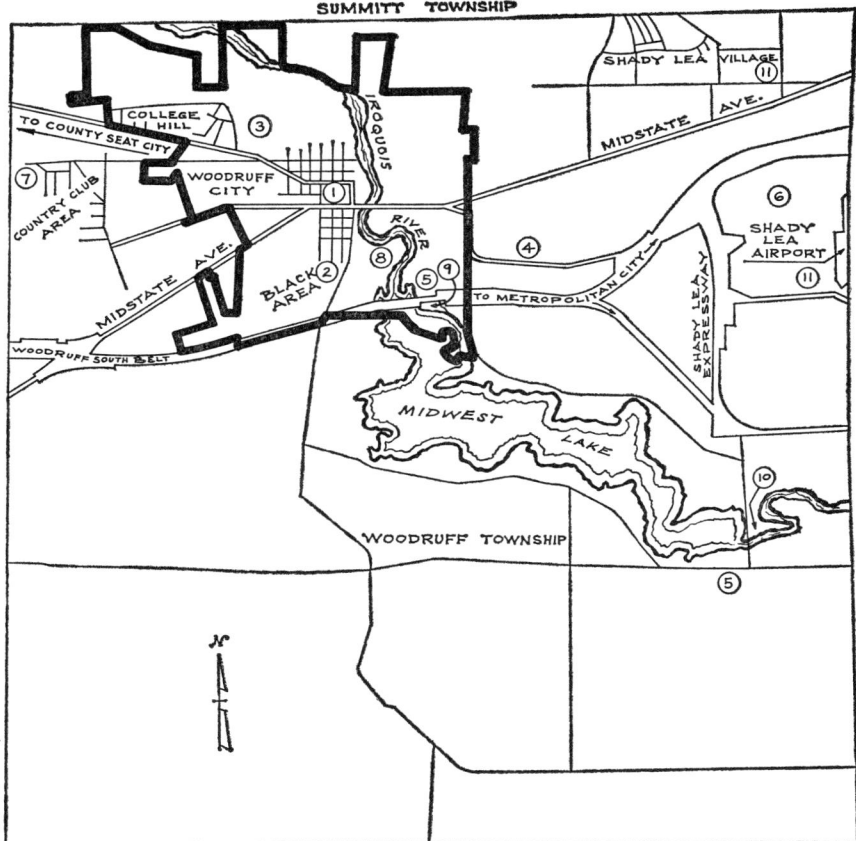

SCALE: 0 ¼ ½ ¾ 1 Mile

LEGEND

City Line
1 Central Business District
2 Black Residential Area
3 Midstate University
4 Township Hall
5 Midwest Motors
6 Universal Motors (Pacific)
7 Iroquois Country Club
8 City Water Treatment Plant
9 City Sewage Treatment Plant
10 Township Water Treatment Plants
11 Township Sewage Treatment Plants

function well and others poorly. Morse asserted that societies vary widely in the degree to which functional prerequisites are met.[6] The conflict between the simultaneous fulfillment of two or more contrary system prerequisites has been emphasized by Sjoberg.[7] The necessity for some degree of preference between such goals as conformity and deviation, equalitarianism and stratification, for Sjoberg, invests every social system with "self-contradictions" manifest in tension and conflict.[8]

Parsons and associates suggest one type of adaptation to the problem of establishing preferences between the system prerequisites, an arrangement whereby each is stressed over the others for a limited time period.[9] The neglect of one prerequisite leads to a buildup of tension that sets in motion a process through which attention and resources are shifted to the area that has been neglected. In time, a pattern of change is established whereby the conflict between opposing system prerequisites is handled by a sequential arrangement shifting priorities and resources from one function to the other. Each prerequisite is fulfilled adequately for a limited time period. This outcome is called "phase movement."

A more pessimistic outcome to this conflict between system prerequisites is suggested by van den Berghe. Social systems can become involved in a cycle of maladjustment that culminates in a revolution.[10] Some social organizations lose their ability to cope with

6. Chandler Morse, "The Functional Imperatives," in Black, ed., *Social Theories of Talcott Parsons,* p. 144.

7. Gideon Sjoberg, "Contradictory Functional Requirements and Social System," in N. J. Demerath III and Richard A. Peterson, eds., *System, Change, and Conflict: A Reader on Contemporary Sociological Theory and The Debate over Functionalism* (New York: The Free Press, 1967), pp. 339–45.

8. *Ibid.,* p. 342.

9. Parsons, Bales, and Shils, *Theory of Action,* Chs. IV, V.

10. Pierre L. van den Berghe, "Dialectic and Functionalism," *American Sociological Review,* 28 (October, 1963), 695–705.

For essays that examine various aspects of structural-functionalism cf. the following: Henry C. Bredemeier, "The Methodology of Functionalism," *American Sociological Review,* 20 (April, 1955), 173–80; Bernard Barber, "Structural-Functional Analysis: Some Problems and Misunderstandings," *American Sociological Review,* 21 (April, 1956), 129–35; Kingsley Davis, "The Myth of Functional Analysis As a Special Method in Sociology and Anthropology," *American Sociological Review,* 24 (December, 1959), 757–72; Carl G. Hempel, "The Logic of Functional Analysis," in Llewellyn Gross, ed., *Symposium on Sociological Theory* (New York: Harper and Row,

system needs, and the rearrangement of social patterns becomes the sole remaining alternative for discharging the imbalances that have accumulated.

This study presents an outcome that is somewhat midway between the models suggested by Parsons and Van den Berghe: the endurance of a social system which is unable to alleviate the sources of conflict and the failure of efforts to do so.

The theoretical model used for analyzing city and township interaction views each municipality as a social system performing simultaneously the four major functions required for system continuity suggested by Parsons. Each municipality also is seen as a unit in the larger society, with specific linkages to the federal government, the national economy, and a national corporation that resulted, early in 1941, in changes that altered fulfillment of the four system requisites and the relations of each municipality to the other. Specific features of the political structure of the Woodruff area intensified a conflict that had existed for many years, a conflict centered around the capabilities of each governmental unit to meet the needs of an expanding population and economy.

The conditions responsible for the conflict existed in the twenties, if not before, but were aggravated during and after the period of wartime industrialization. Two extralocal organizations, the federal government and an automobile manufacturer, selected Woodruff Township for the construction of a huge complex for the production of bombers. The decisions and actions leading to a great increase in industrial activity in the Woodruff area multiplied the demands on both city and township government for those services that a rapidly growing population and economy required for inhabiting a relatively small area. At the time, neither governmental unit was able to meet community needs adequately. Woodruff Township, which hitherto had served a rural population with little need for urban services,

---

1959), pp. 271–305; Ronald Philip Dore, "Function and Cause," *American Sociological Review,* 26 (December, 1961), 843–53; N. J. Demerath III, "Synecdoche and Structural-Functionalism," *Social Forces,* 44 (March, 1966), 390–401.

Collins summarizes the principal postulates of structural-functionalism in Randall Collins, "A Comparative Approach to Political Sociology," in Reinhard Bendix, ed., *State and Society: A Reader in Comparative Political Sociology* (Boston: Little, Brown and Company, 1968), pp. 43–47.

lacked the structure and staff required for meeting the adaptive needs of an industrial economy and labor force. Township government also lacked the right to impose taxes on citizens unless the latter expressly gave consent in an election. The understandable reluctance of elected officials to request that approval made it difficult for the government to gain adequate revenue from owners of industrial facilities and other enterprises. The lack of fiscal inputs operated inevitably to limit the amount and variety of outputs provided by government and therefore to limit effectiveness in serving local needs.

Woodruff City faced a comparable situation. A growing population and economy necessitated an increase in governmental outputs. While city government had the structure capable of meeting these demands, it also lacked access to an adequate industrial tax base. This situation developed from limited territory, two square miles, and few vacant tracts of land suitable for large manufacturing plants. Although city government, unlike that of the township, had the right to levy property taxes, the relatively small tax base was not capable of generating the amount of revenue needed by an aging city with a growing population. Rapid growth of enrollment in Woodruff's university in the sixties aggravated the problem.

Wartime industrialization, and its continuation throughout the postwar era, intensified a serious conflict situation. This consisted of the difficulties each government experienced in acquiring the financial resources needed to adjust output to the needs of a growing economy and population.[11] As the difficulties were occasioned by specific features of government, the conflict involved pattern maintenance, on the one hand, and the instrumental activities of government and the adaptive needs of the area community, on the other.

The difficulty of resolving the conflict depended in part on the degree to which influential groups in each municipality were com-

11. Recognizing that every municipality has difficulty in obtaining the revenue needed for financing operations, this study emphasizes factors over and above those which are universal, namely the pre-emption of the income tax by the federal government and the necessity for local communities to rely heavily on the property tax. In addition to the inadequacies of the property tax, the city of Woodruff was handicapped by having a limited tax base, both in size and in the portion that was industrial. The township was limited in that its government did not have the right to levy taxes. (For further details on the tax base see Chapter 2).

mitted to preserving the basic features of each governmental unit.[12] These attachments were strengthened by several factors, both discussed in later chapters (see Chapters 2 and 5), including the fear of displacement by "alien groups" attracted to the Woodruff area by employment opportunities. These changes involved the growth of the working class and Democratic party and the decline of middleclass property owners and the Republican party. By resisting industrialization the latter groups could seek to restrain the buildup of demands on government and contain the pressures for political change.

Other elements of pattern maintenance and social change complicated the conflict between continuity and adaptation. Each municipality tended to develop mechanisms for protecting itself against actions by its neighbor which would eliminate, at its expense, the structural impediments to improved access to fiscal resources. Annexation of township industry or merger of the two municipalities would greatly increase Woodruff's tax base.[13] Conversely, incorporation of the township as a home-rule city would provide the taxation powers needed to govern an urban industrial municipality.[14] In each instance success for one municipality would be detrimental to the effectiveness of the other. Strong defense mechanisms in each municipality also would operate to strengthen pattern maintenance.

The complex interaction between agents in the larger society stimulating the economic development of the Woodruff area, thereby

12. Parsons expresses this idea in terms of resistance of vested interests to social change. He wrote: "The term vested interests seems appropriate to designate this general resistance to change which is inherent in the institutionalization of roles in the social system. . . . " Parsons, *Social System*, p. 492.

13. For a study of annexation laws in the United States see Frank S. Sengstock, *Annexation: A Solution to the Metropolitan Area Problem* (Ann Arbor, Mich.: The University of Michigan Law School, 1960). For an analysis of factors influencing the occurrence of annexation see Thomas R. Dye, "Urban Political Integration: Conditions Associated with Annexation in American Cities," *Midwest Journal of Political Science*, 8 (November, 1964), 430–46.

14. Preventing annexation and securing of tax advantages are two of the more important factors disposing townships to incorporate as home rule cities. Thomas F. Hady and Clarence J. Hein, "Congressional Townships as Incorporated Municipalities," *Midwest Journal of Political Science*, 8 (November, 1964), 408–24; Henry J. Schmandt, *The Municipal Incorporation Trend, 1950–1960* (Madison, Wisc.: Bureau of Government, University of Wisconsin, 1961).

increasing the community's need for basic services, and the limitations imposed on government performance by features of ecological and political structure represent the substance of this investigation. The efforts to resolve it are traced over a period of approximately three decades. The study examines the factors responsible for the failure of either the emergence of a unified political community or township incorporation. The forces maintaining traditional features of government have dominated the forces seeking to improve the adaptation of the Woodruff area through changes in political structure. The study also seeks to understand the features of the social systems responsible for the absence of more varied approaches to problem solving.

The Decision-Making Pattern

In responding to everyday problems an organization finds it both necessary and economical to develop policies to be followed by officials. Policies set forth the actions to be taken, the programs to be implemented in a particular situation.[15] Where policies are stable, application to a recurrent and relevant situation occurs quickly, with little debate and conflict. Familiarity of executives with the basic policies of an organization also facilitates the co-ordination of the activities of various departments and echelons. Executives and subordinates repeat actions that have been performed many times before. The responses of the organization to the situation are routinized.[16]

15. This definition of the concept "policy" is taken from Lewis A. Froman, Jr., "Public Policy," in David L. Sills, ed., *International Encyclopedia of the Social Sciences,* Vol. 13 (New York: Macmillan Company, 1968), 204. Froman considered two dimensions of the concept, one as a program, the other as its implementation. He concentrated on the content of the program rather than administrative procedures.

Alford gives the concept of policy a broader meaning in terms of consistency in a series of decisions, which presumably includes objectives. Robert R. Alford, "The Comparative Study of Urban Politics," in Leo F. Schnore and Henry Fagin, eds., *Urban Research and Policy Planning* (Beverly Hills, Calif.: Sage Publications, 1967), p. 264.

Policy and policy making, for Etzioni, also is seen in terms of general goals and principles that serve as a basis for reviewing specific decisions. Amitai Etzioni, *The Active Society: A Theory of Societal and Political Processes* (New York: The Free Press, 1968), p. 252.

16. H. H. Gerth and C. Wright Mills, eds. and trans., *From Max Weber: Essays in Sociology* (New York: Oxford University Press, 1946), pp. 214–21.

Certain aspects of the process of developing and implementing policy suggest reasons for the reluctance of an organization to engage frequently in policy reappraisal. These factors therefore contribute to the stability of policy. First, since resources were expended in developing the policy initially, reappraisal requires an additional use of resources. Second, use of traditional policies cuts down argument and conflict among executives, for alternative goals and actions need not be considered.[17] Third, changes in procedures for implementing the policy and therefore alteration in the role behavior of various officials are unnecessary if precedent is adhered to. Fourth, the development of a policy generally involves the development of compromises between various goals and competing bureaus. Raising a policy issue could reopen the conflict between these agencies, as each will strive to improve its competitive position.

Since the policies of each municipality had some measure of stability and continuity, each team of officials was constrained to some degree to adhere to the practices of its predecessor. The extent of the continuity of municipal policy influenced the degree of leadership adaptability to the challenges of economic and social change. Public officials could attempt, by conforming to established policy, to protect the privileges and influence of special interests or, by modification, endeavor to change the locality and the locus of community power. In this sense efforts to preserve and to change policy determine the responses of particular social structures to the changing requirements of each social system. The greater the continuity of public policy, the more closely each municipality adheres to previous responses to industrialization and the less consideration given to alternative courses of action. Where this continuity can be demonstrated by the policy choices of municipal officials, it is possible to speak of a "decision-making pattern" or a set of policies for handling a variety of recurrent problems. This pattern represents an accumulation of precedents that tend to guide and to restrict the decisions of subsequent administrations. The decision-making pattern also may be thought of as a set of guidelines or suggestions for defining particular situations and for selecting appropriate goals and

17. The theory of incrementalism maintains that decision makers generally refuse to consider policies that are thought to produce situations that vary greatly from current conditions. David Braybrooke and Charles E. Lindblom, *A Strategy of Decision: Policy Evaluation as a Social Process* (New York: The Free Press of Glencoe, 1963).

means. By influencing the selection of activities performed by governmental agencies, the decision-making pattern influences the degree to which these structures fulfill the service needs of social units in the municipality.[18]

Frequent application of the decision-making pattern contributes, in time, to the development of a certain measure of internal consistency. The objectives sought in one area of local activity tend to become compatible with those of other spheres. Similarly a tendency exists for policies on means, particularly financial, to overlap from area to area. Opposing pressure groups and variations in situations may produce inconsistencies and incongruities in policy choices concerning different areas of the community. Nevertheless, repeated application of established guidelines may lead to a measure of consistency in terms of an "inner logic" or underlying set of general premises.[19]

18. The concept decision-making pattern resembles concepts used by several scholars to designate certain normative elements of decision making. Banfield and Wilson employ the term "political culture" to designate beliefs about who runs a community, what and how projects are conceived and carried out. They designate two orientations, one stressing the public welfare the other emphasizing private interests. Edward C. Banfield and James Q. Wilson, *City Politics* (Cambridge, Mass.: Harvard University Press and The M.I.T. Press, 1963), pp. 46, 58–60.

Agger, Goldrich, and Swanson considered political ideologies a major influence on decision making. A political ideology consisted of ideas on such subjects as what types of groups should make community decisions, how resources should be allocated to various groups, the role of government and the kinds of interest groupings in the community. Robert E. Agger, Daniel Goldrich, and Bert E. Swanson, *The Rulers and the Ruled: Political Power and Impotence in American Communities* (New York: John Wiley and Sons, Inc., 1964), pp. 14–36.

The manner in which a community responded to various problems was influenced to a large degree by the values or conceptions of the roles of government which were dominant in four cities in Michigan. Oliver P. Williams and Charles R. Adrian, *Four Cities: A Study in Comparative Policy Making* (Philadelphia: University of Pennsylvania Press, 1963).

For a sophisticated examination of the influence of values on decision making see Philip E. Jacob, "The Influence of Values in Political Integration," in Philip E. Jacob and James V. Toscano, eds., *The Integration of Political Communities* (Philadelphia: J. B. Lippincott Company, 1964), pp. 209–46.

19. Nathan Leites developed the concept "operational code" from the writings of Soviet leaders to designate a set of primary assumptions that led to specific policies. Nathan Leites, *The Operational Code of the Politburo* (New York: McGraw-Hill Book Company, 1951).

"Expansionist" and "Restrictionist" Patterns

Policy makers of city and township had to determine the relative importance of improving government operations and preserving the framework of divided political structure. An essential part of this decision concerned the extent to which public officials considered it necessary to provide the kind of facilities preferred by absentee-owned corporations. The priority assigned effective government operations depended on both the importance of pattern maintenance and the extent to which public officials sought to do those things on the local level which could stimulate and maintain a high rate of growth in the local economy.

One strategy for coping with these matters is based on the premise that restraining the demand on government for increases in output of basic services would increase the longevity of forms of political organization by containing the pressures for change. This could be accomplished if the service needs of the municipality grew slowly, which would be the case if the economy and population also were relatively static. This strategy, emphasizing pattern maintenance, could be implemented through a set of policies termed "restrictionist" which seek to hold the line on the municipal budget and tax increases. New plants and residential developments could be discouraged by shortages in basic services and land. Lack of surplus capacity in water and sewage plants and of suitable sites could force corporate executives to bypass Woodruff when seeking a location for a plant or some other type of facility. Officials also would be compelled to refuse services to residents of outlying areas.

An alternative strategy, the "expansionist" pattern, encourages the growth and development of the municipality on the premise that economic growth would produce the revenues needed by government to expand output of essential services. The municipality would become an integral part of the national economy, a locale for the facilities of absentee-owned corporations. To accomplish these ends, the "expansionist" pattern requires frequent and expensive improvements in municipal facilities to develop surplus capacity in wells, water and sewage plants, and in distribution networks. The pattern also includes liberal policies on the provision of services to outlying areas and neighboring municipalities.

The two types of patterns differ in several other respects. Since one encourages and the other discourages community growth, the former is more and the latter less likely to intensify conflict between various interest groups. Economic change often modifies the composition of the population. The restrictionist pattern could minimize changes in the prevailing distribution of political power by holding down the rate of growth by making the local area unattractive to industrial organizations. Implementation of the expansionist pattern would increase the likelihood of changes in the political structure of the municipality by encouraging growth of the economy and population.

Each type of pattern also includes policies on methods for eliminating the structural factors restricting the government's fiscal inputs. Several direct methods are available for accomplishing this objective. A vigorous policy of annexation might have enabled the city to acquire much if not all of the township's industrial tax base and, ultimately, merger of the two municipalities. The fiscal limitations of township government could be eliminated through separate incorporation as a home-rule city. Either change would have dysfunctional consequences for some or many groups in the neighboring municipality. Annexation and merger would put an end to the political identity of the township and the loyalties of township residents; it also could lead to dismissal of some municipal employees. Incorporation of the township, on the other hand, could solidify the boundaries of the two municipalities, for it is exceedingly difficult for the land of one incorporated municipality to be annexed by another.

The restrictionist pattern with its emphasis on confining the demands for government services and preventing change in the distribution of political power does not favor annexation or other forms of territorial growth. The expansionist pattern requires such policies to secure the revenue needed for aligning the adaptive needs of the community and the output of government services. Adoption of the expansionist pattern by the city would have led to an aggressive program of territorial expansion. Adoption by the township, with its large reserve of undeveloped land, could lead to separate incorporation. Whether such policies were successful would depend in part on the efforts of the neighboring municipality to prevent changes it considered injurious.

This discussion does not intend to imply that policy makers of each municipality rationally and consciously considered all of these problems, related each to the other, and selected either the restrictionist or the expansionist decision-making pattern. The patterns evolved by trial-and-error, from consideration of more immediate matters, such as by how much, if at all, the budget of a municipal department should be increased. As each generation of public officials wrestled with taxation, the budget, capital improvements, essential services, welfare, and many other problems, policy preferences were registered on the basis of such general characteristics as the amount of risk involved, short-run as opposed to long-run gains, and orientation to social change. These general preferences when applied to a host of specific problems, those confronting a governing body of a municipality, led to a determination of preferences on growth in the economy, pattern maintenance, and instrumental activities of government, all of which fall within the decision-making pattern. Much of this study concerns the factors responsible for the particular configuration of patterns in the two municipalities, the manner in which each influenced the activities of government and the political structure of the Woodruff area over a period of approximately three decades.[20]

Influential Organizations

The origins, continuity, and change of a decision-making pattern depended in part on the influence of those groups supporting and those opposing it. Strata, political parties, and interest groups adhere to and advocate particular beliefs, and they all seek policy outcomes thought consistent with these viewpoints.[21] The dominance of a

20. The amount of time covered in this study varies with the area of the community under consideration. Since mention is made of the annexation attempts of the twenties, this phase of intermunicipal relations spans roughly fifty years. Sanitary services in the city spans over forty years; for the township, almost thirty years. Activities of the Chamber are reviewed since its inception in 1920; of the banks, since the early years of this century; for the newspaper, since the twenties; in contrast, quantitative data on leaders and on banking officials pertains to the late fifties and early sixties.

21. Max Weber, *Economy And Society*, Guenther Roth and Claus Wittich, eds., Vol. 2 (New York: Bedminster Press, 1968), pp. 468–518, 839–42, 848–50. For a discussion of Weber's theory of status groups, beliefs and social structure see Reinhard Bendix, *Max Weber: An Intellectual Portrait* (Garden City, N.Y.: Doubleday and Company, 1960), pp. 265–70.

particular decision-making pattern can result from the influence of those interest groups that endorsed and expounded it. The life span of each pattern, the nature of the changes that occur in the pattern, if any, also depend on the relative influence of the groups favoring and opposing it.

The top officers and the directors of banks are among the local groups capable of shaping a community's decision-making pattern. The nature of banking as a business provides these persons with a strong interest in the local economy and in influencing decisions concerning this sphere of the system. The volume and profitability of the banking business depends to a considerable degree on the spending and borrowing activities of economic, political, and social organizations. The views of bankers on economic growth, and also on the importance of maintaining certain forms of governmental structure, may influence many local leaders. This influence derives not only from the functions of the bank for the economy but from the fact that many officers and directors are among the community's larger property owners and from families that possess a long and distinguished record of achievement in local affairs.

The Chamber of Commerce offered all local businessmen (see Chapter 6), managers of enterprises, and certain professional people the opportunity to exercise collective influence over the activities of various social and political organizations. Through the efforts of the executive secretary and his staff the organization oversees the activities of city and township governments and expresses the collective opinion of members. As spokesman for some of the most respectable and affluent groups in the community, business and professional, the organization could shape public opinion on important issues. In times of crisis, the Chamber also provides a form of collective leadership should political and other leaders, for one reason or another, falter or lose confidence (see Chapter 6).

Public opinion often influences the actions of government officials. *The Woodruff Press,* as the community's sole newspaper and, for many years, the only locally owned, formal medium of communication serving the entire Woodruff area, played a major role in distribution of information to local residents. Editorial policies and news accounts of strategic happenings could either encourage or possibly prevent public officials from following the guidelines of the decision-making pattern. Change could result from the mobilization of public opinion by agencies of mass communication favoring or opposing courses of action recommended by the mayor or other officials. The positions of the newspaper on a number of critical issues reaching as far back as the twenties are considered in Chapter 7.

Individuals who held positions of leadership in the organizations cited above and in local government were the actors most likely to make or to influence decisions on intermunicipal affairs.[22] Informa-

22. The pioneering study of leadership concerned the morphology of leadership in a southern metropolis. Floyd Hunter, *Community Power Structure* (Chapel Hill, N.C.: The University of North Carolina Press, 1953). Paul Miller studied action in the field of health in over 200 communities. Paul A. Miller, *Community Health Action: A Study of Community Contrast* (East Lansing, Mich.: Michigan State College Press, 1953). Hunter applied his reputational technique to a study of national leaders with less success than in his earlier work, Floyd Hunter, *Top Leadership, U.S.A.* (Chapel Hill, N.C.: The University of North Carolina Press, 1959). A study of a New England community emphasized the dynamics of establishing a health center, Floyd Hunter, Ruth Connor Schaffer, and Cecil G. Sheps, *Community Organization: Action and Inaction* (Chapel Hill,: The University of North Carolina Press, 1956). A political scientist studied leadership in Regional City by methods differing from those used by Hunter but the data, in general, support Hunter's findings; see M. Kent Jennings, *Community Influentials: The Elites of Atlanta* (New York: The Free Press of Glencoe, 1964). Hunter's method was tested in a study of changing race relations in a southern city by M. Elaine Burgess, *Negro Leadership in a Southern City* (Chapel Hill: The University of North Carolina Press, 1962).

In the thirties and forties several community studies provided limited but suggestive information on leadership. The Lynds concluded that one family dominated Middletown; see Robert S. and Helen M. Lynd, *Middletown in Transition: A Study in Cultural Conflicts* (New York: Harcourt, Brace and Company, 1937). In his study of Yankee City, W. Lloyd Warner recognized the serious consequences for community leadership of the transfer of ownership of several shoe factories from local families to absentee-owned corporations; see W. Lloyd Warner and J. O. Low, *The Social System of the Modern Factory: A Social Analysis* (New Haven: Yale University Press, 1947). Several co-workers of Warner applied his stratification approach to a Mississippi community. In their report, the authors indicated that a "ring" of upper-middle-class-businessmen and politicians "ran" the town; see Allison Davis, Burleigh B. Gardner, and Mary R. Gardner, *Deep South: A Social Anthropological Study of Caste and Class,* rev. ed. abr. (Chicago: The University of Chicago Press, 1965). In his study of Elmtown, Hollingshead showed that the two top classes controlled the school board and dominated the administration of the high school; see August B. Hollingshead, *Elmtown's Youth* (New York: John Wiley and Sons, Inc., 1949).

Robert Dahl's study of New Haven stakes out a view of leadership that

tion on the socioeconomic characteristics of city and township leaders illuminate some of the conditions that influenced the reactions of these persons. Differences between city and township leaders on economic and political positions, place of birth, and length of residence, to name but a few factors, suggest how various groups of leaders might react to proposals for changing the political structure of the Woodruff area (see Chapter 3).

---

places it in the context of a specific form of political institution, a democratic polity. Dahl is concerned both with the morphology of leadership and the influences of political processes and procedures on leaders; see Robert A. Dahl, *Who Governs? Democracy and Power in an American City* (New Haven: Yale University Press, 1961). A number of recent studies used a comparative approach. A study of four cities in Michigan emphasized the values of leaders along with forms of local government; see Williams and Adrian, *Four Cities.*

Robert Agger and associates studied four communities in different parts of the country. Considerable attention was given to the ideologies of particular cliques of leaders within each community, and the competition among these cliques for control over the making of public policy; see Agger, Goldrich, and Swanson, *Rulers and the Ruled.* Presthus tested the validity of the pluralist theory in two communities in New York; see Robert Presthus, *Men at the Top: A Study in Community Power* (New York: Oxford University Press, 1964).

Floyd Hunter emphasized the elitist aspects of community leadership in *Community Power Structure.* His point of view has been supported by Delbert C. Miller, "Industry and Community Power Structure: A Comparative Study of an American and an English City," *American Sociological Review,* 23 (February, 1958), 9–15, also "Decision-making Cliques in Community Power Structures: A Comparative Study of an American and an English City," *American Journal of Sociology,* 54 (November, 1958), 299–310; Burgess' data [in *Negro Leadership*] on white and Negro leadership in Crescent City, in general, were consistent with elitist suppositions. Presthus (in *Men at the Top*) found dominance of economic leaders in one town and of political leaders in the other. A study of one small town in New York State reported domination by a small clique of leaders, an "invisible government," which included or represented the interests of successful businessmen and farmers; see Arthur J. Vidich and Joseph Bensman, *Small Town in Mass Society: Class, Power and Religion in a Rural Community* (Princeton, N. J.: Princeton University Press, 1958). Although he did not use the reputational technique, Baltzell felt that a group of top businessmen dominated Philadelphia; see E. Digby Baltzell, *Philadelphia Gentlemen: The Making of a National Upper Class* (Glencoe, Ill.: The Free Press, 1958). On the national level the Hunter thesis has been ardently supported by C. Wright Mills, *The Power Elite* (New York: Oxford University Press, 1956).

Advocates of a position that, in varying degrees, conforms to pluralism include the following: Dahl, *Who Governs?;* Robert O. Schulze, "The Role of Economic Dominants in Community Power Structure," *American So-*

Longitudinal and Comparative Framework

Since the alternatives for each municipality to change these features of political or ecological structure limiting the government's tax potential would have a decisive effect on the interests of the other, each had developed a defensive strategy. Whether the city could grow territorially or the township incorporate as a home-rule city depended in part on the countermoves by its neighbor. Similarly, the development of one municipality could lead officials of the other to reappraise policies and make adjustments in goals and means. Strategy could be developed to anticipate and prevent those actions in the neighboring municipality which might harm local interests.

---

ciological Review, 23 (February, 1958), 3–9, and "The Bifurcation of Power in a Satellite City," in Morris Janowitz, ed., *Community Political Systems* (Glencoe, Ill.: The Free Press, 1961); Herbert Kaufman and Victor Jones, "The Mystery of Power," *Public Administration Review,* 14 (1965), 205–12; although concerned solely with a controversial public housing plan the authors contended that Chicago did not have an elitist type of leadership structure in Martin Meyerson and Edward C. Banfield, *Politics, Planning and the Public Interest: The Case of Public Housing in Chicago* (Glencoe, Ill.: The Free Press, 1964). In a subsequent study of six controversial issues, Banfield found that many of Chicago's leading businessmen lined up on opposite sides of issues; see Edward C. Banfield, *Political Influence* (Glencoe, Ill.: The Free Press, 1961). A study of a variety of issues in Syracuse also found strong evidence of pluralism in Roscoe C. Martin et al., *Decisions in Syracuse* (Bloomington, Ind.: Indiana University Press, 1961). A study of the city manager in eight Florida communities found some with an elitist and others with a pluralist type of leadership structure; see Gladys M. Kammerer et al., *The Urban Political Community: Profiles in Town Politics* (Boston: Houghton Mifflin Company, 1963). For a critical analysis of elitist studies and a sturdy defense of the pluralist approach see Nelson W. Polsby, *Community Power and Political Theory* (New Haven: Yale University Press, 1963).

For articles that review the field of community power see the following: Peter H. Rossi, "Research on Decision-Making in American Local Communities," *Administrative Science Quarterly,* 1 (March, 1957), 425–43; Arthur Kornhauser, ed., *Problems of Power in American Democracy* (Detroit: Wayne State University Press, 1957); William V. D'Antonio and Howard J. Ehrlich, eds., *Power and Democracy in America* (Notre Dame, Ind.: University of Notre Dame Press, 1961); Charles M. Bonjean and David M. Olson, "Community Leadership," *Administration Science Quarterly,* 9 (December, 1964), 278–300; William Spinrad, "Power in Local Communities," *Social Problems,* 12 (Winter, 1965), 335–56; John Walton, "Substance and Artifact: The Current Status of Research on Community Power Structure," *American Journal of Sociology,* 69 (January, 1966), 430–38, and "Discipline, Method and Community Power: A Note on the Sociology of Knowledge," *American Sociological Review,* 31 (October, 1966), 684–89.

As long-term solutions to the problems occasioned by economic development would require action by both municipalities, this study focuses on the interaction of city and township. It also includes those features of each municipality, such as forms of government, public policy, and demographic characteristics, which have a bearing on that interaction.

The critical events in the interaction of city and township are studied developmentally. Complex changes in social structure seldom are accomplished quickly. The circumstances leading up to such innovations usually build up slowly, over an extended time period. Interest groups committed to the maintenance of certain forms of social structure seldom are brushed aside by groups committed to change. Usually a long sequence of interaction has preceded such developments, wherein the inadequacies of traditional policies have become ever more noticeable, and the citizenry has been educated in these matters, usually under the auspices of both political leaders and the mass media.

To determine the existence and influence of decision-making patterns a number of strategic situations must be examined spanning a variety of circumstances—depression, wartime, peacetime, prosperity, recession. The actions of officials would vary with these changes if situational elements are decisive; otherwise actions should conform to traditional policies despite variation in situations. Application of a restrictionist decision-making pattern should evoke policies during prosperity similar to those during a depression.

A longitudinal framework also permits consideration of the feedback of information on the results of previous policies of action on a current problem. A restrictionist pattern in the city, for example, should not be modified as officials observe the growing viability of the township or even the extension of utility mains around Woodruff. For these conditions are consistent with the inward-looking character of the restrictionist pattern. Similarly, the expansionist pattern of the township would not be modified as the chances of city territorial growth declined, for this condition is consistent with the objectives of the pattern.

A developmental framework also permits a more adequate analysis of the merger campaigns, by making it possible to determine the major functions performed and the extent to which the outcome resulted from actions of participants or from conditions antecedent to each campaign. These data permit a more accurate analysis of the campaigns than a cross-sectional analysis.

The impact of decision-making patterns is studied in a number of different situations, classified either as recurrent or nonrecurrent.[23] The former pertains to events or problems that occurred repeatedly and for which the decision-making pattern provides specific policies. This permits the routine application of the pattern, with little thought given to alternative courses of action. Since officials are familiar with the standard procedure for disposing of a matter, leaders outside the government arena seldom become involved in discussions. The absence of outside involvement may give the appearance of a leadership vacuum. Application of the decision-making pattern to recurring situations may enable the community to be administered in accordance with the objectives of the dominant interest groups without the overt involvement of the leaders of these groups. Many of these situations are presented in Chapter 4.

The nonrecurring problem often had the appearance of a "once-in-a-lifetime opportunity." Each municipality had a chance to acquire facilities or to engage in activities that normally were prohibited by cost considerations. Since customary fiscal restrictions were not operative in these situations, officials had options that hitherto had not been available and were not likely to be available again. The opportunity to acquire certain utility facilities had this character. Acquisition by the city would enhance while acquisition by the township would greatly diminish prospects for changing area political structure.

The decision-making pattern played a major part in assisting officials to choose a course of action. Where utilization of an option ran counter to the pattern, inactivity was an appropriate reaction.[24]

23. For somewhat different approaches to the significance of this distinction the reader should consult March and Simon on the one hand and Selznick. James G. March and Herbert A. Simon, *Organizations* (New York: John Wiley and Sons, Inc., 1958), pp. 26–28, 140, 172–86; Philip Selznick, *Leadership In Administration: A Sociological Interpretation* (New York: Harper and Row, 1957), pp. 29–89.

24. For a brief discussion of inertia in the context of social-system theory see Parsons, Bales, and Shils, *Theory of Action*, pp. 223–33. For Catton inertia is the normal condition of social units and social change is the circumstance requiring explanation. William B. Catton, Jr., *From Animistic to*

Officials were unwilling to initiate and engage in actions that could move the organization along a path different from that which had been customarily followed. More specifically, nondecision making refers to the nonresponse of organizations to situations involving either advantage or threat in which the right and the authority but not the obligation to act existed. Where the organization was a municipality, nondecision making was manifest in the unwillingness, usually spontaneous, of officials to come together at an appropriate time to review traditional policies in the light of the current situation and to decide on an appropriate course of action. Nondecision making by officials of one municipality coupled with affirmative action by leaders of the other municipality had major consequences for the continuity of area political structure.

Negative decision making produced a result similar to that of nondecision making, for an organization did not alter current activities. It differed from nondecision making in that a formal decision not to act on a specific proposal or request was made by officials and recorded in the proceedings.

Inactivity, on the other hand, refers to the nonresponse of individuals to requests for help, assistance, or to suggestions for action. Each individual brushed aside or ignored the request without first discussing the matter with others.

Each of these three modes of responding to certain situations generally occurred when few persons had knowledge of either the opportunity or the request for action. Officials were able to dispose of the matter with little direct or indirect interference from outside agencies. This factor increased the effectiveness with which these techniques were used in Woodruff.

Merger Campaigns

State statutes provided procedures for changing area political structure, either through annexation or merger of the two municipalities.

Naturalistic Sociology (New York: McGraw-Hill Book Company, 1966), pp. 225–37. For a discussion of inaction in terms of the "costs" of action for an organization, March and Simon, *Organizations,* pp. 175–77. As applied to leadership behavior, the concept is carefully analyzed by Peter Bachrach and Morton S. Baratz, "Two Faces of Power," *American Political Science Review,* 56 (December, 1962), 947–52. For a briefer discussion with a somewhat different twist see Peter Bachrach and Morton S. Baratz, "Decisions and Nondecisions: An analytical Framework," *American Political Science Review,* 57 (September, 1963), 641–42.

Statutes also set forth the steps by which an unincorporated municipality could become a home-rule city. Merger would combine two municipalities, governmental bureaucracies, and revenue systems into one. The Woodruff area would acquire a new political identity. Incorporation of the township would provide the municipality with the taxing powers it long had needed and facilitate the development of the governing apparatus. Incorporation also would stabilize the boundaries of the two municipalities by virtually eliminating the possibility of Woodruff's acquiring township land.

Three campaigns for reorganizing area political structure took place during the thirty years covered in this investigation. One proposal in 1957 called for the merger of the two municipalities, while the other two, in 1950 and 1963, sought to annex a very large amount of township land. Since the territory to be annexed was considerable and the amount remaining to the township small, the proposals are classified as merger. In addition to initiation of these efforts, township leaders, on several occasions, expressed interest in separate incorporation. A number of annexation elections also were held. Each of these strategies—merger, annexation, and township incorporation—could improve the functional effectiveness of at least one of the local governments.

Two merger campaigns, that of 1957–58 and of 1963–64, receive extended treatment in Part III, and the third, in 1950, is discussed briefly. The emphasis on merger rather than annexation is the result of several factors. First, as attempts to carry out a major change in area political structure, incidence of the three movements suggests the existence of an expansionist pattern in Woodruff. To demonstrate the validity of the analysis presented in Chapter 4, the factors triggering each campaign must accord with the city's restrictionist pattern. Second, analysis reveals the groups and conditions responsible for efforts to revamp area political structure.[25] Third, the dy-

25. The last of the three campaigns discussed in Part III asked the voters to approve the annexation of township territory not the merger of the two municipalities. Since the area to be annexed had approximately 90 percent of the residents and all the factories of the township, the proposal would have "merged" the urban portion of the Woodruff area within the framework of city government.
The literature on efforts to unify local units of government and on the governmental problems of metropolitan areas is extensive. Several studies of campaigns to establish metropolitan governments are discussed by Norton Long, *The Polity* (Chicago: Rand McNally and Company, 1962), pp. 196–

namics of the campaigns indicate the relative effectiveness of nonpartisan and partisan governments in an intermunicipal election contest. Fourth, concentration on merger campaigns also reveals the factors in the township conducive to separate incorporation.

Initiation of the merger campaigns differed in at least one respect from most of the policy-making situations concerning sanitary services. Each campaign broadened the "scope of conflict,"[26] as private citizens participated in the movement and voters expressed a judgment on the proposal. This expansion of political involvement

---

214. For another review of these campaigns see John C. Bollens and Henry J. Schmandt, *The Metropolis: Its People, Politics, and Economic Life* (New York: Harper and Row, 1965). For an analysis of the "metro" campaign in St. Louis see Scott A. Greer, *Metropolitics: A Study of Political Culture* (New York: John Wiley and Sons, Inc., 1963); for an account of the campaign in Miami see Edward Sofen, *The Miami Metropolitan Experiment* (Bloomington, Ind.: Indiana University Press, 1963); for a brief account of the effort to merge two Illinois cities see Phillip Moneypenny and Gilbert Y. Steiner, "Merger? The Illinois Consolidation Case," in Richard T. Frost, ed. *Cases in State and Local Government* (Englewood Cliffs, N.J.: Prentice-Hall, Inc., 1961, pp. 267–79; for a study that reviews efforts to change forms of government in a number of metropolitan areas see Roscoe C. Martin, *Metropolis in Transition: Local Government Adaptation to Changing Urban Needs* (Washington, D.C.: Housing and Home Finance Agency, 1963).

For a critique of several studies of metropolitan areas see Charles R. Adrian, "Metropology: Folklore and Field Research," *Public Administration Review*, 21 (Summer, 1961), 148–57. Robert Wood recommends metropolitan government as an antidote to the provincialism and uniformity of life in suburbia. See Robert C. Wood, *Suburbia: Its People and Their Politics* (Boston: Houghton Mifflin Company, 1958). A contrasting view is provided by Edward C. Banfield, who emphasizes the function of balkanized government in reducing conflict where the population of the central city and of the outlying areas have opposing political loyalties; see Edward C. Banfield, "The Politics of Metropolitan Area Organization," *Midwest Journal of Political Science*, 1 (May, 1957), 77–91. Some scholars argue, in contrast to the viewpoints represented by both Banfield and Wood, that governmental units in metropolitan areas have already achieved a substantial measure of interlocal organization. As an example of this viewpoint see Vincent Ostrom, Charles M. Tiebout, and Robert Warren, "The Organization of Government in Metropolitan Areas: A Theoretical Inquiry," *American Political Science Review*, 55 (December, 1961), 831–42.

For a detailed "overview" of relations between various levels of government see W. Brooke Graves, *American Intergovernmental Relations* (New York: Charles Scribner's Sons, 1964).

26. E. E. Schattschneider, *The Semisovereign People: A Realist's View of Democracy in America* (New York: Holt, Rinehart and Winston, 1960), pp. 2–3.

endangered the positions of public officials and the influence of the decision-making pattern. A successful campaign could put men in public office who were committed to a different decision-making pattern.

The outcome of the three merger campaigns was influenced by a number of factors. One set of conditions was antecedent to the campaign itself, such as the degree of dependence for services of township neighborhoods on the city and the distribution of registered voters between the two municipalities. These and similar conditions were partially the product of previous decisions and nondecisions of municipal officials. Their significance became manifest when the ballots had been counted.

A related set of factors pertains to the preparations for waging the election battle. Election outcome depended partially on the degree of readiness of both supporters and opponents, the formulation of campaign strategy, establishment of a campaign organization, and the support obtained from such influential persons as the editor of the local newspaper and public officials. Another set of variables concerns the degree to which election strategy reflected the lessons gained from previous efforts to modify area political structure. Implementation of complex structural change may require several attempts.[27] Information from previous campaigns should lead to improvements in the election proposal and in plans for conducting the campaign. The side that learns from past experience would have the best chance of winning.

Vertical and Horizontal Patterns[28]

Although several societal institutions and nationwide organizations have influenced events in the Woodruff area for many years, this study concentrates on internal structures and processes. While no

27. Martin (in *Metropolis in Transition*) presented several cases in which adoption of a proposal to modify some aspect of area government was preceded by changes in the original plan to take account of the objections of particular interest groups.

28. Warren uses these terms in a theoretical context to illuminate relations of the local community to the larger society. Roland L. Warren, *The Community in America* (Chicago: Rand McNally and Company, 1963), Chs. 8, 9, and "Toward a Typology of Extra-Community Controls Limiting Local Community Autonomy," *Social Forces*, 34 (May, 1956), 338–41.

systematic effort is made to delineate the linkages between local and extralocal organizations apart from interaction between the two municipalities, the data indicate that external agencies have both intensified and provided resources for handling various conflict situations. The conclusion of several community researchers that local leaders have lost or abdicated control over the community to external centers of power does not apply here.[29] On the other hand, had the involvement in Woodruff area affairs of several extralocal organizations differed from those mentioned below, the events and difficulties would have varied from those presented in subsequent chapters. Among the more important external factors were the following:

1. The statutes of Midstate made annexation and merger difficult to accomplish. The laws required the approval of residents of the area to be annexed and the approval of residents of the two municipalities involved in the issue. Consolidation likewise required the approval of voters in each municipality. Developing a favorable public opinion was a prerequisite for governmental change. Some states, by contrast, remove the issue from the voters and delegate it to a judicial panel. Others permit an incorporated municipality to decide which areas to annex and when the change should be made.[30]

2. The federal government and Midwest Motors made the decision to construct the bomber factory and housing for defense workers in Woodruff Township. The events set in motion by these decisions and the facilities constructed in the township greatly accelerated trends that had been operative in the Woodruff area for at least twenty years. These included the establishment of plants, the acquisition of locally owned facilities by absentee-owned corporations, and the gradual specialization of local manufacturing in automotive products. The relations of the local college to the factors in the metropolitan community which expanded student enrollment and necessitated increasing investment by the state legislature also contributed to community growth, especially in the sixties.

3. The change in the ownership of the local newspaper from the

29. Warner and Low, *Social System of the Modern Factory;* Vidich and Bensman, *Small Town in Mass Society.*

30. For a discussion of various annexation procedures see Bollens and Schmandt, *The Metropolis,* pp. 400–438.

family that had published it for more than half a century to a newspaper group led to improvements in staff, news reporting, and to modifications of editorial policy.

4. Both the County Seat City and Metropolitan City housed a variety of specialists who were prepared to render various types of assistance, for a fee, to local groups and organizations. The skills and expertise of these specialists were resources for supplementing and guiding the efforts of local officials in seeking to cope with a variety of problems. Specialists from outside the Woodruff area who, at various times, played an important role in local affairs included the following: consulting engineers, bond consultants, attorneys, and representatives from the state's Township Association. Other specialists who could have provided assistance but who did not, for a number of reasons, included a research organization specializing in public administration and, during the war, a representative of the National Resources Planning Board.

Conclusion

This study concentrates on the factors responsible for a "bottleneck" situation and the failure of efforts to ease the ensuing tensions by changing features of social and ecological structure. The situation in the Woodruff area was analogous to a private company forced to provide products despite the refusal of customers to pay a reasonable price. The ecological structure of the city and the absence of taxing powers of the township were largely responsible for the inability of both units of government to obtain the revenues needed for accommodating the growing economy and population. Neither municipality could cease to operate; the basic services had to be provided in some manner. As the gap between demand and delivery of services became wider, the tensions and conflicts intensified.

The dynamics of this conflict situation are analyzed from the World War II period to the mid-sixties. The central problem concerns the factors responsible for the persistence of the conditions resulting in the "bottleneck" and the reasons underlying the failure of efforts to improve the situation through social change.

2. The Woodruff Community

History

The community of Woodruff, located on the Iroquois River, was settled in 1823. It is in the middle-western United States, in southeastern Midwest state. The latter is a synthesis and contrast of heavy industry and profitable farming, metropolitan city and remote unsettled wilderness, old ethnics and new, homogeneous immobile and heterogeneous mobile population groupings. Woodruff City and Woodruff Township reflected this divergence.

The city, which consisted of a little over four square miles, had been caught in a viselike grip by its thirty-two square-mile township on the east, south, and west and by Summitt Township to the north. Thirty miles to the east lay Metropolitan City, whose region encompassed Woodruff. A few miles to the west was County Seat City. The center of a major university and industrial research complex, its residents tended to be more cosmopolitan and socially prominent than the Woodruff counterpart.

For over a hundred years Woodruff served Woodruff Township as a trade center. Township residents came to the city to shop, to bank, and for church, cultural events, and nonfarm organizational participation. Some came to city schools, and others came for off-the-farm employment. In 1920, the population of the city and township was 7,413, and 1,083, respectively. By 1960, the township had outdistanced the city, with 25,950 residents to the city's 20,957.[1]

In the latter decades of the nineteenth and the early years of the twentieth century, the economic base of the city consisted of diverse manufacturing enterprises, paper, textile, carriages and carriage parts, agricultural implements, and a variety of wood products. While many of these businesses employed fewer than two dozen persons, the Woodruff economy was controlled by local manufacturers, merchants, property owners, and bankers.

In 1849, a number of Woodruff businessmen and prestigious citizens, through the offer of a sizable tract of land, accomplished the location of a college in their community. A century later this institution had become a university in name and aspiration. In the years that followed, it grew rapidly from an enrollment of approximately 4,000 students in 1956 to about 16,200 twelve years later, with expectations for 25,000 by 1975.

The presence of a college influenced both the economy and image of the city. The rapid growth in students, faculty, buildings, and equipment since 1955 boosted the local economy, particularly the retail, construction, and financial segments. The impact on the community image was suggested by the Chamber of Commerce's pithy description of Woodruff as the town where "education and commerce meet." For a century or more Woodruff residents believed that their town provided the type of environment suitable for the education of young men and women. Woodruff was distinguished by its middle-class morality, respectable and sober, free of the dinginess and rowdiness of industrial cities. The schoolhouse and mercantile enterprise were preferred to the factory smokestack as symbols of Woodruff's way of life.

The development of the automotive industry in Metropolitan City early in the twentieth century, at first gradually and later more rapidly, strengthened conditions contradictory to this image. By the twenties several locally owned companies produced parts for Metropolitan City automotive companies such as Midwest Motors and

1. U.S. Bureau of the Census, *U.S. Census of the Population: 1960. Number of Inhabitants, Midstate.* Final Report, PC (L)–24A (Washington, D.C.: U.S. Government Printing Office, 1961), p. 13, and *Fifteenth Census of the United States: 1930. Population, I, Number and Distribution of Inhabitants* (Washington, D.C.: U.S. Government Printing Office, 1931), p. 532.

Universal Motors. Midwest Motors had extensive land holdings throughout the Woodruff area, including land in Woodruff purchased in the twenties. These holdings led to the construction of a small plant in the city in the thirties and to the erection of a bomber plant in the township in the forties. By mid-century the local economy had become integrated into the manufacturing functions of Metropolitan City and dependent upon the activities of two major corporations, Midwest Motors and Universal Motors.

In the late thirties, Woodruff's labor force seldom exceeded two thousand. By 1943, when employment at the bomber plant reached its peak, over forty thousand persons were on the payroll. From that year until the middle of 1946, area employment declined to approximately 7,600.[2] Pacific Motors, a west coast company, purchased the bomber plant in 1946 to produce automobiles and then, during the Korean War, to manufacture cargo planes. In 1953, a devastating accident in a Universal Motors plant northeast of Woodruff combined with the desire of Pacific Motors to withdraw from the automotive industry resulted in the plant's sale to Universal Motors. The company produced automobile transmissions in one part of the former bomber factory; the remaining part had become the airport for the metropolitan region. A few years later Universal Motors built body and assembly plants in the township. Following the trend, Midwest Motors built a township plant to produce parts and to serve as a warehouse. By 1965, area industrial employment reached 22,000 and the Woodruff area's principal economic function focused on the manufacture of automobiles and automotive parts. Vitality of the area economy depended on levels of automobile production and employment in the plants of two absentee-owned corporations.

The rapid growth of manufacturing in the Woodruff area virtually eliminated agriculture from the area economy. In 1930 the township had 156 farms valued at over $2.5 million. Summit Township, immediately north of Woodruff Township, had 153 farms, valued at slightly more than $2 million.[3] During the depression, farming in

2. Reports on employment in Woodruff were made public annually by the local Chamber of Commerce and published in *The Woodruff Press.*

3. U.S. Bureau of the Census, *Fifteenth Census of the United States: 1930. Agriculture, I, Farm Acreage and Farm Values by Townships or Other Minor Civil Divisions* (Washington, D.C.: U.S. Government Printing Office, 1931), p. 290.

Woodruff Township appeared to gain in scope as it did elsewhere in the country. The 1940 census reported the presence of 223 rural farm homes, 21 percent of the dwellings of the municipality.[4] Only eight farmers and farm managers and six farm laborers remained in the township's labor force ten years later.[5] The municipality had become industrial.

The transformation in the area economy left many Woodruff residents with ambivalent reactions. While the manufacturing plants of both municipalities were appreciated and valued, many in the city, especially members of, and those close to "old families," preferred a community with the social characteristics and prestige of County Seat City. With its nationally recognized university and complex of research organizations, County Seat City had the elite population elements that many in Woodruff desired. Instead, Woodruff's greater accessibility to Metropolitan City and the abundance of land in the eastern half of the township had contributed to the rise of a manufacturing complex and of a sizable blue-collar population. Only Woodruff's university enabled the locality to retain many features of a middle-class community. As a locality the Woodruff area was subordinate in status to County Seat City while economically it was part of Metropolitan City's automotive industry. Limits on the extent to which Woodruff could emulate County Seat City were firmly set by its dependence on Metropolitan City.

Population Trends

The change in number of inhabitants for city and township in recent decades reflects the influence of wartime and postwar industrialization. In 1920 the city had a population of more than 7,400 inhabitants (Table 1), while the township had a population of about 1,000. Twenty years later the township had become more urban, with a population of 4,153, while that of the city stood at 12,121. In

4. U.S. Bureau of the Census, *Sixteenth Census of the Population: 1940. Housing, I, Data for Small Areas, Part I* (Washington, D.C.: U.S. Government Printing Office, 1943), p. 685.
5. U.S. Bureau of the Census, *U.S. Census of the Population: 1950*. Vol. *II, Characteristics of the Population, Part 22* (Washington, D.C.: U.S. Government Printing Office, 1952), p. 94. These data provide a general indication of agricultural activity since they apply to the Shady Lea area and not to the entire township.

the succeeding two decades the population of the township increased rapidly, reaching 14,630 in 1950 for a gain of 252 percent and climbing 77 percent in the following ten years to slightly under 26,000. Woodruff's gains in population for the two decades were much smaller than that of the township, 51 percent and 14.5 percent, respectively, to just under 21,000 in 1960.

The rate of growth would have been even smaller had not the Census Bureau, in 1950, initiated the practice of counting college students living on campus as residents. In any event, township population exceeded that of the city in 1960 by about 25 percent.

Over the years Woodruff City had a sizable black population while, as recently as 1960, that of the township has been quite small. In 1940, Negroes comprised 13.8 percent of Woodruff's population, and by 1960, the proportion had increased to more than a fifth, 23 percent.[6] In that same year the black population of the township

Table 1. Population of Woodruff City and Township, 1960–1920, and Percentage Change[a]

| | Woodruff | | | |
| | City | | Township | |
Year	Number	Percent Change	Number	Percent Change
1960	20,957	14.5	25,950	77.4
1950	18,301	51.0	14,630	252.3
1940	12,121	19.5	4,153	58.6
1930	10,143	36.8	2,618	141.7
1920	7,413		1,083	

a. Sources: U.S. Bureau of the Census, *U.S. Census of the Population: 1960. Number of Inhabitants, Midstate.* Final Report, PC(1)–24A (Washington, D.C.: U.S. Government Printing Office, 1961, p. 13; and *Fifteenth Census of the United States: 1930, Population, Vol. I. Number and Distribution of Inhabitants,* p. 532.

6. U.S. Bureau of the Census, *Sixteenth Census of the United States: 1940. Population, II, Characteristics of the Population, Part 3* (Washington, D.C.: U.S. Government Printing Office, 1943), p. 883, and *U.S. Census of the Population: 1960. General Population Characteristics, Midstate.* Final Report PC(1)–24B (Washington, D.C.: U.S. Government Printing Office, 1961), p. 83.

was 3 percent.[7] This seems unusual in that the township experienced the more rapid growth in industrial employment. The preference of Negroes for city residence may be caused by the existence of a black "ghetto" on the south side, while the township traditionally had been white.

The religious composition of the area has been predominantly Protestant. Catholics made up approximately 20 to 25 percent of the population. The largest Catholic church was situated in downtown Woodruff, while another was located in the northeastern part of the township. A third parish was established in the southeastern part of the township early in the sixties. The number of Jews living in the Woodruff area was too small to support a synagogue. For religious worship, the Jews of Woodruff went to County Seat City.

As a result of the influx of migrants from southern states during World War II, southern whites have been an important minority group in both city and township. For a number of reasons the township has been more closely identified in the popular mind with the southern "hillbilly." During the war many lived in Shady Lea Village, the defense housing area built in the northeast section of the township. In the fifties and sixties, various leaders of the southern whites had gained positions on the Shady Lea School Board, and in township government and political parties. By contrast, few had achieved political prominence in the city. Nevertheless, evidence from census tracts, although limited to a brief time period, suggests that both municipalities had similar proportions of whites born or raised in the South. Approximately 5 percent of Woodruff's inhabitants five years old and above in 1960 resided in a southern state in 1955 compared with 4 percent for the township.[8]

Spatial Organization

Most communities are divisible into a number of geographical parts that separate its residents socially from each other. The physical basis maintaining each area may be the stereotyped railroad track, a road or highway, a hill or valley, a river or body of water, and

7. *Ibid.,* p. 112.
8. U.S. Bureau of the Census, *U.S. Censuses of Population and Housing: 1960. Census Tracts,* Final Report PHC(1)–7 (Washington, D.C.: U.S. Government Printing Office, 1962), pp. 15–16.

suggestively, zoning regulations and land use. The principal divisor in the Woodruff community is the Iroquois River, which bisects the city and the township in its northwest to southeast course and leaves two clearly defined areas, east and west, in its wake.

Disecting the community from east to west were two highways, one a limited-access expressway and the other a town-to-town artery, leading eastward to Metropolitan City. The expressway fell along the city's southern boundary and divided the township on both the east and west sides. On the east it separated the Woodruff Township Hall area to the north from a more expensive housing development area to the south. The expressway, on the west, divided the populated, better housing areas located in the northern township and bordering the city with the sparsely populated rural areas to the south. The arterial highway, Midstate Avenue, located to the north of the expressway and in a line cutting through the center of the city, refined the community's distinctive living arrangement further. Within the city, it separated the black housing areas and some low income housing from the white; higher income areas clustered about the college and west toward the Iroquois Country Club. In the township it segregated most of the wartime housing development, known as Shady Lea, into a separate northeast section. Woodruff City and the township never has had, clustered in one area, high-prestige housing in the $50,000 to $100,000 range. Here and there about the College Hill—Country Club area one finds an extremely expensive house close to modestly priced dwellings.

East-West Division

The status distinction between "east" and "west" was symbolized by the location in each of these areas of certain institutions. The "country club" and "university" were in the western half of the Woodruff area, while most factories and the railroad depot were on the east side. Construction of the bomber factory and Shady Lea Village in the eastern part of the township solidified the status differentiation between these two segments of the area community.

Census tract data for 1960 on the population of the city and township reflect the consistency between the status connotations of neighborhoods and the spatial distribution of the social classes. While the eastern and central tracts of Woodruff in 1960 had approximately 26 percent of its men employed in white collar occupations, the two western tracts had over 53 percent. Although the difference was not as pronounced for the township, the association between area and class remained strong. The eastern tracts of the township had 31 percent of their men engaged in white-collar occupations while those in the west had 40 percent.[9] In addition, over 70 percent of the owner-occupied dwellings valued at $22,000 or more were in the western part of the city and township. These facts explain the presence of over 80 percent of Woodruff area community leaders, businessmen, and professionals on the west side of the Iroquois River, in both city and township.[10]

The consequences of annexation for Woodruff would vary with the geographic direction in which growth took place. Expansion in the direction of prestigious County Seat City, seven miles to the west, would not augment Woodruff's industrial tax base, although valuable commercial property would be brought within Woodruff's jurisdiction. The advantages of westerly expansion would be largely political, in terms of strengthening the upper classes and the Republican grip on the city. Eastward expansion, on the other hand, would tend to have the opposite consequences. While the marked increase in industrial tax base initially would permit tax reductions for city property owners, the population of the annexed area would tend to strengthen the working classes and the Democratic party. These differential consequences of city expansion played an important part in Woodruff's responses to area economic and social development.

Government and Politics

Since the Civil War, the Woodruff area and the county and state within which it was located had a strong, relatively unchallenged, Republican tradition. The large, rural farm population, the small local industries, and the town merchant group that serviced them were devoted to that party. With the magnitude of industrial development in the state during World War I and World War II and

9. *Ibid.,* pp. 33–34.
10. This fact was obtained from a tabulation made by the authors of the area of residential location of the various leaders, businessmen and professionals.

the staggering growth of Metropolitan City thirty miles away, the Democratic party in Woodruff's county grew. The influx of war workers from the South during World War II promised further changes in the party-influence pattern in Woodruff. After the war, a large number of these men and women settled in Woodruff City and the township. The resentment that had been directed toward them as newcomers, with alien cultural values and interests, less economic means, and little or no transferable family status, placed the group in a minority position. By the mid-fifties this group began to contribute candidates (and Democratic votes) to township elections. An all-Democratic board was elected in 1957 for the first time in the history of Woodruff Township. Throughout the sixties, with the exception of one two-year term, Democrats have held seats, usually the majority, on the township board.

The small and relatively ineffective Democratic party in the city of Woodruff also received a boost from the war influx. The city had a large Negro population located in one ward, during the fifties and sixties, which voted overwhelmingly Democratic. A number of Woodruff City Democrats became active on a county basis; several served on the county committee and one became county Democratic party chairman. While the city Democrats became somewhat more important, the township party increased more rapidly in membership and effectiveness. The relative strength and independence of each, combined with their real and imagined status differences, resulted in conflicts among township, city, and even county Democrats.

Unlike the Democratic party, Woodruff Republicans in the city and township maintained one organization until it was split into two groups in the mid-fifties. By 1960 and 1961, the township Republican chairman felt that a serious rift divided his group and city Republicans. The county organizations of both political parties recognized a difference between the membership and political experiences of their group and that of the township contingent. Observations over a six-year period indicated that as Democratic residents of the township secured economic and educational advantages they often changed their party affiliation to the Republican persuasion. This was true also of the mobile southern white group. A manifestation of this change was the reaction of other county Republicans toward the township group. By word and action Iroquois County and Woodruff City residents conveyed to Woodruff Township residents their belief that status differences existed between them.

Both city and township, before 1946, held partisan elections. City voters adopted a nonpartisan form of government in 1946 with at-large elections, with indirect election of the mayor and the city manager. By contrast, the form of township government, with partisan elections to fill seven seats on the governing body on an at-large basis, did not change. This divergence in the form of city and township government, which complicated the difficult task of expanding Woodruff's territorial boundaries, is discussed in Part III.

Nonpartisan city government was adopted after the end of World War II despite the opposition of many older political leaders who had participated in the previous form of government. These men succeeded in defeating the proposed city charter in the spring election of 1946. Similar proposals were approved in the subsequent election held in the fall of the same year.[11] The results of these changes appear to conform with experiences of other communities with this form of government.[12] Three aspects of the change, nonpartisanship, at-large elections and selection of the mayor by the city council contributed to the continued political pre-eminence of Woodruff's upper classes. Members of minority groups, who generally were loyal to the Democratic party, tended to have considerable difficulty winning elections against well-known, middle-class, Republican candidates. This tendency was strengthened by the influence of the two wards with the largest voter turnout whose votes often were indispensable for victory. Voters of these wards on the west side of Woodruff tended to vote for those Democrats and minority-group members who had demonstrated in their past civic

11. For a discussion of the change in Woodruff's government see Robert O. Schulze, "The Bifurcation of Power in a Satellite City," in Morris Janowitz, ed., *Community Political Systems* (Glencoe, Ill.: The Free Press, 1961), pp. 53–66.

12. For a review of the literature on nonpartisanship and a discussion of the major conclusions see Edward C. Banfield and James Q. Wilson, *City Politics* (Cambridge, Mass.: Harvard University Press and The M.I.T. Press, 1963), pp. 151–67. The authors also examine the operations of the council-manager form of city government, pp. 168–86.

behavior reasonableness and flexibility rather than militancy. While it is not possible to stipulate the party allegiance of all persons elected to the city council under the nonpartisan arrangement, one indication is gained from party affiliation of those selected by the city council as Woodruff's representatives to the County Board of Supervisors. Over the years, the ratio of party representation generally has been three Republicans and two Democrats; at times the ratio has been four to one or all Republican. A Democratic city council doubtless would have appointed more Democrats than Republicans to the County Board of Supervisors.

Elimination of the direct election of the mayor and stipulation of a one-year term of office weakened that position at a time when the city needed strong leadership. Election of the mayor did not require a strong popular following but satisfactory personal relationships with fellow council men. For the most part the mayor accomplished his objectives through a coalition with fellow council members. The absence of veto powers provided additional assurance that the mayor could gain little by using public opinion as an ally in any conflict with the city council. These arrangements strengthened the incentive to make and implement policy on important issues privately, without the overt intervention of an interested public opinion.

The establishment of the city manager was intended to provide initiatives based on principles of public administration rather than partisan politics. Cumulatively, down through the years, successive city managers have accomplished some changes in long established policies and views on local government (see Chapter 4). Many of these changes came too late to affect the course of area political and economic development.

In the decades following World War II Woodruff's government was run, for the most part, by a committee-like structure whose members owed their position to the votes of friends and acquaintances in the middle classes. The forms of city government—nonpartisanship, at-large elections, and indirect election of the mayor—discouraged persons from seeking a career in local politics. Strength in one's party and a large following did not guarantee election to the community's highest political office. Since one could do very little as mayor, strong and able men were not encouraged to seek that office. By contrast, as demonstrated in the chapters that follow, township political parties provided the framework and the leadership for enabling a limited form of government to operate with a surprising degree of effectiveness. Partisan politics in the township encouraged the participation of citizens in governmental affairs, thereby facilitating the integration into the community of hundreds of recent arrivals. This differential appeal of township and city politics for energetic and ambitious young men is suggested by two facts. First, that two representatives to the state legislature, elected in 1964 and in 1966, from the district that included city and township, had both held full-time elected positions on the township board, i.e., township supervisor and township clerk. Formerly the office had been filled by two members of a Woodruff family, father and son, both Republican, for more than sixty years. A second indicator is provided by the differential participation of office holders of township and city government in the merger campaigns discussed in Part III. While township office holders were vigorous and leading opponents of the proposal, the mayor and councilmen, with a few exceptions, were either inactive, lukewarm supporters or hostile.

Economic Trends and Fiscal Problems

Data on changes in tax base and millage rates for city and township since 1940 reveal both the difficulties confronting each municipality and some of the sources of innovation in area political structure. The township's rapidly growing tax base provided a strong incentive for some leaders to promote annexation or merger, while, as a defensive and fiscal move, township leaders hopefully considered the establishment of a home-rule city.

From 1940 to the late sixties, Woodruff Township experienced a remarkable expansion of economic activity. Although the tax base of the city also increased during this period, the rate of growth was much smaller than that of the township. In 1940, before the construction of the bomber plant, the township's tax base was approximately $3.3 million compared with $10.3 million for Woodruff.[13]

13. Data on the value of property in each municipality were obtained from the offices of the city assessor and township supervisor. The data were taken from annual summaries of the value of property on the assessment roll. These summaries generally were published each spring in *The Woodruff Press*.

A decade later the tax base of the township was more than 50 percent greater than that of the city, $34.3 million as compared to about $22 million. The value of assessed property in the township in 1967 exceeded $90 million, more than double that of the city, which was slightly more than $43 million.[14] Since Woodruff's tax base increased slowly in value between 1956 and 1967 and the township had ample land available for future industrial development, the difference in value of assessed property between the two municipalities should widen in the years ahead.

In the years immediately following the end of World War II, the councilmen, under the new form of government, distributed benefits to all property owners in the form of reduced millage rates. After reaching a peak of more than 22 mills per thousand dollars of assessed valuation in 1942, the rate was reduced annually to 14 mills by 1950. The millage rate was held at this low level throughout the Korean War and it was not increased until 1955, when it was pegged at a little more than 15 mills. The rate doubled in the next eleven years, reaching 28 mills in 1966 and 29.8 mills in 1967. Soon thereafter the level of property assessment was increased from about 29 percent to 50 percent of the market value. The millage rate for 1969–70 was set at 16.5 mills.

Composition of the tax base affects a city's capacity to support municipal services. A higher proportion of taxed industrial property usually allows a municipality to provide a higher level of services. Since two-thirds of the township tax base was industrial property,[15] the township had a substantial capacity for supporting an urban population. Woodruff's prospects in this regard were limited. From 1953 to 1963, one-third of Woodruff's tax base consisted of industrial, one-fifth of commercial, and more than two-fifths of residential

14. For the first time in over a decade, Woodruff's tax base increased appreciably in one year, gaining nearly 8 percent between 1966 and 1967 to $43,253,580. At the same time the value of assessed property in the township increased to more than 90 million dollars. *The Woodruff Press,* March 23, April 24, 1967.

Use of figures based on assessed instead of equalized valuation of property minimizes the ratio of township to city property valuation. Since the end of World War II the level of property assessment has increased from approximately 21 percent to 25 percent in the township and from 25 percent to 29 percent in the city. During this period the equalization factor usually has been 1.6 for the city and 1.9 for the township.

15. Dittoed report of local government expenditures compiled by the Woodruff League of Women Voters, 1963.

property.[16] Since the proportion of industrial tax base decreased slightly during this ten-year period while that of residential increased from 43 to 47 percent, prospects for improvement did not seem bright.

A limited territory presented the city with prospects more serious than that of a static tax base. The shortage of industrial sites within the city could lead to a reduction of Woodruff's industrial tax base. If local plants required land for expanding operations, the absence of sites could force relocation to another community. City officials also had no guarantee that local plants would remain operating indefinitely. Competitive factors might require the closing of a factory or the transfer of some functions elsewhere. These eventualities could compel officials to reduce city services, increase taxes, or both. To heighten the anxiety of city officials, incorporation of the township would diminish prospects for territorial and industrial expansion.

Township tax rates had changed little in recent decades. Township voters approved a special levy of about one mill in 1962 for garbage collection, and the county tax rate was increased from 15 to 18 mills in 1964. Despite these small increases and the rapid growth in industrial tax base, township government did not possess a sound fiscal position. Although township population in 1960 was about one-fourth larger than that of the city, government expenditures in 1961 were about 40 percent of Woodruff's, $500,000 and $1.25 million, respectively. This fact suggests the restrictiveness of the township's fiscal powers. State law prohibits township government from levying taxes without the expressed approval of voters. Approval, if granted, is limited to a specific time period. If officials wish to renew a tax levy, another election must be held. The bulk of township revenue came from a one-mill rebate from county government[17] and a return of sales tax revenue by the state on a per capita basis.

Inability to levy taxes compels township government to live on a

16. Woodruff data for 1953 were obtained from a report by the city manager in 1953 to the chairman of a Chamber of Commerce committee. The report for 1967 was written by the city assessor. Information for both municipalities for 1963 was obtained from the report of government finances prepared by the Woodruff League of Women Voters, 1963.

17. Dittoed report on local government finances compiled by the Woodruff League of Women Voters, 1963.

limited budget. The municipality cannot furnish many of the services Woodruff City provided its residents. While Woodruff has a police department the township depended on the county sheriff's department and the state highway patrol. County government also provided maintenance and snow clearance for township roads. The township did not have a professional planning staff, although it had been growing rapidly for more than two decades over a relatively large geographical area. In addition to facilities for these services, the city had departments of public works, forestry, and engineering, which the township lacked. On the other hand, township government provided fire protection throughout the municipality, and in more recent years it supported a public library and a recreation program. Over the years, despite fiscal limitations, the township board made a determined effort to provide services requested by influential groups of property owners. This sensitivity to interest groups increased the strain on budgetary resources.

Both municipalities experienced a fiscal crisis in the spring of 1967. As the city millage rate neared the statutory limit of 35 mills, it became evident that measures had to be taken to increase the government's fiscal inputs. Two alternatives were considered: an income tax and a change in the level of property assessment. The latter had risen gradually in the past few years, from 25 to 29 percent of market value. In the spring of 1967, the city council ordered the reassessment of all property at the 50 percent level. In so doing, the city council doubled the amount of revenue that the tax base could produce. At the same time, councilmen warned that, should this measure fail to produce sufficient revenue, adoption of an income tax would be unavoidable.

Some indication of the inadequacies of municipal services in Woodruff emerged from city council discussion of the 1967–68 budget. A request from the fire department for additional manpower elicited this comment from the city manager: "The number of men available for first-call response today is less than 20 years ago . . . and the number of buildings and people in the city have increased greatly. . . . A similar situation has existed in the police department," he added. [18] The chairman of the local Civil Service Commission told the councilmen that personnel in the fire department had increased

18. *The Woodruff Press,* May 2, 1967.

by only four men in the past twenty-three years.[19] Population over this period of time increased by approximately 60 percent.[20]

The difficulties in the township were equally serious. The revenue provided by approval in 1962 of a .6 mill levy for garbage collection had proved inadequate, and the needs of the fire department no longer could be met adequately from the general fund. The township board scheduled an election in the spring of 1967 for a special levy of 3.3 mills per thousand dollars valuation to run for five years. Following defeat of the proposal, the township board reduced the scope of fire department activities and terminated the township-financed collection of garbage. Voters subsequently approved a 5-mill levy, with funds earmarked for the fire department, garbage collection, and the general fund. The increase in revenue led to a rapid increase in the budget. For the 1969–70 fiscal year, the township budget was $1.6 million, or 64 percent of the city's budget of $2.5 million.

These events in city and township made many citizens more aware of fiscal and service problems that stemmed from the pattern of area distribution of tax base and the structure of local government.

Territorial Expansion and Occupational Structure

Although both municipalities long have suffered from fiscal difficulties while the economy of the area prospered, few attempts to remedy the situation either on a piecemeal or wholesale basis have succeeded. From the twenties to the sixties, Woodruff doubled in size from two to four square miles of territory. Most of the annexed land was on the west side and residential, with the exception of a small tract on the south side. The largest parcel annexed at one time consisted of 610 acres.

Failure of efforts to grow territorially at the expense of Woodruff

19. *The Woodruff Press,* May 16, 1967.

20. To ease these fiscal problems the city council requested voters in late 1969 to adopt a 1 percent income tax on residents and corporate profits and 0.5 percent on nonresidents who worked in the city. This request was coupled with another to reduce the maximum millage rate by 5 mills. In the election held on December 2, 1969, the proposal lost by 115 votes. If the city council accepted the outcome of this advisory election, it would be compelled to hike the millage rate to close to the 20-mill limit for the 1970 fiscal year. *The Woodruff Press,* December 3, 4, 8, 1969.

Township have been numerous, although no annexation elections were held between 1930 and 1956. Three elections were held in the twenties, two involving land on the west side and one of land on the east side. A few acres of land on the west side came into the city in 1924. From 1950 to 1953, an effort to annex most of the township's eastern territory was tied up in the courts; the petition finally was dismissed. While annexation of 610 acres early in 1958 succeeded, merger of the two municipalities was defeated a few months later. A large-scale annexation was voted down in 1964, and an effort to annex 1,500 acres in Summitt Township was rejected in late 1966.

During this four-decade period, city and township citizens voted consistently on the issues of annexation and merger. City voters always supported and township citizens opposed Woodruff's territorial growth. While data in subsequent chapters suggest consistency in the views of township voters and leaders, the views of city voters and officials appeared to differ at certain critical times.

The relatively static boundary lines of the city had important consequences for the occupational and class composition of the two municipalities during the years of extensive industrial development and population growth. Despite its middle-class aspirations and pretensions, Woodruff, by 1940, was largely working class in terms of occupational structure. Roughly 58 percent of the employed males were in blue-collar and one-third in white-collar occupations.[21] Construction of the bomber factory and subsequent industrialization threatened to enlarge the working class numerically and politically. The reaction of city officials and leaders to the rapid economic development of the area early in the forties is understandable. Local leaders could not separate political considerations from the problems of fulfilling the adaptive needs of an expanding urban area.

Woodruff's inability to expand eastward and the few successes in annexing westside parcels had an important pay-off. Between 1940 and 1960, Woodruff City became more middle class in occupational structure. The proportion of men employed in white-collar occupations rose from 32 percent in 1940 to 37 percent in 1960

---

21. U.S. Bureau of the Census, *Sixteenth Census of the United States: 1940. Vol. II, Characteristics of the Population, Part 3,* Kansas-Midstate (Washington, D.C.: U.S. Government Printing Office, 1943), p. 888.

while that for blue-collar dropped from 58 to 47 percent. Operatives, the mainstay of the working class, declined from about 28 percent in 1940 to about 22 percent two decades later. On the other hand, service workers, many of whom are oriented toward middle-class values, increased in that twenty year period from 7 to 13 percent. The proportion engaged in the craftsmen and kindred-worker category declined slightly from 19 to 17 percent.[22]

While percentagewise these changes are small for a period of twenty years, increasing the proportion engaged in middle-class occupations during an era of steady growth in manufacturing activity cannot be dismissed lightly. A better appreciation of this trend can be gained from examining the occupational structure of the township in 1960, which resembled that of the city in 1940. About 58 percent of the employed men were engaged in blue-collar and 33 percent in white-collar occupations. Approximately 30 percent were in the operatives and kindred-worker category, and less than 6 percent were service workers.[23]

Occupational differences notwithstanding, data on income and education for 1960 suggest that the populations of city and township were quite similar. The township bulged more in the middle of the income distribution while the city had higher concentrations at both ends. More than a third of city families, 36 percent, had annual incomes below $5,000 as compared with 19 percent for the township. In the $5,000 to $10,000 bracket the city had 45 percent and the township 63 percent. The city had a higher proportion of affluent families, 5 percent had incomes in excess of $15,000 in contrast to 2 percent for the township.[24]

The picture for educational attainment of persons twenty-five years old and over resembled that for income. A third of the city residents had not gone beyond elementary school and 40 percent

22. U.S. Bureau of the Census, *U.S. Census of the Population: 1960. Vol. I, Characteristics of the Population, Part 24, Midstate* (Washington, D.C.: U.S. Government Printing Office, 1963), p. 247.

23. U.S. Bureau of the Census, *U.S. Censuses of Population and Housing: 1960. Census Tracts.* Final Report PHC (1)–7 (Washington, D.C.: U.S. Government Printing Office, 1962), pp. 33–34.

24. U.S. Bureau of the Census, *U.S. Census of the Population: 1960. Vol. I, Characteristics of the Population, Part 24, Midstate* (Washington, D.C.: U.S. Government Printing Office, 1963), p. 265, and *U.S. Censuses of Population and Housing: 1960. Census Tracts,* pp. 15–16.

had attended or completed high school. A fourth, 26 percent, had been to college. Comparable figures for the township are 30, 49, and 21 percent, respectively.[25]

Similarities of population in the two communities may be as, if not more, significant than the differences. The city seemed to have both a higher proportion of low income and of affluent families, while the township appeared to have a larger concentration in the upper ranks of the working class and in the lower levels of the middle class. A major difference, apart from occupation, was the size of the black minority group, which represented 23 percent of the city's and 3 percent of the township's population.

Conclusion

The extensive and sustained industrial growth of the Woodruff area since World War II led to at least two persistent sources of strain, one institutional and the other social psychological. First, both municipalities experienced the limitations of certain features of government. The city suffered from a shortage of land and industrial tax base. Acquiring township industry or vacant land suitable for economic development were the most obvious means for achieving that end. Township government, to support its more rapidly expanding population, industrial economy, and demand for services, needed more adequate powers of taxation. Incorporation as a municipality would permit local officials to more effectively utilize the industrial tax base. Since the strategy of one municipality would be detrimental to the other, the two municipalities were locked into a "zero-sum" conflict situation.

Traditional views of each municipality as a "community" complicated efforts to resolve the conflict. Despite the many similarities in the socioeconomic composition of the population of the two municipalities, traditional images stressed differentiation. Realistically, the basic line of demarcation was the east-west division in each municipality, which corresponded generally with the blue-collar and white-collar distinction. Many city residents continued

25. U.S. Bureau of the Census, *U.S. Census of the Population: 1960. Vol. I, Characteristics of the Population*, p. 238, and *U.S. Censuses of Population and Housing: 1960, Census Tracts*, pp. 15–16.

to think of the whole township as socially subordinate to the city. The identification of the township with Shady Lea Village was the result of the older association of the municipality with the rural and undeveloped area. These associations reinforced its inferior-status ranking. The views, although unrealistic, induced considerable ambivalence among many city leaders. They preferred to avoid territorial expansion of Woodruff for as long as possible. Some of those who had come to recognize the advantages of a larger industrial tax base could not go along with plans for annexing working-class neighborhoods. This bias did not generate workable alternatives to the status quo (see Chapter 10).

Township residents, who greatly resented the "superior air" of city inhabitants, took a different view of their municipality's manufacturing functions. Recognizing the advantages that these facilities conferred on the township and the city's need for land and additional industry, township citizens regarded their municipality as superior to the city. It was dynamic, growing, and youthful, albeit somewhat boisterous at times, while Woodruff was a decaying, dying city. By voting against annexation and unification proposals, township residents reminded city inhabitants that "the worm had turned." It provided great satisfaction for many township residents to even old scores.

The desire on the part of influential citizens to enhance the psychological distinctiveness of each municipality, despite the many similarities in the existential base, strengthened the forces for continued governmental autonomy.

3. Woodruff's Leaders

Conceptual Framework

At the time the research began in the fall of 1957, Hunter's *Community Power Structure* was the single most important study of community leadership.[1] Hunter conceived of the "power structure" as an informal unit, separate from formal associations and institutions, largely unnoticed by the mass media and thereby able to operate covertly and effectively. Hunter sought to explain certain changes in the community as the product of the efforts and resources utilized by the men who occupied positions in the power structure and who were able to control the actions of persons in various organizations and institutions.[2]

During and in the months immediately following the first consolidation campaign, the authors tended to see leadership in Hunter's terms. The fund-raising meetings were viewed as an activity of the power structure (see Chapter 8). Certain actions were thought to be indicators of the relative power of various participants. The election outcome could be construed as a measure of the strength of each municipality's leadership structure. When attention turned

1. Floyd Hunter, *Community Power Structure* (Chapel Hill, N.C.: The University of North Carolina Press, 1953).
2. *Ibid.*, Chapters 3, 4, 7, 8.

to a comparison of each of the three campaigns, it became apparent that this approach could not explain certain uniformities and that each campaign was launched with little advance preparation and only after a group in the township talked openly of separate incorporation as a home-rule municipality. As the researchers delved more deeply into the history of the area, they became aware of a tradition of municipal independence in responding to local problems. The effort to comprehend the factors responsible for the development and persistence of this pattern of intermunicipal relations required consideration of factors other than the properties of the leadership structure.

When the scope of the research broadened to include preceding and subsequent merger campaigns and some of the critical events of the thirties and forties, an awareness developed of the importance of variables that some studies of leadership structure neglected. As ideas developed in the process of data collection and analysis, they came closer to the views subsequently expressed by several critics of community leadership investigations. These critics, mentioned below, called attention to both the limitations of the model used by Hunter and others and to variables that had been overlooked. As our research proceeded, features of the community were included which did not fit the traditional framework of leadership analysis. The outcome of the 1957–58 campaign could not adequately be explained by the strengths and weaknesses of the leaders for and against the merger proposal or by any other type of event occurring during the campaign. It was necessary to include certain antecedent conditions, some of which were the outcome of actions and inactions of government officials extending as far back as the thirties and forties. These factors, especially certain uniformities in decision making by city and township government, permitted us to interpret several features of the merger campaign which had been puzzling, e.g., the fact that relatively young and inexperienced men assumed responsibility for the campaign, holding it unchallenged to the bitter end, and the appearance of support from so-called "top leaders." To explain these events as the result of weak or misguided leadership did not square with other situations in which certain leaders had acted decisively.

A comparison of the first merger campaign with a 1950 effort that was tied up in the courts for three years and with the campaign of 1963–64 indicated that these efforts served purposes other than those intended by their initiators and supporters. These purposes were consistent in essence with the ends served by the policies of city officials in handling a multitude of problems relevant for area growth and intermunicipal relations. Several critical events had to be considered, critical in the sense that, at the time, prospects were bright, either currently or in the near future, for accomplishing changes in area political structure. Recognition that these decisions lessened the probability of these innovations strengthened the conclusion that the merger efforts, although important, were somewhat anticlimatic. One important factor at work in all these situations was the set of policies employed by decision makers in each municipality, the expansionist and restrictionist patterns. The analysis focused on these patterns, their influence on policy choices, the situational factors that explained their rise and continuity, and their impact on the social organization of the Woodruff area.

Having delineated some of the important opportunity situations, the next step involved examination of the actions and inactions of those organizations that may have played some part in the policy outcome, especially the Chamber of Commerce, the newspaper, and the banks. The first awareness of their importance was shown by the role played in the merger campaign by representatives of these organizations. Analysis of the involvement of each organization in some of the important events in the recent history of the area led to a view of leadership that has had a long and distinguished place in the social sciences, that of interest groups and conflict, as expounded by Bentley, Herring, Garceau, Latham, Truman, and McConnell, among others.[3] According to this view, it was far more

3. Arthur F. Bentley, *The Process of Government* (Chicago: University of Chicago Press, 1908); E. Pendleton Herring, *Group Representation before Congress: Public Administration and the Public Interest* (New York: McGraw-Hill Book Company, 1936); Oliver Garceau, *The Political Life of the American Medical Association* (Cambridge, Mass.: Harvard University Press, 1941); Earl Latham, "The Group Basis of Politics: Notes For a Theory," in Heinz Eulau, Samuel J. Eldersveld, Morris Janowitz, eds., *Political Behavior: A Reader in Theory and Research* (Glencoe, Ill.: The Free Press, 1956), pp. 232–45; David B. Truman, *The Governmental Process: Political Interests and Public Opinion* (New York: Alfred A. Knopf, 1951); Grant McConnell, *Private Power and American Democracy* (New York: Alfred A. Knopf, 1966).

important to ascertain the influence of selected organizations and interest groups in the problem-solving efforts of city and township government than to delineate the relative power position of each of the persons designated as influentials.

Finally, the effort to understand the continuity of area political structure during an era of economic and urban growth prohibited analysis of events such as the merger campaigns cross-sectionally. Each campaign had to be recognized as one event in a long chain of interactions between the two municipalities. Issues, decisions, and campaigns exist within an historical matrix of social structure and past problem-solving efforts. For example, the character of the two unification campaigns would have been quite different had city officials in the forties followed a more aggressive policy on utility expansion.

Decisions and nondecisions are partly conditioned by precedent and by the conditions brought into existence by past actions. Among the more important of these historical factors are the traditional modes of defining specific situations which the leaders accepted from their predecessors. While recognizing that communities vary in the degree of importance of the "political culture," we endeavor to demonstrate that expansionist and restrictionist decision-making patterns were critical factors in influencing both the development of city and township relationships and the area political structure during an era of rapid industrialization. Norton Long seemed to endorse this viewpoint when he said, in a discussion of ideology and leadership structure, "The monism that counts may be that of the 'definition of the situation' rather than the elite structure. . . ."[4]

By deciding not to concentrate on delineating the properties of the leadership structure of city and of township, we were able to do the following: first, analyze the historical sequence of events responsible for the continuity of area political structure, to select and concentrate on those critical decisions that had a decided effect on this outcome; second, analyze the characteristics and influence of certain normative elements of decision making; third, concentrate on the activities and influence of certain organizations and interest

4. Norton E. Long, "Political Science and the City," in Leo F. Schnore and Henry Fagin, eds., *Urban Research and Policy Planning* (Beverly Hills, Calif.: Sage Publications, 1967), p. 250.

groups in the campaigns, on critical decisions, and on the decision-making patterns.

In the meantime, students of leadership had become somewhat disenchanted with the controversies over elitist and pluralist leadership structures and over the proper methods to be employed—reputational, decisional, and positional. Assessments of these studies emphasized certain failings. Despite the voluminous research on these subjects, Polsby insisted that the conclusions of many researchers on features of the leadership structure usually are inadequately supported by the facts.[5] Norton Long goes even further and questions the value of these studies: "The question 'Who Governs?' has proved in the end rather less interesting than expected. In a sense it has been a blind alley arising from the obsession with when can it be shown that 'A' has power over 'B' and the understandable desire to refute the social science fiction of C. Wright Mills and Floyd Hunter. . . ."[6]

Clark, who was kinder than Long in his review of community leadership studies, chose to emphasize what these investigations neglected: ". . . most studies in the community power tradition have nevertheless remained more concerned with the identity of actors in different issue areas, and their overlap across issue areas than with the actual outcomes of decisions. . . ."[7]

Alford emphasized a similar point in developing a conceptual scheme for analyzing decision making. He differentiates the structural and cultural features of a community from the situational factors impinging directly on concrete policy-making processes.[8]

5. Polsby has expressed this view in several publications, most recently in Nelson W. Polsby, " 'Pluralism' in the Study of Community Power, or, Erklärung before Verklärung in Wissinssoziologie," *The American Sociologist*, 4 (May, 1969), 121. He developed his argument in a more complete and systematic form in an earlier work. Polsby reviewed and criticized a group of studies of community leadership that he considered to be based on a theory of social stratification. He contended that the findings of these studies did not verify the initial assumptions. Nelson W. Polsby, *Community Power and Political Theory* (New Haven: Yale University Press, 1963).

6. Long, "Political Science and the City," in Schnore and Fagin, eds., *Urban Research and Policy Planning*, p. 252.

7. Terry N. Clark, ed., *Community Structure and Decision-Making: Comparative Analyses* (San Francisco: Chandler Publishing Co., 1968), p. 68.

8. Robert R. Alford, "The Comparative Study of Urban Politics," in Schnore and Fagin, eds., *Urban Research and Policy Planning*, pp. 263–71.

Variables in the former categories both influence and are influenced by policy decisions. Failure to differentiate these categories leads to a neglect of some of the most important variables. Such features of the community as organizations, decision-making patterns, and differences in the characteristics of city and township leaders shed light on the interaction between social structure and decision making.

The information presented below on the men and women selected by respondents as leaders are not part of an effort to determine the type of leadership structure that operated in each municipality. The data permit a comparison of the characteristics of persons in the city and in the township said to be leaders. The data indicate differences in the requirements for gaining a reputation for leadership in each municipality and shed some light on the factors influencing the development of each municipality's decision-making pattern. At the end of the chapter short vignettes are provided for a number of city, township, and nonresident leaders. They serve to identify participants in events described in succeeding chapters and make more meaningful the selection of courses of action by the leaders.

Methodology

Sixty-eight Woodruff men and women, forty-six in the city and twenty-two in the township, filled important leadership roles in Woodruff area development in the early sixties. Each was identified through a synthesis of the positional, reputational, and decisional approaches. Lists of officers, board members, pertinent committee chairmen and members in official organizations and private associations connected with community development were compiled in the early years of study. Additional lists for organizations that had played significant decision-making roles in this area, e.g., the Chamber of Commerce, Rotary, the banks, the newspapers, political parties, township and city governing bodies, were assembled and scrutinized for years preceding the field-work period. Although persons holding positions of authority may not have made key decisions, possession of this resource afforded the actor a leadership opportunity that he might not exercise.

During the first and second years of field work the list of positional leaders was supplemented by the names of several men who had played important roles publicly and behind-the-scenes in the consolidation campaign. The final list of men were interviewed, utilizing a four-page, two-part schedule (see Appendix 1). The first part contained a series of general but interrelated questions on the prevailing problems and problem-solving efforts within the community, questions pertaining to specific problems of historical interest and questions concerning the identity of the "top" leaders in the city and township. The second part consisted of eighteen personal background questions. The schedule was designed to assist in ferreting out leaders who may have played or were playing a more covert, less visible leadership role than our access to fund-raising and decision-making groups had indicated.

The initial interviewing served as a dragnet to provide names of other high level leaders. The use of reputation[9] as a survey tech-

9. The literature on the methodology of leadership studies is too complex to be summarized in one footnote. Some of the important items can be cited. The reputational technique was developed and used by Floyd Hunter, *Community Power Structure.* Subsequent studies that utilized this technique and articles that defend its use include the following: William A. Gamson, "Reputation and Resources in Community Politics," *American Journal of Sociology,* 72 (September, 1966), 121–31; Baha Abu-Luban, "The Reputational Approach in the Study of Community Power: A Critical Evaluation," *Pacific Sociological Review,* 8 (Spring, 1965), 35–42. Presthus used both the reputational and decisional methods for identifying leaders. See Robert Presthus, *Men at the Top: A Study in Community Power* (New York: Oxford University Press, 1964), pp. 33–63; M. Elaine Burgess, *Negro Leadership in a Southern City* (Chapel Hill, N. C.: The University of North Carolina Press, 1962), pp. 76–107, 210–16; William V. D'Antonio, Howard J. Ehrlich, and Eugene C. Erickson, "Further Notes on the Study of Community Power," *American Sociological Review,* 27 (December, 1962), 848–54; William V. D'Antonio and Eugene C. Erickson, "The Reputational Technique as a Measure of Community Power: An Evaluation Based on Comparative and Longitudinal Studies," *American Sociological Review,* 27 (June, 1962), 362–76; Howard J. Ehrlich, "The Reputational Approach to the Study of Community Power," *American Sociological Review,* 26 (December, 1961), 926–27.

For critiques of the reputational method see the following: Raymond E. Wolfinger, "A Plea for a Decent Burial," *American Sociological Review,* 27 (December, 1962), 841–47; Nelson W. Polsby, "Community Power: Some Reflections on the Recent Literature," *American Sociological Review,* 27 (December, 1962), 838–41; Raymond E. Wolfinger, "Reputation and Reality in the Study of Community Power," *American Sociological Review,* 25 (October, 1960), 636–44; Nelson W. Polsby, "How to Study Community Power: The Pluralist Alternative," *Journal of Politics,* 22 (August, 1960),

nique provided, at an early stage in the field work, the names of an additional half dozen leaders whose part in Woodruff decision making later proved to be substantial. The interview also presented an opportunity for a first formal meeting and the establishment of rapport that, in most cases, led to informal meetings and discussions in subsequent years.

Leaders were not asked to rank selections, nor were the number of nominations each received utilized to devise a general structure of community leadership. The number of nominations permitted rough differentiation between the "more" and the "less" important leaders. Each of the sixty-eight nominees was mentioned as a leader by at least 15 percent of their number. This was an arbitrary cutoff point selected because the next lowest percentage for the leaders on the positional lists dropped to 4 percent. The percentage high for selection as a leader was 72 percent.

The final selection criteria that resulted in the sixty-eight specific city and township leaders came as a result of their recorded activity in decision making and policy formation within the context of area development. Although the decisions selected for study were within the framework of area development, they represented a variety of subareas, such as change in form of city government, fund raising, the development of banking policy, promotion of business in the central business district, plant placement, and annexation/consolidation attempts.

All of the sixty-eight leaders had participated in some level of decision making in one or more of the subareas listed above. Several of the leaders participated in area development by nonresponse or inaction, which took the form of withholding overt support or financial assistance necessary for issue success. This type of inaction, sometimes visible, sometimes concealed, was considered to be an important form of leadership behavior. Each of the sixty-eight city

---

474–84; Nelson W. Polsby, "The Sociology of Community Power," *Social Forces,* 37 (March, 1959), 232–36; Robert A. Dahl, "A Critique of the Ruling Elite Model," *American Political Science Review,* 52 (June, 1958), 463–69.

In a comparative analysis of thirty-three studies of community power, Walton found that the methods used for studying leaders varied with the professional training and commitment of the researcher. John Walton, "Discipline, Method, and Community Power: A Note on the Sociology of Knowledge," *American Sociological Review,* 31 (October, 1966), 684–89.

and township men and women met all three of the following criteria:

1. Held positions of importance in their municipality—offices and board positions in public or private organizations.

2. Were known and mentioned as "top" leaders by at least 15 percent of their number.

3. Were observed by the researchers or known to function as decision makers.

Admittedly, these procedures, a combination of the positional, decision making, and reputational approaches, may not have differentiated precisely the more from the less influential leaders. The pool of city and of township leaders provided by these techniques was sufficiently representative to permit accurate and meaningful comparisons of city and township influentials. Although the authors' interest, as stated, was drawn to area development decisions and, in turn, to leaders who participated in this sphere, no man whose name had been mentioned as a top city leader, a top township leader, a part of "the power structure," the man/men on top in the city or township, or the "downtown boys" during the course of the years of data collection failed to appear on this list. In addition, during the fall of 1965 through 1966, *The Woodruff Press* published an editorial series appearing once every several weeks honoring an outstanding Woodruff leader. Out of some twenty-five tributes only one man, whose accomplishments were in the field of music, had not appeared on the list of sixty-eight. The sixty-eight leaders who held positions of importance, who were known as leaders also included those men who were considered and referred to as top community leaders.

Characteristics of Area Leaders

In examining the background of men and women reputed to be leaders the concern was with those factors which would illuminate the following: whether the basis of leadership reputation in city and township were similar or different and, if the latter, in what respects; whether features of leadership had any bearing on the characteristics and continuity of each municipality's decision-making pattern and on the ease or difficulty of accomplishing area political reorganization. In addition to data on the socioeconomic background of city and township leaders, information was gathered on such items as age, family background, length of residence in the community, and patterns of organizational involvement in local affairs.

Birthplace, Age, and Length of Residence
In communities where stratification systems are fairly rigid and where population movement, particularly immigration of ethnic or racial groups have occurred, community birth or length of residence and age levels are important indicators of inclusion and exclusion patterns. A leadership that emphasizes local birth or long community residence handicaps the newcomer. A leadership weighted on one end or the other of the age continuum reflects the length of time required for leadership training. It also indicates the opportunities afforded younger men to train and function in established, prestigious organizations.

The opportunity for gaining a position of leadership in the township was greater than in the city for the person born outside the community. However, the majority of city leaders also had been born outside the community. The basic difference concerned the area from which the leader had come, since most of the city leaders were natives of Midstate while almost half of the township leaders had been born in other states. Approximately 82 percent of the city leaders were born either in Woodruff or in the state, and 18 percent were born out-of-state. Almost half of the township leaders, 43 percent, were born out-of-state. A substantial minority of city leaders, 30 percent, were born in the community, in contrast with 14 percent of township leaders. With few exceptions, township leadership consisted of persons who had moved into the area from relatively distant communities. City leadership consisted of persons who either were raised in Woodruff or in nearby localities. This difference is reflected in the fact that more than a fifth of township leaders, 22 percent, were born below the Mason-Dixon line, compared with less than 3 percent of city leaders. Recent arrivals would have been the sole source of leadership for the township. The 1960 U.S. Census indicated that the population of both municipalities was equally mobile.[10] Of those persons five years and over living in the city and township in 1960, 26.4 percent and 22.3

10. U.S. Bureau of the Census, *U.S. Census of Population and Housing: 1960. Census Tracts.* Final Report PHC (1)–7 (Washington, D.C.: U.S. Government Printing Office, 1962), pp. 15–16.

percent, respectively, lived outside the county metropolitan area in 1955. In addition, the proportion of Woodruff area residents five years and older who were living in the South in 1955 is about the same for both municipalities, approximately 5 percent in the city and 4 percent in the township. Since these data do not include persons moving to the Woodruff area before or after 1955, they serve only as "rough" indicators of migration characteristics. Together with the data above, they suggest that persons who moved into the community from outside the state are more handicapped in seeking a position of leadership in the city than in the township.

Accessibility of leadership positions to newcomers also is indicated by length of community residence. Within the city leadership groups, 68 percent came to Woodruff before 1940, and 34 percent came before the depression. The situation was reversed in the township. Among the township leadership group, only 26 percent came before the depression. Only 31 percent of city leaders compared with 74 percent of township leaders came to Woodruff after 1940.

Most township leadership positions were filled by persons who came to Woodruff in the forties and fifties when the change from a rural to an urban environment occurred. The farmers of the twenties and thirties whose age and family background was similar to Woodruff City leaders had sold their holdings; only one of the township leaders was a farmer. Township leadership since World War II was more transient, fluctuating with changes in the size of the area's industrial labor force. By contrast, the careers of the city's leaders were less likely to be directly affected by productivity in the area's absentee-owned industrial plants.

The differences between city and township leaders in year of community arrival were reflected in age patterns. City leaders were much older than township leaders. Approximately 72 percent of Woodruff City and 28 percent of Woodruff Township leaders were over forty-five years of age. Another indication of the youthfulness of township leaders was the fact that more than 36 percent were thirty-five years of age or under, and only 18 percent were age fifty-six and above. The corresponding figures for city leaders were less than 7 and 41 percent, respectively.

Variations in age and year of arrival indicate that it was more difficult to become known as a leader in the city than in the township. This fact suggests that the training and prerequisites for leadership reputation differed between the two municipalities. Data on occupation and organizational participation shed further light on these matters.

Organizational Participation
The number of organizations in the community to which leaders belonged and the number of offices held, past and present, reflect the kinds of responsibilities these persons have fulfilled and the sources of their reputation. Membership in a local organization was important for both city and township leaders. There were no leaders in either municipality who failed to belong to at least one association. City leaders were much more involved in local organizations; 52 percent belonged to five or more associations, in contrast with 14 percent of the township leaders.

City and township leaders did not seem to perform at the same level of responsibility in local associations, although holding at least one office was important for both leadership groups; 59 percent of city and 46 percent of township leaders belonged to local associations. Consideration of past activity indicated that city leaders exercised the responsibilities of office for many years. In previous years, 88 percent of the city leaders and only 55 percent of the township leaders held one or more offices. A far greater proportion of city than of township leaders held positions as directors of such organizations as the banks, the local hotel, service clubs, the United Fund and its various member units; 67 percent and 22 percent, respectively. Furthermore, 39 percent of city leaders and 9 percent of township leaders held two or more board positions.

These differences in organizational involvement reflect a number of factors. First, that many of the organizations in which leaders participated were located in and thought of as "city" associations although in some cases, such as the United Fund, responsibilities were for the entire area. Second, associations in the township were fewer in number, and consisted primarily of political organizations and neighborhood civic associations. Since persons chosen for offices and board positions tended to be thought of as having primary allegiance to the city, and the township had few comparable associations, considerable disparity in positions held had to exist between city and township leaders. Third, more of the city than township leaders were wealthy or had been long associated with an important economic organization, by Woodruff standards, such as the banks or a local manufacturing concern. Hence these people tended to have a better chance of being selected as an officer or board member of these organizations. Fourth, skills and abilities in managing an organization probably were more important for gaining a reputation as a leader in the city than in the township. Fifth, reflecting on the patterns of age distribution, gaining recognition as a leader was more difficult and time-consuming in the city than in the township.

Occupation

What a man does in the workaday world determines, to a large extent, how much time and money he will or will not be able to devote to community service, how much interest in community affairs he will or must take, areas of interest that would seem to be most beneficial to him, and often, the level of prestige he may reach within the confines of community life. The occupation of the sixty-eight leaders were classified under seven headings:

1. Professional—lawyers, educators, doctors
2. Local industry and commerce—proprietary
3. City-county-state government—appointed or elected officials
4. Housewife
5. Outside community—those employed outside the community, one in public relations and one a top level labor union executive
6. Absentee industry—management level
7. Retired

Both city and township leaders were predominantly employed in local industry or commerce, 45.7 and 40.8 percent, respectively. The local industry and commerce category consisted of retail and wholesale store owners, managers, presidents and owners of the several small local industries, realtors, and bankers. It is noteworthy that differences did exist between city and township residents who fell into this classification. Five or six men in the city were bankers; there were no bankers in the township. Four city leaders were realtors while one township leader was so employed. Retail establishments in the city were larger and more specialized than those in the township, e.g., furniture, gift and large general department stores as compared with grocery, garages, gasoline stations in the township. Whereas the city was the center of a locally owned paper manufacturing plant and a step ladder company, the township had only a locally owned milk production and manufacturing plant.

Professionals in both residential groups were important; 34.8 of the city leaders and 18.2 percent of the township leaders were professionals. Government positions were far less important in the city leadership group, accounting for only 6.5 percent of the leaders, while in the township 18.2 percent held political positions. A handful of township officers and residents aspired to be full-time professional politicians; only one city leader had devoted his life to a professional career in politics.

Education
Since city leaders were older, more had reached maturity at a time when less importance was attributed to formal education. As a result, a lower percentage of the city leaders, 39.1 percent, had had some college work compared with 50.0 percent of the township leaders. However, city leaders had higher percentages of their members who had postgraduate training, 41.3 percent, compared with 22.7 percent of township leaders.

Opportunities within the city for the professional with postgraduate training were greater than in the township. Professional services are usually clustered in a focal geographical and economic center that requires and facilitates their use. Second, Woodruff City leadership, with more favorable economic positions, fostered and supported a range of middle-level professional leaders with specialized advanced education: law, medicine, architecture, accounting. The higher percentage of township leaders with some college training was symptomatic of the importance and use of education as a factor in economic and class mobility within the township's leadership and industrial structure.

Church Affiliation
City leaders in comparison with township leaders enjoyed more prestige and status. This in turn was reflected in their church affiliation. The city-located Congregational, Methodist and Episcopal

churches, in rank order, were considered to be the most prestigious. Within the city and township of Woodruff, there were approximately sixty-two churches. The sixty-eight Woodruff leaders belonged to nine city, four township, and one County Seat City church.

The largest proportion of city leaders were Congregational and Methodist, 20 and 17 percent respectively, while township leaders proportionately favored the Catholic, Methodist, and Baptist persuasion, 22.7, 18.1, and 13.7 percent, respectively. Denominational affiliation in Woodruff tended to be used as a factor of social differentiation and was less important as a selector and measure of leadership importance or potential. However, membership in a fundamental sect would have been subject to criticism in the city and doubtless would have affected the mobility of the individual to high city-leadership positions. The latter would have been true to a lesser extent in the township.

Summary

City leaders were older, had resided for a considerably longer period in the community, and their reputations as leaders were more firmly anchored to a record of successful exercise of responsibilities in a variety of organizations. Differing further, the city had a core of old families who retained positions as leaders and were passing their positions on to sons, e.g., Chamber of Commerce committees, United Fund directorships, Rotary offices. This limited the number of positions open to newcomers. The township did not have a comparable core of old, established leaders with sons to maintain even a semipermanent leadership hierarchy. Many of the large farm owners who might have developed a semblance of family continuity had sold their holdings with the industrialization of the area.

The role of the family in assisting younger members to gain recognition as a community leader and the variations by age between city and township may have affected the respective decision-making patterns. Since city leaders were older than township leaders and tended to have resided in the community for a longer period of time, many more had undergone leadership training in the twenties and thirties. Municipal policies emphasized caution and frugality. In a good many cases the fathers of current city leaders may have personally recommended or advised certain policies for handling recurrent problems. Many city leaders tended to view the city and its problems in a manner similar to that of the previous generation of leaders.

Township leaders, on the other hand, date mainly from the post-war period, from the era in which the township assumed responsibility for its industrial and political development. Unhindered by recollections of how matters were handled in previous decades, these leaders, although younger and less expert at managing certain types of organizations, saw the township's growth potential and developed the policies for fulfilling that objective. Youthfulness also may have made township leaders more willing than city leaders to assume the financial and political risks involved in aggressive pursuit of economic growth (see Chapter 4).

Township leaders were a much more mobile group than city leaders. In fact, most of the persons regarded as leaders in 1958 no longer were leaders by 1963. By 1966, with only a few exceptions, leadership changes had again occurred. Since leadership structure clustered about the political institutions, changes in office holders resulted in rapid turnover. Success in terms of vote getting elevated the office holder to higher leadership levels commensurate with the office held, e.g., supervisor, clerk.

City leaders held positions in organizations that offered them status and potential for exercising influence. With the dearth of township-centered organizations, township leaders had to accept the "crumbs" of organizational affiliation designated to them by their city counterparts. Over half of the township leaders stated that they did not feel "comfortable in city organizations" or they had not been "made to feel at home." As a result, most of the township opportunity for leadership derived from participation in political parties, township government, or in the approximately ten civic organizations related to specific township neighborhoods.

Township residents had a much greater opportunity for gaining position and reputation as leaders in the township than city residents had in the city where apprenticeship was lengthy. One must qualify that a status differential existed between the organizations used to obtain leadership mobility in the city and those used for this purpose in the township. Nevertheless, the township newcomer could find suitable avenues for his talents in a shorter period of time, at least within the township.

The difference between channels of leadership mobility in city and township had serious consequences for efforts to reorganize local government. If the city and township were united politically, township leaders would have had greater difficulty maintaining positions in the leadership structure than city leaders. Lesser wealth, occupational status, and years of organizational experience may have placed the township leader at a considerable disadvantage. The greater opportunities for leadership mobility open to lower-middle-class and working-class persons in the township induced a fierce desire to preserve township autonomy. The struggle for autonomy was, to a considerable degree, an attempt to keep open the channels of mobility in the township leadership structure. The hostility of township leaders toward city leaders was intensified by fears of political subordination in the event of governmental reorganization. Surprisingly, many city leaders did not feel confident of their ability to dominate township leaders should merger occur (see Chapters 4, 5 and Part III).

Whatever the differences in the power of city leaders relative to township leaders, they had a clear superiority in most of the resources indispensable for power—wealth, prestige, contacts, and organizational know-how. Ultimately, leadership decision-making success must be measured in terms of the aims of community leadership itself. Regardless of the differences in the characteristics of city and township leadership structures, each was successful for a fourth of a century or longer in maintaining governmental autonomy and the retention of its own dominant features.

Vignettes

During the years of field work, certain city and township men and women were observed as they performed leadership roles within the sphere of area activities. A description of some of the most influential participants will make their functions more meaningful. A number of additional leaders who acted as important decision makers are analyzed in detail in subsequent chapters, i.e., the Chamber of Commerce executive secretary, the newspaper owner and editor, and governmental officials. The vignettes of seven city and five township leaders are not intended to expose the personalities of the several leaders—as interesting as they may be. They highlight pertinent facts that should enable the reader to comprehend their position and opportunity for decision making in Woodruff.

City Leaders

MICHAEL DAVENPORT was a local industrialist from an old and socially prominent family. He was born in 1903. Davenport's grandfather had settled in Woodruff shortly after the Civil War and had quickly prospered with the economic development of the area. The Davenport family, through an advantageous marriage and the accumulation of a fortune, was considered "old family" in Woodruff. Davenport's grandfather had helped organize and sustain the First National Bank, which had existed until 1933. His grandfather and father had served as bank president. The Davenports had helped organize the Country Club. Mike was president of the paper manufacturing company founded by his grandfather. He was a member of the Episcopal church, had served a term as president of the Woodruff Chamber of Commerce, belonged to many community organizations, and had served as the first mayor of Woodruff after the change to the city manager and nonpartisan forms. He served in that capacity for five years and as councilman for an additional three years. Davenport had attended Midstate University for several years.

ROBERT SAMPSON, as contrasted with Davenport, was a self-made local businessman and oil distributor who had been born in a small Iroquois County village in 1900. Sampson first came to work in Woodruff in 1917. After a series of business failures that forced him temporarily to leave Woodruff, he settled permanently in the city in 1926. Sampson, through hard work and acumen, had developed a lucrative and varied business enterprise. By investing much of his earned resources in real estate throughout the metropolitan area, he had become one of the wealthiest men in Woodruff. He was believed to be one of the few Woodruff millionaires.

Sampson was a member of the prestigious Presbyterian church, president of his own company, had served a term as president of the Woodruff Chamber of Commerce, and belonged to many community organizations. He had served as one of the Woodruff City representatives to the Iroquois Board of Supervisors for twenty-two years, 1943–65. In the early sixties he chaired a successful finance drive to purchase and construct a new campus and buildings for a local business college. Soon after, although possessing only a high school education himself, he assumed the position of college president. Sharply contrasting with Davenport, Sampson was "new" family, "new" business, and "new" money.

HAROLD SCHEIBLE came to Woodruff in 1889 at the age of three. His father established a prosperous hardware business which he continued. As an important merchant during the early years of the century, he had invested in local real estate, had participated in local government, been an active vigorous leader in the Chamber of Commerce, and held long time positions on the boards of the National Bank and the local Savings and Loan Association. Scheible held more board positions in Woodruff's economic organizations than any other leader in the community. His son, an attorney, gave up a position in an old and distinguished New York law firm to join the family business. By 1966, Scheible had launched his son into community and board service.

THOMAS MCDOWELL was born in 1880 and was the owner of a Woodruff furniture store that had been family owned since the early 1900's. His grandfather helped organize the Woodruff Savings and Loan Association. A member of the McDowell family had been on the board of the First National Bank in the twenties and McDowell was on the board of the National Bank of Woodruff. He was a member of the Congregational church, the Chamber of Commerce, and many other community organizations. McDowell's son, like Scheible's, had been launched in the late fifties and early sixties into community services that complemented the family's economic interests. McDowell's leadership activities and economic interests were similar to Scheible's.

R. JASON LOCKWOOD was born in Woodruff in 1905. His father had been a local merchant. He graduated from Midstate University's law school in 1927, practiced law for several years in another Midstate community, and in 1931, returned to Woodruff to open his own office. During the depression years he participated in the reorganization of the Country Club and helped organize the National Bank of Woodruff after the closing of its predecessor, the First National Bank. He served as attorney for the bank since the thirties, became a director in 1950, and president in April, 1963.

Lockwood also served as consulting attorney for the Woodruff

Township Board from 1941 to 1949. During the forties he also was local attorney for Pacific Motors. In these two capacities he assisted the township in the purchase of the federally owned water and sewer system. He also developed the legal plan to contest the 1950 annexation of Pacific Motors' plant and Shady Lea. In the early sixties he was elected a delegate to Midstate's Constitutional Convention. In this position he headed a successful Woodruff area campaign to support the new document.

Lockwood was active in the state and county bar associations, a past director of the Rotary Club, and a University regent. He was a member of the First Congregational church.

CARL ERICKSON came to Woodruff from a northern Midstate community when he was twenty-four years old. He established an office supply and gift store which prospered. Under his leadership the Jaycees campaigned for and won voter approval of the city manager—council form of government. Erickson served as a city official in several appointed capacities. He was a city representative with Sampson to the Iroquois County Board of Supervisors from 1941 to 1951. He chaired the city's first planning commission during 1951–60. Erickson was active in the Midstate Retail Association, the Woodruff Lions Club, the Chamber of Commerce, and was a member of the Methodist church. He was appointed a director of a Federal Savings and Loan Association in the Metropolitan City area that had a Woodruff branch. It was through his behind-the-scenes encouragement with another leader, Gerald Harding, that the abortive consolidation attempt of 1957–58 was made.

Township Leaders
JOSEPH ZELLER, a native of Woodruff, returned to the community after World War II and proceeded to build business interests in the township. By 1957, he owned a tavern, a gasoline station, a fuel-oil distribution center, a grocery store, and had several real estate ventures in progress. The tavern became the meeting place of political leaders during the 1957 township election and continued to fill that function until its sale by Zeller in 1960. During the consolidation campaign he received much publicity as an active leader of the opposition. He established a short-lived Township Businessmen's Association as the township's answer to the Woodruff Chamber of

Commerce. After an unsuccessful bid for a school board seat and his failure to provide the leadership required to maintain the township service club on a firm footing, Zeller's leadership position declined. By 1964, his name was seldom mentioned.

RONALD PASTER, born in Woodruff in 1920, was the owner of a large local dairy established by his father. A college graduate, he devoted much of his organizational energies to professional associations: National Holstein Association of America, Midstate Dairy Association, and Midstate Milk Producers. His only official governmental position was as a member of the Township Planning Board in 1943. Over the years he had played a behind-the-scenes leader role advising political aspirants of both political parties, using his money and influence to function in as free a manner as possible. For many years, as the township industrialized, he held one of the few stable positions in the township leadership structure, linking the rural leadership of the past with the transient leadership of the industrial present. He contributed a semblance of continuity to a fluid leadership structure. He was Catholic and had been a member of the Woodruff Chamber of Commerce. In 1965, after the sale of his extensive dairy land holdings, Paster moved to County Seat City.

RONALD PARKER, born in 1913, was not a native of Woodruff. He came to the township in 1947 to work as a skilled tool-and-die man at Pacific Motors. He and his wife had worked for many postwar years in township Democratic party circles. With a small nucleus, Parker helped to maintain the township Democratic party organization during the years of Republican majority. He had been instrumental in keeping Democratic party views before the Republican township officers. Parker ran an unsuccessful primary race for township supervisor in 1957. He was a very active member and strategist of the Save the Township Committee during the consolidation campaign. His wife was elected to the township board in 1961. The family belonged to the First Baptist church.

GARY JONES, born in the South in 1924, a graduate of Midstate University, came to Woodruff in 1951 as a metal specifications specialist at Midwest Motors. He was a member of the Church of Christ. With a group of other young township industry men he organized a study group that focused on township problems. In 1958, he became an important member of the Save the Township

Committee and its self-appointed tax expert. The recognition and success he gained during the consolidation campaign won him election to the position of township supervisor in 1959 and election to the state legislature in 1966.

BILL E. STRITE, a Baptist, was born in MacDowell, Kentucky, in 1933. He first came to Woodruff with his family with the wave of Appalachians seeking industrial employment. Strite went back to Kentucky in 1951 and returned again to Woodruff in 1956. In 1959, he left college in his senior year and ran a successful race on the Democratic ticket for township clerk. In 1961, he again won the clerk's office, showing more voting strength than he had in 1959. In 1963, he ran against Gary Jones for supervisor. His slate won but Strite lost. In 1964, he was elected township clerk for the third time.

Nonresident Leaders

Several persons named as leaders because they performed important functions in the Woodruff area did not reside in either the city or the township. Three were managers of the local facilities of absentee-owned corporations: the city plant of Midwest Motors, Universal Motors' township plant, and the Woodruff office of the electric utility company. In addition to the position as manager for absentee-owned corporations, these three men shared a number of additional characteristics. Each had been born in Midstate and lived in County Seat City. Each had held his present position in the Woodruff area for a relatively brief time. The manager of the utility company came to Woodruff in 1952, the official for Universal Motors came the following year, and the third manager in 1956. Of the three, the first devoted the greatest amount of time to community affairs. He was the only one of the three to attend any of the fund raising meetings for the first merger campaign. Each of these men belonged to the Woodruff Chamber of Commerce. Committee participation for the automotive officials was largely delegated to their lower-level executives. These men concentrated on company business but kept in touch with local occurrences pertinent to plant operations through reports from subordinates, some of whom resided in either the city or the township.

A fourth man, Donald Nelson, who received nominations as a

township leader, had been in continuous association with township affairs for approximately two decades. The few nominations that he received were not indicative of the influence he exercised on township policy and economic development.

Nelson was a partner in a County Seat City firm of sanitary engineers that was asked to plan the utility network for Shady Lea Village during World War II. Nelson performed much of the engineering work and subsequently was asked to advise the township board on the vital issue of whether or not to acquire the utility plants constructed in the township by the federal government. Nelson participated actively in the lengthy negotiations leading to the acquisition, and he subsequently was employed to establish the townships utilities department. When this task had been completed, the township board insisted that he serve as manager, a highly unorthodox arrangement since Nelson retained his position as partner in the engineering firm. This arrangement continued until 1963, when Nelson resigned as manager of the utilities department.

Conclusion

Gaining the reputation of a leader in the township required patterns of activity and possession of resources that differed in some ways from those required in the city. These differences had some bearing on patterns of intermunicipal relations. While acquiring a leadership reputation in the township seemed less difficult than in the city and more open to persons of lesser resources, retaining the reputation for an extended time period was more problematic.

Acquiring a reputation as a leader in the city depended, to a greater extent than in the township, on whether one's family had been active in local affairs. Personal reputation was partly a function of family reputation, in terms of a history of economic success and civic involvement. "Newcomers" who had acquired a leadership reputation without benefit of family background likewise had demonstrated some measure of success in a business or profession. The reputation for leadership skill often had been acquired from participation first in the Jaycee organization and then in the Chamber of Commerce. For both groups, leadership reputation was strengthened during the individual's mature period, in his mid-forties and above, by election to top offices in the Chamber, Rotary, the church, and selection for the boards of the three local fiscal institutions and to boards of local and county government.

In only a few instances did family play a corresponding role in the career of reputed township leaders. The prominent farm and small-business families that had dominated township affairs in the twenties and thirties were swept aside by the currents of industrial growth of the forties and fifties. The men with reputations as township leaders had come during and after this era, and they owed their status to hard work and skills acquired in the activities of political parties, government elections, and civic associations. Economically these men were settled in blue-collar occupations and small businesses or were junior-level executives in area manufacturing plants who hoped to attain higher statuses in industry. Election to a position on the township board, especially to one of the three full-time positions, often capped the individual's career as a local leader. The loss of an election, either in the primary or the main event, dimmed the individual's reputation. Even for those who had managed to retain their elected position for five or six years, the intense competition within each and between the two parties combined with the pressures of raising a family often led to a shift in interest to more private concerns. Usually the two or three persons whose positions rested more on a substantial business enterprise and covert involvement in politics, but not on an elected political office, retained their reputation as leaders for a longer time period. Turnover among township residents with a leadership reputation appeared higher than among city leaders. The greater fluidity of township as opposed to city leadership partly accounts for the considerable importance in township government of employed professionals, especially the consulting attorney and the manager of the utilities department.

Differences in the organizational base of city and township leadership may also have influenced the evolution of intermunicipal relations. The men and women who enjoyed reputations as township leaders did not have the positions in the organizations which reputed city leaders held. The occasions on which accomodations of area problems could be evolved and patterns of intermunicipal cooperation developed were thereby restricted largely to contacts between political officials. The meetings of the banks, of the Chamber, and of the top prestige service clubs did not provide an opportunity for friendships and mutual trust to develop among city and township leaders, nor did they provide occasions for mutual discussion of area problems and for developing agreements on co-operative action. Instead, the problems tended to be handled by government officials whose first consideration often was the probable reaction of the electorate.

The municipality with the more stable leadership patterns may appear to have a decided edge in any annexation or merger contest. The superiority of prestige, wealth, and organizational know-how might appear to confer considerable advantages in any "all-or-none" contest. This conclusion fails to consider two factors: first, the policies that guided municipal operations in city and township over the years; second, the skills that township leaders acquired from involvement in local politics. The importance of the first factor is examined in Chapters 4, 5 and 6, while the latter is taken up in Part III.

4. Municipal Sanitation and the Decision-Making Pattern

The decision-making record compiled in the area of environmental sanitation is a key by which social scientists may gauge the seriousness of leaders concerning community growth and development. While many leaders give lip service to such a commitment and may even encourage the development of industrial recruitment committees or the setting aside of land for an industrial park, these overt actions may not be indicative of actual priorities. Committees are easily organized and one risks little by setting aside land that may be unsuitable for industrial development. To support industrial growth and the consequential increase in population, a community must develop the sanitary facilities and capacities required to meet anticipated demands. A community must anticipate need and must act to meet that need. Sanitary facilities are costly and their anticipatory development is a clear monetary indication of the faith and interest of leadership in future community growth.

An additional measure is the level of sanitary services that have been developed to meet the day-to-day and crisis needs of the present population. A community that has failed to develop a level of services that can effectively care for existing residents and plants cannot provide sufficient services for outlying areas or new industries on a temporary basis until expanded facilities may be con-

73

structed. Purposeful or otherwise, this limitation will weaken a community's potential for industrial and geographical expansion.

Geographical Expansion

Residents of outlying areas often choose to become part of a city to obtain services essential for health and welfare. The success of Kalamazoo, Michigan, with extensive annexation was attributed in part to the refusal of the school board to accept students from outlying areas unless these sections joined the city. The value placed on education and also on sanitary services facilitated an increase in the city's territory of 143 percent in three years.[1] Voters in East Ann Arbor decided to join Ann Arbor, Michigan, in the fall of 1956 to obtain a number of city services, including water and sewage disposal.[2] Ostrom and associates report that Los Angeles compelled adjoining communities to accept annexation to obtain water.[3] The communities surrendered their identities as political entities to obtain this service. After examining the factors responsible for annexations in the San Francisco Bay area, Bollens concluded that the availability of city services for suburban areas often was decisive. He wrote, "The need for adequate sewer connections has largely determined the success of many recent Bay area annexation elections. . . ."[4] Refusal of the city to extend water mains and provide police and fire protection before annexation also contributed to electoral decisions to join the city.[5] Roscoe Martin summed up the role of sanitary services in the relations of municipalities. He hypothesized that the probability of outlying areas choosing to merge with a central city varies directly with the degree of their self-sufficiency for sanitary services, as indicated by the amount of investment in the requisite facilities.[6]

1. Clarence H. Elliott, "Kalamazoo Cited for Annexation Efforts," *Michigan Municipal Review,* 30 (October, 1957), 219–20.

2. "Favorable Vote Consolidates Two Michigan Cities," *Public Management,* 39 (January, 1957), 12.

3. Vincent Ostrom, Charles M. Tiebout, and Robert Warren, "The Organization of Government in Metropolitan Areas: A Theoretical Inquiry," *American Political Science Review,* 55 (December, 1961), 840.

4. John C. Bollens, "Elements of Successful Annexation," *Public Management,* 30 (April, 1949), 99.

5. *Ibid.,* p. 100.

6. Roscoe C. Martin, *Metropolis in Transition: Local Government Adap-*

A city can obtain concessions from suburbs in exchange for basic services. Salt Lake City used its water supply to control the development of the county. Grand Rapids, Michigan, established subdivision regulations in areas outside the city in exchange for providing sewerage disposal, water, and other services.[7] Where cities do not seek or cannot annex outlying areas, availability of needed services provides leverage for obtaining some measure of control over suburbia.

These considerations operated in the Woodruff area with special force. Since the city was surrounded on almost all sides by the township, territorial growth would be at the expense of the adjoining municipality. Prospects for success would depend greatly on whether the need for sanitary services could be satisfied by township government or by city hall. City and township were locked into a competitive situation. Neither municipality could plan for the future without taking into consideration the plans and resources of its neighbor. If city officials had high hopes for territorial, residential, and economic growth, they had to develop the facilities for serving township neighborhoods before township government acquired these capabilities.

---

tation to *Changing Urban Needs* (Washington, D.C.: U.S. Government Printing Office, 1963), pp. 103–4.

There are a few case studies of efforts to cope with water and sanitation problems. For an account that emphasizes the difficulties of gaining the co-operation of various governmental bodies in a metropolitan county see Roscoe C. Martin et al., *Decisions in Syracuse* (Bloomington, Ind.: Indiana University Press, 1961), Chs. IV, V.

Wildavsky discusses the factors leading to a choice among three plans for adequate provision of water for Oberlin, Ohio. Aaron Wildavsky, *Leadership in a Small Town* (Totowa, N.J.: Bedminster Press, 1964), Ch. 4.

For an interdisciplinary and quantitative approach to the organization of water systems see Arthur Maass et al., *Design of Water-Resource Systems: New Techniques for Relating Economic Objectives, Engineering Analyses, and Governmental Planning* (Cambridge, Mass.: Harvard University Press, 1962).

7. Edward C. Banfield and Morton Grodzins, "The Desirable and the Possible," in Edward C. Banfield, ed., *Urban Government: A Reader in Politics and Administration* (New York: The Free Press of Glencoe, 1961), pp. 86–87.

Winston-Salem adopted a plan whereby it not only extends utility mains to new subdivisions but pays part of the cost of these extensions if developers agree to observe the city standards on the design and construction of streets. "Suburban Utilities Plan Foresees Annexation," *Metropolitan Area Problems*, 5 (February, 1962), 7.

Woodruff's Industrial Potential

At the time that city officials planned the construction of the municipality's water treatment and sewerage disposal plants in the mid-thirties, there was an acute awareness of a shortage of land for economic and residential growth. This shortage had played some part in the loss of an enterprise that later grew and prospered elsewhere in Iroquois County. Efforts had been made in the twenties to annex township land, in which the availability of city services played an important part (see Chapter 7). Given the circumstances described below, development of surplus sanitary facilities to be used for carrying out a program of annexation could have been given a high priority in the planning of the sanitary facilities.

The shortage of land for industrial development was mentioned and discussed by Chamber of Commerce directors and some local leaders. Early in 1937 the chairman of the Chamber's Industrial Development Committee wrote of the problems of bringing industry to the community in the Chamber newsletter.[8] The Chamber received an average of one inquiry per week from firms expressing an interest in moving to Woodruff. It was difficult to accommodate these firms, the committee chairman wrote, since the city did not have suitable sites. The chairman expressed faith in the industrial future of the city because of the proximity to Metropolitan City. He made no proposal, however, for obtaining land suitable for industry.

Two years later, the shortage of land was considered at a meeting of Chamber directors.[9] The organization went on record as prepared to assist a "reliable and worthy manufacturer" to obtain an industrial site. The value of this resolution was negligible as directors felt that little could be done about the lack of land in the city. No mention was made of a program of annexation and related policies on water and sewerage.

During the depression, some Woodruff leaders were disturbed by the shortage of land for manufacturing enterprises. They expressed

8. "Industry At Highest Peak," *Publication of the Woodruff Chamber of Commerce,* 1 (January, 1937), 1.
9. Proceedings of the Board of Directors of the Woodruff Chamber of Commerce, January 10, 1939.

belief in the community's potential for economic expansion. Quite possibly the severity of the depression in the community had given leaders an appreciation of a sizable industrial payroll and tax base (see Chapter 5). Chamber members may have recalled the loss of a small manufacturing plant that had moved to another community in the county and was prospering. The firm moved after failing to find a location for an expanded facility. Not only did the enterprise prosper in its new home, a smaller and more receptive community, but in later years the owners acquired a much larger company and traded the stock of the firm on the New York Exchange. Over the years the company repaid its community backers handsomely for the interest shown during the first years of settlement.[10] The relocation of this firm cost Woodruff leadership talent along with tax base and payroll: the company maintained its national headquarters in the small town to which it had moved. The loss of a plant because of lack of land also might have led to higher priorities for surplus sanitary facilities.

The character of basic health services as a "means" for accomplishing the goal of territorial expansion provides the opportunity to study the influence of the two patterns of decision making. The decisions on the construction and expansion of utility plants and on extension of services to outlying areas indicate the nature of the goals that leaders pursued. Studying the sequence of these decisions over a period of time reveals the stability and duration of the decision-making patterns. If the goals of the decision-making pattern prescribed territorial expansion and industrial development, utilities would be used to facilitate annexation and merger. If wartime events increased the likelihood of annexation on a large scale, exploitation of these situations would be consistent with expansionist aspirations. Decisions limiting utility facilities over an extended time period under varying fiscal circumstances would indicate the strength of the goals of preserving Woodruff as a small city.

Previous discussions indicated that a number of factors influenced decision making (see Chapter 1). Leaders may be prevented from seeking certain goals because of a lack of resources. For this reason comparisons are made of decisions made in times of prosperity with comparable decisions made during the depression. Decisions made

10. Interview with a company director, March 9, 1961.

during a crisis may differ from decisions on the same matter made under more normal circumstances. The review of decisions since the thirties takes this factor into account, along with changes in the organization of Woodruff government and in the economic functions of the area. The difficulty of fully comparing events that occur at two or more points in time with different historical contexts is recognized. Data on decision making in utility development is presented separately for each unit of government before comparisons between the two are made. This order of presentation was selected to afford the reader the opportunity of judging, in a less confusing manner, the extent to which each unit has evolved a consistent pattern of decision making.

The City Utility Program

Utility Development in the Thirties

During the twenties and thirties pressures intensified on city officials to improve sewerage and water facilities. The sewerage disposal system, consisting of storm and sewer drains that emptied into the Iroquois River, did not provide for the treatment of wastes. The water system, built in 1889, included several wells, pumps, and an inadequate distribution network. Facilities were lacking for purifying water and reducing water hardness. The state health department, in the mid-twenties, took cognizance of the hazards created by these deficiencies and ordered city officials to end the pollution of the Iroquois River.

For over ten years city officials and leaders grappled with the problems of constructing the necessary facilities. Innumerable committee meetings and negotiations with federal agencies for financial assistance were held while placating impatient state health officers. The plans prepared by the city's firm of consulting engineers were reviewed carefully. The firm recommended a water purification plant with a rated capacity of 4 million gallons per day (m.g.d.) and a sewerage treatment plant with a capacity of 2 m.g.d. The recommendation for the water facility would give the city a capacity twice that of the present system. The engineers "talked themselves blue in the face" to convince city officials of the need for such a facility.[11] The latter responded by scaling down the plans. A sewer-

11. Interview with advisors of Woodruff administration, December 14, 1961.

age disposal plant with a rated capacity of 1.5 m.g.d. was built in 1938 and, in the following year, a water plant with 2 m.g.d. The years of effort and discussion that entered into the planning of the utility plants resulted in a water treatment plant with the same capacity as that of the fifty-year-old facility that it replaced.

The decisions of the mayor and the councilmen did not generate opposition. The decision that aroused the wrath of some local leaders concerned the vote of the city council to save $7,000 by excluding the equipment for reducing the hardness of the water. The Chamber of Commerce succeeded in persuading the city council to hold a referendum on the issue. The Chamber also led a successful fight for voter approval. The failure to wage a fight for utility plants with the capacities recommended by the engineers can be attributed to a lack of funds brought on by the depression. Conservation of fiscal resources had a far higher priority than territorial and economic growth.

The Wartime Boom
Woodruff entered the wartime era with sanitary facilities adequate for the city's current population and level of use, with very little surplus capacity. This circumstance was to play an important role in the decision to construct large and modern sanitary plants in the township.

The announcement early in 1941 that Midwest Motors, on behalf of the federal government, would construct a plant a few miles east of Woodruff for the manufacture of four-engine bombers seemed unbelievable to city leaders and area inhabitants. The residents were accustomed to factories with several thousand square feet and a labor force of several hundred. Employment at the local plant of Midwest Motors, the city's largest employer, was slightly more than 800 in 1936.[12] Initially employment at the township bomber factory was expected to reach 100,000.

Overnight the township acquired an industrial park, a huge industrial labor force and facilities that guaranteed industrial growth in the postwar era. The bomber plant had 3 million square feet and a peak labor force in excess of 40,000. Factory and equipment cost $57 million. An airport suitable for testing the aircraft was built

12. *Publication of the Woodruff Chamber of Commerce,* 1 (January, 1937), 1.

next to the factory. An expressway to Metropolitan City and local access roads were constructed at a cost of $16 million.[13] In a matter of months an enormous industrial plant, with rail, highway, and air transport facilities was constructed in what had been a rural township. The community experienced more industrial growth in one year than leaders could have achieved in a lifetime.

The decision to build the bomber plant in Woodruff Township was finalized without knowing where an adequate supply of water and housing would be found. Before construction of the factory, consulting engineers for Midwest Motors met with Woodruff officials to ascertain the amount of water, if any, the city could make available for factory use. The inquiry from Midwest Motors provided the opportunity to explore the possibility of obtaining federal assistance for financing utility expansion in exchange for providing the bomber plant with a large quantity of water. The risks to city taxpayers were negligible since federal, not local, funds would be used. Possession in the postwar period of utility plants with capacities sufficient to serve the factory and adjoining neighborhoods would enhance Woodruff's ability to control the development and political structure of the area.

If the availability of funds in the late thirties determined the decisions on the capacities of the two utility plants, the opportunity to obtain federal assistance during the early years of the war should have led Woodruff leaders to exploit the situation to the utmost. Federal agencies were willing to do what was necessary to expedite defense production and to meet the needs of the population engaged in the manufacture of strategic products. If Woodruff aided the bomber factory, its labor force, or both, there was every likelihood of obtaining federal funds for improving its utility systems.[14] Woodruff officials could have developed the two systems in accordance with the recommendations of their consulting engineers.

The primary concern of city officials at the meeting with the engineers representing Midwest Motors was protection of Woodruff's water system. Recognizing the limitations of a treatment plant

13. These facts were obtained from an article published during World War II in the *American Political Science Review*. An exact reference would reveal the identity of the community since the authors refer to it by name.

14. Interview with advisors of Woodruff administration, December 14, 1961.

that was barely adequate for local needs, city officials thought in terms of delivering an amount of water that would not overtax their facility.[15] They did not explore the possibility of expanding the city's water supply and treatment plant as the means for serving both the bomber factory and Woodruff's clientele. The maximum amount of water that officials could provide, 0.25 m.g.d., would meet the needs of the bomber plant during the initial construction phase. The federal government agreed to pay the cost of installing a pipe line to connect the treatment plant and the factory. The meeting ended with city officials having made clear to the engineers that water for the bomber plant would have to be obtained elsewhere.

Company engineers searched the township for an adequate source of water. An area suitable for wells was found about a mile west of the factory site. The engineers prepared plans for construction of wells and of a water treatment plant with a capacity of 6 m.g.d. At a subsequent meeting this plan was chosen over several others including a proposal by Woodruff's firm of consulting engineers. The firm, at the request of the federal government, prepared a plan for serving the bomber plant. The city's water supply would be increased by tapping a well source near County Seat City and piping it to an expanded treatment plant.[16] The essentials of this plan were implemented by city officials in 1964. It was just as feasible in 1941 as it was twenty-three years later.

The federal government also financed construction of a sewerage disposal plant in the township. It had primary and secondary treatment, and a capacity of 4.5 m.g.d., adequate for a population of 60,000.

The water facilities built in the township served the factory throughout the war. This arrangement may have been the most feasible and expeditious way to meet the urgent need for uninterrupted production of bombers. Whether alternative arrangements would have worked as well or better may never be known. The situation facing officials of Midwest Motors and their engineers might have looked different had the city been able to provide more than 2 m.g.d. This would have been the case if the recommenda-

15. Interview with a member of the firm of consulting engineers employed by Midwest Motors, October 31, 1961.
16. Interview with advisors of Woodruff administration, December 14, 1961.

tions of their engineers had been followed a few years earlier. Under these circumstances, serving the bomber plant from the city's plant, or from the latter and a smaller plant in the township, might have appeared more advantageous.

Water for Shady Lea Village

Hope of obtaining funds for expanding the two utility plants was not yet lost. A year after the decision had been made to build utility plants in the township to service the bomber plant, city officials were given a second opportunity. Officials of federal agencies requested permission to use the city water temporarily supplied to the bomber factory for the residents of the Shady Lea housing to be constructed in Woodruff and Summitt Townships. When the waterworks was completed in the township, the factory no longer would need city water. If permission were granted, it would be unnecessary to build water facilities in the village. Acquiescence by city officials would increase the need for expansion of the water plant and strengthen the case for federal financing.

The leaders and officials of the city allowed other considerations to outweigh the postwar industrial and fiscal needs of the municipality. When the announcement was made of the decision to construct a housing village near the factory, County Seat City officials, the County Board of Supervisors, and Woodruff City leaders protested vigorously. For months these groups had argued that defense workers should be housed in nearby communities. It was felt that if the problems of adapting to a rapid influx of thousands of persons could be distributed among many communities, the basic character of the county and of Woodruff would remain intact.

Fears of change focused on a handful of considerations. The idea of a housing village in one area was identified with the United Automobile Workers whose president had advocated a "model" village as the solution to the problem of housing the defense workers. A high administration official, who had been a powerful union leader, had spoken in favor of this proposal to President Roosevelt.[17] Local leaders feared that a heavy influx of defense workers would strengthen the Democratic party and UAW locals, also. As two observers expressed it, "Underlying the opposition was the fear

17. *The Woodruff Press,* November 14, 1941.

that a bomber city . . . would be a CIO city, therefore Democratic, and a menace to Republican control of the county. . . ."[18]

Woodruff residents feared that low-cost government housing would depress property values and create slum conditions in the township, and this concern had some justification. Hundreds of trailers and shacks appeared in the eastern part of the township while the bomber plant was under construction. Babies were born in tents in below zero weather. Young children played in dirt contaminated by leakage from septic tanks.[19] City and county leaders envisioned the village area as a permanent slum. In a "white paper" that expressed the attitudes of county officials, the county prosecutor described the proposed housing project as "a concentration of low-cost, uniform dwellings which, after the cessation of abnormal industrial activity in the region, will become an eye-sore attracting solely the lower class of inhabitants. . . ."[20]

The prospect of a sprawling slum in the northeastern part of the township inhabited by a horde of rural folk unaccustomed to urban living appalled most local residents. Fear that these people would be the bulwark of a militant, union-controlled Democratic party inspired deep anxiety in the minds of community leaders. The economic needs of the city during and after the war were difficult to remember while considering the political implications of urbanization.

The necessity to determine the type and scope of responsibility for the township was forced on Woodruff in the fall of 1942, when federal officials requested the transfer of the water supplied the plant to Shady Lea Village. This request was made several months after city officials had submitted proposals for close to a million dollars of federal money for the expansion of water and sewerage facilities. City officials had been informed by the Federal Works Agency that approval was delayed pending clarification of the anticipated housing needs of the community.[21] Presumably the grant

18. Article published in the *American Political Science Review*. See note 13 above.
19. Interview with the county health officer, August 3, 1961.
20. County prosecutor, "Outline Statement of Position of Iroquois County on Proposed New Federal City at Shady Lea," May 12, 1942.
21. Letter from regional project control officer of Federal Works Agency to manager of Woodruff Water Department, September 4, 1942.

would be approved if the need for additional utility services could be demonstrated.

Woodruff would have benefited from expansion of its two utility systems. Woodruff would gain options that it did not possess and that it might not obtain in the years ahead. By providing assistance to the Village, a sizable area of the township would be dependent upon the city for basic services. The area served could be expanded in postwar years to keep pace with residential, commercial, and industrial developments. The city would have demonstrated concern for and ability to handle the needs of outlying areas. These circumstances taken together would have improved the possibility of annexing the area after the war had ended. From the standpoint of future growth, Woodruff had nothing to lose by granting permission to use the water for Shady Lea Village.

Officials of the Federal Public Housing Agency met with the Board of Public Works on September 18 and September 24, 1942, to obtain permission to divert city water from the bomber factory to the village. At the second meeting the request was framed in these terms: ". . . the Federal Works Agency asked the Board . . . (to grant) use of water for said Federal Housing Project up to 250,000 gallons a day for 3,000 dormitories and 480 2-family trailers on foundations. . . ."[22]

City officials, at the initial meeting, did not approve the request. They asked instead for federal approval of its plans for expansion of the water system. The response of city officials at the second meeting was even more tentative, suggesting that approval of the request from the agency depends on the "flow of water shown by new well developments."[23] In essence, city officials did not explicitly and definitively turn down the request but made demands that federal officials were unwilling or unable to meet. City officials showed little disposition to co-operate with federal agencies in meeting the pressing needs of the bomber plant workers, their families, and the township. Federal officials responded not by scrapping plans for the housing of defense workers but by financing construction of wells and water mains to serve village residents.

A few weeks later, on October 16, 1942, city officials were noti-

22. Proceedings of the Woodruff Board of Public Works, September 24, 1942.
23. *Ibid.*

fied that the proposal for expansion of the *sewerage* disposal system had been placed in a "deferred classification." The door was left open for reviewing the proposal. If conditions changed and the need for service increased, city officials could request reconsideration of their application. Nothing was said about the proposal for improvement of the waterworks system.[24]

If this notification was intended as a warning, city officials ignored it. No effort was made to reopen negotiations on providing water for the village. Early in 1943, the Federal Works Agency approved a small grant of $34,000 for waterworks improvement in Woodruff. This amount was not sufficient to undertake the program suggested originally by the firm of consulting engineers.

Woodruff received little or no financial aid from the federal government for its utility systems during the war although it was the center of a major defense production area. Since the community had made little or no contribution to housing defense workers, either within or without the city, the need for utility improvement was considered less urgent by federal officials than those of nearby cities.

Woodruff officials ignored the opportunity to control the postwar development of the area and to remedy the city's land shortage and the inevitable fiscal problems it had faced in the past and would face in the future because of an inadequate tax base. Perhaps never again in the history of the community would an opportunity present itself to acquire funds for doubling or trebling the capacities of the water filtration and sewerage disposal plants.

The dangers of overcommitment might explain the actions of city leaders. At least it provided an excellent rationalization. No one in 1942 knew the future use of the bomber plant. While Midwest Motors had an option for its postwar purchase, city leaders had no knowledge of corporation plans. It is doubtful that company executives knew in 1942 whether or not the plant would be purchased. Furthermore, it was widely believed that the postwar problems of reconverting to peacetime production would bring on a serious recession. City residents could well imagine what that would do to their community. Investment of capital in unneeded utility facilities might have been considered wasteful.

This explanation must be rejected for an obvious reason. Im-

24. Proceedings of the Woodruff Board of Public Works, October 16, 1942.

provement of the utility systems would have been financed by federal money. Consequences of violating the marginal cost rule would have been minimal for the community.[25] The inaction of city officials was directed at preserving control of the city by the higher income, property-owning, Republican families and maintaining the *status quo* in governmental structure. City leaders hoped to prevent the transfer of political power to the UAW and "hillbillies." Presumably these goals could be attained by not encouraging the continued operation of the factory and of Shady Lea Village in the postwar period. If the village became a "ghost town" at the end of the war, the threat to Republican control would be ended. City officials, as the consultant for the National Resources Planning Board put it, "didn't seem to realize that the bomber plant was there."[26]

In rejecting requests for services, Woodruff officials created a reservoir of ill will among township citizens. By opposing construction of the housing village in the Woodruff area, by attacking the original suggestion of permanent housing in preference for temporary housing, and by rejecting requests for water for the village, city leaders conveyed an impression of disinterest if not antagonism toward township needs. City officials had no intention of "being a good neighbor," of extending a helping hand to those in need who, at the same time, were producing an important military weapon. During the merger campaigns that occurred fifteen and twenty years later, township residents were constantly reminded of Woodruff's antipathy to the needs of their municipality.

City leaders may be credited with one dubious distinction. The community survived the boom of the war years with no additions to the two utility plants, although they operated for periods of time beyond design capacity. A report in *The Woodruff Press* on July 29, 1942, stated that the water plant had pumped over 2 m.g.d., the design capacity, on the previous day. On August 1, 1942, the local paper stated that a water shortage had seemed imminent sev-

25. Manuel Gottlieb, "The Milwaukee Waterworks Expansion: A Case Study in Urban Investment Planning," *Public Administration Review,* 24 (December, 1964), 224. The rule states that the expenditure of revenue for improvements in facilities is not justified unless the change produces funds sufficient to meet the costs involved.

26. Interview on February 2, 1962. The consultant had made numerous visits to Woodruff to meet with and advise local officials in 1941 and 1942.

eral times during July. The gravity of the situation was revealed in a March 12, 1942, report to the Board of Public Works by their consulting engineer who urged preparation of a request for federal funds. The engineer stated: "Woodruff is in the so-called 'defense area' and regardless of where the main Federal housing project may be located the Woodruff utilities, both water and sewer, will be sorely taxed to meet the new situation. This condition is now indicated by the increased pumpage at the water works plant and by the increased flow at the sewage disposal plant. The fact is . . . the water works plant at the present time has already exceeded its capacity. . . ."[27] When the war ended, Woodruff faced the future with utility systems that were incapable of meeting the needs of a growing population and economy.

Postwar City Utility Developments: Disposal of
Township Utility Plants
The lack of concern of city officials for residents and industrial operations in the township could have been caused by fears of overcommitment. If substantial improvements in its utility facilities had been made and the area reverted to its prewar economy, city government might have difficulty in financing operations of a water and sewerage system with more capacity than was needed in the foreseeable future.

If these factors were uppermost in the minds of Woodruff's officials, action should have been taken as soon as the war had ended to gain control over the development of the city's hinterland. The industrial future of the area received a substantial boost in the fall of 1945. After Midwest Motors refused to exercise its option to purchase the bomber plant, Pacific Motors acquired it to manufacture automobiles, and Midstate University purchased the airport. The corporation also operated the water and sewerage plants, which it leased from the federal government. During the period that these arrangements were made, there were no signs of interest from city officials in exploring the possibility of city ownership or city operation of the utility plants in the township.

Soon thereafter, the legal staff of Pacific Motors made a discovery that led to the decision to discontinue operation of the utility plants.

27. Proceedings of Woodruff Board of Public Works, March 12, 1942.

Leasing the utility plants made the company subject to regulation by the state utilities commission. While seeking a solution to this problem, the executive in charge of the utilities for Pacific Motors, T. F. Vanderpoole, discovered that regulations of the War Assets Administration provided for the sale of surplus property at virtually a 100 percent discount if health problems existed which these facilities could alleviate.[28] Vanderpoole brought these matters to the attention of the township attorney, R. Jason Lockwood, who presented them to the township board. The board employed Donald Nelson and his firm of consulting engineers to determine whether ownership and operation by the township was feasible. After weeks of careful study, at a special meeting on Friday evening, April 12, 1946, the township board authorized the supervisor and treasurer to go to Washington to "confer with officials of the Excess Property Corporation and the officials of Pacific Motors Corporation relating to the leasing or purchasing of the Public Utilities connected with the former Shady Lea Bomber Plant."[29] Negotiations were consummated two years later. The township board purchased the two utility plants, distribution systems, and wells for the token price of $75,000. Officials also promised to finance the improvement of the distribution system to alleviate the health problems in the heavily populated areas east of the city. With this agreement, the township gained control of its future.

Woodruff officials may have had little opportunity to acquire the utility systems. First, since the facilities were leased, operated, and used by Pacific Motors, the company's preference would be given considerable weight. Second, the company aroused and encouraged the interest of township officials in acquiring the facilities. Third, city officials in the recent past had not shown any disposition to help meet the pressing problems of the township. City officials had provided minimal assistance for the bomber plant and none for Shady Lea Village.

In light of these factors, one would not expect knowledgeable informants to assert that Woodruff officials had an "opportunity" to purchase the utility plants. Nevertheless, several persons who

28. Interview with a former top executive of Pacific Motors, August 15, 1961.
29. Proceedings of the Woodruff Township Board, April 12, 1946.

held responsible positions in city government in 1946 and 1947 mentioned that the city had had this opportunity.

The city's opportunity grew out of the disagreement between federal officials and township representatives over the purchase price. Since the township had little capital with which to purchase the facilities, its officials emphasized the health needs of the area in an effort to force the price down to the lowest possible level. At one point, federal officials asked $95,000 and township officials offered $40,000.[30] The decisive factor enabling the township to acquire the facilities at a lower price was the report of the county health officer on the health hazards existing in the township. This report, according to township attorney Lockwood, referred to the "germs in effluence flowing along open drainage ditches, not respecting boundaries."[31]

The purchase price was emphasized by a former member of the city administration. Woodruff officials refrained from bidding for the utility systems to avoid "jacking up the price."[32] Competition with the township would not benefit either municipality. By refusing to enter the negotiations, Woodruff officials simplified the township's problems in acquiring the facilities, since the federal government had no other purchaser. At a later stage in the transaction, the executive secretary of the Chamber of Commerce and other local leaders flew to Washington in a Pacific Motors plane to actively endorse the township's bid for the facilities.

Whether Woodruff would have been offered the facilities if it had outbid the township is problematic. The evidence suggests that the city did have a definite "opportunity" to acquire the facilities, and officials deliberately refrained from utilizing it. A member of the Woodruff Planning Commission at the time of the negotiations reported several meetings devoted to preparation of a bid for the township utilities. The matter was dropped precipitously and no additional meetings were held on the subject.[33]

The inaction of city leaders is partially explained by the condi-

30. Interview with former township supervisor, August 11, 1961.
31. Interview with former township attorney, September 28, 1961.
32. Interview with former member of Woodruff administration, May 19, 1961. The informant was given the opportunity to explain city inaction on legal grounds, declined to use it, and volunteered the above version. These facts increase confidence in the validity of the explanation.
33. Interview with former Planning Commission member, April 6, 1961.

tions of the sale of the utilities. The health problems in the eastern section of the township had to be rectified. This required development of a water distribution system for heavily populated areas. To accomplish this objective, township officials promised to issue bonds totalling $600,000. City officials would not increase municipal debt to alleviate township health problems and assist township residents. If Pacific Motors folded, the area might become "a ghost town," and Woodruff would be "stuck" with a large bonded indebtedness.

City leaders did not seem to envision the city and urbanized part of the township as one municipality. Confirmation is provided by Vanderpoole, the Pacific Motors executive, who lived in Woodruff from 1945 to 1951. In his opinion, the decisions of city officials were based on the assumption that ". . . the bomber plant and the population influx were passing phenomena. City leaders gave no thought to long-range planning for the future. They expected the community to return to the quiet town that existed before the war."[34] A long-term member of the city administration unknowingly agreed with this viewpoint when he said, with some feeling, that the postwar reasoning of city officials would have been correct if a fire in 1953 had not forced Universal Motors to purchase the bomber plant from Pacific Motors. Had it not been for the fire, the factory would have stood empty, and members of its labor force would have left the community.[35]

City officials failed to take positive steps toward acquiring the utility systems. An official of the General Services Administration stated: ". . . our records do not indicate that there was any communication between the War Assets Administration and the City of Woodruff concerning the water and sewage systems serving the Shady Lea Bomber Plant or that the City was interested in acquiring the systems."[36]

City officials had short memories. In the late thirties, members of the Chamber of Commerce were convinced that locational advantages assured the community's future as an industrial center. A few years later, with facilities that no one in Woodruff in 1937 possibly could have envisioned—a vast manufacturing plant, a modern and

34. Interview with former Pacific Motors executive, August 15, 1961.
35. Interview with Woodruff administration official, May 28, 1962.
36. Letter from Curtis A. Roos, Director, Disposal and Acquisition Services, Public Buildings Service, General Services Administration, Washington, D.C., May 25, 1961.

spacious airport, utility plants with surplus capacity, and an expressway that connected the area to Metropolitan City—community leaders were convinced that corporations would not locate plants in the Woodruff area. Any justification for this assumption disappeared when Pacific Motors acquired the factory in the fall of 1945.

Woodruff officials and leaders refused to recognize the significance of the legacy of the community's wartime role. They preferred to believe that the township would revert to its rural, open-country, undeveloped condition. Shady Lea Village would be deserted, a mere reminder of the community's role in World War II. Thus merger with the township would be illogical, unnecessary, and wasteful of the taxpayer's money. Divided government would continue to be functional for the area.

Expansion of City Utility Plants
The township's acquisition of the water and sewerage disposal systems altered relationships between the two municipalities. Township government could influence the rate and degree of economic and population development. It could deprive Woodruff officials of the one major inducement for annexation of township land, provision of sanitary services. Aggressive development of the utility systems and extension of services to all developed areas would encircle Woodruff with trunk-line utility mains. This development would virtually terminate Woodruff's prospects for territorial expansion. The probability of city encirclement by township mains was enhanced by the willingness of Pacific Motors to pay higher utility rates to permit rapid amortization of the township revenue bonds. The utility department would enjoy a higher than customary level of profitability during its first years of operation.

The Woodruff City administration could not avoid a contest with the township board involving which municipality would first extend utility mains west of the city. If city leaders had any hope of winning the race, the capacities of the two utility plants had to be expanded. Woodruff's first city manager, who took office in 1947, calculated the cost of the improvements in 1948 and in 1950 to be approximately a million dollars.[37] He decided, after consultations

37. Report from the Woodruff city manager to the mayor and councilmen, March 5, 1951. In this report the city manager disagreed with the recommendation of the consulting engineer that the waterworks plant be expanded immediately. He preferred a piecemeal program of improvements.

with Mayor Davenport and the councilmen, that the "voters" would not endorse the program. As an alternative he proposed, early in 1951, a number of stop-gap measures. These included acceptance of the offer from the township engineer to sell water to the city up to 1 m.g.d., an offer that was put forth only a few months after the city had filed petitions to annex most of the eastern half of the township, including the utility plants. Viewing this offer to augment the city's supply of water as a justification for delaying expansion of the utility plant, the city manager urged acceptance of the township bid. This was done and improvement of the water plant was delayed.

Fiscal capability could not have dictated this response since the property tax, after 1946, had been cut repeatedly, with no increase in assessment levels. The rate dropped from 20.76 mills in 1946 to about 14 mills in 1950, the lowest since 1936. The millage rate remained at this low level for five years, when it was raised to 15.12 mills. Maintaining the millage rate at the 14 mill level from 1950 to 1954 was made possible by a 36 percent increase in the value of assessed property and by the sale of several municipal facilities.

The consulting engineers for Woodruff repeatedly urged expansion of the utility plants. In 1948, if not before, and again in 1950, efforts were made to persuade city leaders to improve the facilities.[38] The nature of the situation was clearly indicated in a letter dated March 28, 1952, from the consulting engineer to the city manager:

> We know that you realize full well the fact that for the last four years your present plant (waterworks) has been operating under an annual average load that is in excess of its design capacity and that during this period there has been several months in which the load has been twenty-five percent over capacity and many days in which the load has been fifty percent over capacity. It is too much to expect any plant to continue to function satisfactorily under these conditions and we hope that some relief might be provided before there is a serious breakdown in these facilities.[39]

City officials responded by postponing expansion until 1955. In that year voters were asked to approve a bond issue for the expansion of the water and sewerage plants. However, the bond issue had been reduced in scope from the level recommended by the consulting engineers. The capacity of the water plant was to be doubled rather

38. Proceedings of the Woodruff City Council, July 10, 1950.
39. City manager's file, March 28, 1952.

than trebled. The superintendent of the water department, when informed of the reduction in the bond issue, told the city manager that the expansion would merely "enable the city to catch up with demand."[40] Surplus capacity for handling increased demands still would be lacking.

Postponement of improvements in the two utility plants limited Woodruff's ability to take advantage of opportunities for annexation which later became available through no effort of the city leaders. In 1953, representatives of the Country Club area requested water from the city council. The wells developed and owned by their property owners' association were no longer adequate for a growing neighborhood. City officials refused to provide service prior to annexation. Residents of Country Club, with the help of Nelson, developed new wells that sufficed until a trunk-line main from the township water plant reached the neighborhood some years later.

The consequences of Woodruff's responses became even more apparent in 1957. A serious pollution problem had existed in the Country Club area for several years. Annual epidemics of infectious hepatitis and diarrhea endangered the health of residents. Although the city's sewerage plant was seriously overburdened, the state health department granted Woodruff permission to extend a sewerage main to the Country Club area. At the time this represented the best and most expedient solution. The thrift propensities of the decision-making pattern led to a negative response. Since the main would pass through undeveloped land before reaching the neighborhood, the cost of the extension could not be levied entirely on the families to be served. The municipality would have to bear part of the cost until such time as reimbursement could be obtained from those who settled on the vacant territory. Woodruff officials considered the expense too great and refused to authorize construction of the line. If city officials had gambled, if they had taken the risks entailed by providing water in 1953 and sewerage disposal in 1957, an area already tied to the city by social and political interests would have been dependent for the most basic of all services. Not only would chances of annexation have greatly improved, but the township engineer might have been unable to justify to state authorities the extension of a trunk-line main to the area several years later. If

40. Interview with member of Woodruff administration, June 14, 1962.

this had happened, the township board, in effect, would have abandoned hope of preventing the city from annexing much of the west side.

In the spring of 1959, the pollution problem on the west side had not been eliminated despite the order of several years standing from the state health department to the county drain commissioner for remedial action. City officials offered to provide services to Country Club if annexation occurred. Plans for annexation were developed, and in October of 1959, *The Woodruff Press* reported the impending publication of a booklet presenting the advantages of this change.[41] During an interview a few months earlier, the mayor confidently predicted a successful outcome. Again Nelson defeated the plan. He sought and obtained permission from the State Health Department to extend a trunk-line sewer main to the west side. After the township board announced plans to provide this service, the city council abandoned its annexation plan. Petitions were not filed, and the booklet citing the advantages of joining the city was not published.

Defeat of the plan to annex the Country Club area reveals the close connection between city spatial growth and availability of utility services. The addition of 610 acres the previous year, in 1958, can be attributed to this relationship. It was difficult for the township to service the extreme northwest corner of the municipality because of the necessity of pumping water against the force of gravity. Since Woodruff could service the area before the township, the principal land owners, who hoped to develop residential neighborhoods, pushed successfully for annexation.

The proddings of the consulting engineers and city manager produced partial results in the late fifties and decisions in 1964 appropriate for a city with hopes of growth. The administration accepted the recommendation in the late fifties to construct a sixteen-inch trunk-line water main around the periphery of the city. The size and location of the mains would permit extension of service to outlying territory. The plan that the consulting engineers had proposed in 1941 for water supply and treatment plant expansion also was implemented. The city council approved a bond issue without first seeking voter approval. The city council finally exercised initiative

41. *The Woodruff Press,* October 21, 1959.

on fiscal policy for the utility system. Funds were used to construct a pipeline to a source of water near County Seat City and to expand the capacity of the water plant to 8 m.g.d. For the first time in over twenty years Woodruff had sufficient surplus capacity in its waterworks plant. Since the improvements were completed after the township board had extended water and sewerage mains west of the city, the city had little chance to use its surplus for territorial expansion. The plant expansion might never have occurred as long as a dependency relationship existed between city and township which could result in township demands for city services.

The Township Utility Program

Acquisition of Wartime Facilities

Township leaders faced the same uncertainties at war's end which confronted city leaders. If Pacific Motors failed, the township board would be unable to meet the payments on any large bond issue. Continued industrial development of the township would strengthen the Democratic party and undermine Republican control of local government. For these reasons and those mentioned below, township officials did not hasten to purchase the utility systems.

Reluctance of township officials to acquire the utility plants could be attributed in part to factors not applicable to city government. The township board had little experience in providing services requiring the operation, maintenance, and financing of valuable equipment. Officials were unfamiliar with the money market and the intricacies of floating a bond issue. The amount of money required for managing an urban municipality seemed enormous. The absence of a utilities department for managing the facilities and the lack of office space intensified doubts on the advisability of acquiring the water and sewerage systems. Once the acquisition was made, township officials would have problems whose solution required extensive change in the organization and activities of local government.

Township officials rejected several alternatives to township ownership and operation of the utility plants. Purchase and operation by a private company would have maintained the autonomy of the township, without requiring township government to manage a complex enterprise. Township officials rejected this alternative since a private company might place profits ahead of the interests of the municipality.[42]

A procedure that received some consideration was continued operation of the facilities for township government by Pacific Motors. The evidence indicates that this arrangement was suggested initially by executives of Pacific Motors.[43] After township officials expressed interest, executives urged government operation and ownership. The urgings of Pacific Motors executives and of Donald Nelson, consulting engineer, led to the acquisition. Nelson assured board members that the financial and technical problems of utilities operations could be handled. With the aspirations for independence of the municipality, the discount in price offered by the federal government, and the township supervisor's belief that the purchase would prevent the city from annexing township land, acquisition was assured.[44]

Growth and Development of Facilities

The arrangement that the township board made with Donald Nelson facilitated the economic development of the municipality. It gave considerable authority to a man who understood fully the relationships between utilities development, municipal growth, and political autonomy. Nelson was determined to use his powers, both as manager of the combined sewerage and water department and as partner in a firm of consulting engineers, to achieve these objectives. He functioned both as a planner and an administrator.

Solvency of the utility systems depended initially on the ability of Pacific Motors to pay service rates that allowed rapid amortization of the bonds. In the long run, the profitability of the water and sewerage department depended on the market; department operations encouraged rapid growth of demand for water and sewerage services. This required, in contrast with Woodruff's policies, expan-

42. The private holding company that owned the water company serving Onondaga County, New York, was concerned primarily with maximizing short-run gains and deferring capital improvements. Martin et al., *Decisions in Syracuse,* pp. 113–14.

43. Review of the proposed contract between Pacific Motors and Woodruff Township Board by consulting engineer, July 1, 1946.

44. Interview with former member of Township Board, August 11, 1961.

sion and improvement of the systems in advance of need, *before* the plants operated in excess of rated capacity. Wherever possible, trunk-line mains were to be extended to areas before development. The engineer's recommendations usually were accepted by the township board with few revisions.

After the township acquired the utility systems in 1948, bonds were sold and mains were extended to the heavily populated areas. Seven years later, a bond issue of close to a million dollars was sold. The proceeds were used to redeem the bonds issued in 1948 and to finance expansion of trunk-line mains on East Midstate Avenue. Less than three years later another million-dollar bond issue financed new trunk-line extensions and doubled the capacity of the filtration plant to 12 m.g.d. Early in the sixties a million-dollar bond issue financed expansion of both water and sewerage mains to areas west of Woodruff. When this program was completed in 1963, the city was virtually encircled by the township's utility mains. In 1965, the capacity of the sewerage disposal plant was increased to 8 m.g.d., and exploration began for new sources of water.

In the sixties, Woodruff Township arranged to provide utility services to neighboring townships. An area in the township west of the city purchased water and sewerage services. Negotiations with Summitt Township were initiated after Woodruff City filed petitions in 1965 to annex 1,500 acres of its territory. The township to the south became interested in utilities services after a corporation decided to build a cement plant within its borders. Officials of Woodruff Township and of the township to the west announced, in 1966, the formation of an area sewerage authority. The authority could issue revenue bonds for utility development at a low rate of interest.[45] Woodruff Township was becoming a bulwark of balkanized government in the County Seat metropolis.

The decision-making pattern of the township responsible for these and related developments contrasted sharply with that of the city. While city leaders advocated a restricted community role for local government, township leaders saw the governmental apparatus as the principal mechanism for achieving continued industrial and population growth. The risks entailed in meeting the financial needs of the utility systems, occasioned by fluctuations in the auto indus-

45. *The Woodruff Press,* August 10, 1966.

try, were to be undertaken with the best possible safeguards for the solvency of the water and sewerage department and the township government. But the risks were to be endured, not avoided. The objective of growth was pursued despite the fact that, if successful, a large proportion of the newcomers to the area would be operatives in the automobile plants, members of powerful unions, and sympathetic to the Democratic party. The pursuit was initiated by a Republican township board and members of the local Republican party although it was inevitable that the Democratic party, which only barely existed in the township until after the war, would gain strength sufficient for controlling some if not all of the township political offices. If redistribution of political power was the price for continued township autonomy and for economic and population growth, it would have to be paid. The overriding objective, to which all others were subordinated, was the maintenance of township autonomy and independence. Township government had to meet the needs of a growing and varied clientele.

The degree of risk that township leaders accepted with the purchase of the utility systems and that city leaders avoided should not be minimized. In 1953, Pacific Motors planned to abandon the former bomber plant and transfer operations to another city. Nelson had some sleepless nights, and bank officials worried over loans to employees of the automobile concern. A major fire in a plant in another city led Universal Motors to purchase the factory. In a few months, the economic health of the Woodruff area improved dramatically.

Analysis

Both city and township governments were subject to factors limiting availability of the fiscal inputs needed for effective operation. A small territory restricted the growth of Woodruff's industrial activity and tax base. This limitation proved especially serious when conditions created by the wartime emergency resulted in the construction of facilities needed by the city in the adjacent municipality. The tension created by this situation was intensified by restrictions imposed on township officials by regulations specific to the township form of government. Taxes could not be levied without first obtaining the approval of the voters. While a rural township never might need to levy a tax, this stipulation would seriously limit the availability of funds for an industrial municipality.

These features of city and township produced a state of conflict that became increasingly serious as population and industrial activity grew. As the two municipalities became more urbanized, the demands made upon each unit of government for provision of essential services also increased. At the same time, industrialization of the township contributed minimally to that municipality's treasury and only indirectly helped that of city government. The imbalance in each municipality between output for services and input of fiscal resources led to a growing concern and recognition of the need for change.

With construction of the bomber factory and utility plants in the township, relationships of the two municipalities assumed greater importance. While in the past growth had been the obvious solution to Woodruff's problems, the opportunity to annex both factories and utility plants made expansion even more appealing. City government would have taxing power over lucrative sources of revenue and control over the sanitary services needed to guide further growth.

The opportunity for the township was no less significant. Operating a utilities department on a self-supporting basis offered freedom from the normal restrictions of township government. User charges, not taxes, would be the principal source of income. Voter approval also could be bypassed in financing improvement of sanitary facilities through issuance of revenue bonds. A proper rate schedule and a substantial rate of growth in industrial demand virtually would guarantee the self-sufficiency of the utilities department. If this proved correct, township government also would expand, both in output of services and in manpower. By functioning effectively to provide services essential for life and health and for a growing economy, township government could demonstrate its viability and sustain its claim to legitimacy.

The principal flaw in this strategy derived from the limitations in the taxing power of township government. The growth of population, economy, and institutions inevitably would increase the strain on township government for services that could not be financed by user charges but would require more revenue than that provided by rebates from county and state governments.

In considering industrialization as the means for adjusting amount of fiscal input with demand for municipal services, several matters had to be considered. One set pertained to the factors that would facilitate industrial growth. These included for both municipalities adequate sanitary facilities, and for the city, annexation or merger with the township. This circumstance required, in turn, a concern by city officials for those events in the township which affected the city's opportunity for serving outlying neighborhoods. Township officials likewise had to be concerned with events in the city, for the danger of losing territory to the city was proportional with Woodruff's surplus sanitary capabilities. The second set of circumstances pertained to the consequences of sustained industrialization for social structure. Increasing numbers of blue-collar workers and members of minority groups concentrated in the working class would modify the class structure, the power of various interest groups, and the political parties. Sooner or later the groups that traditionally controlled government in each municipality—the Republican party, larger property owners, and "old families"— would be challenged by organizations representing the blue-collar workers.

Officials had to decide whether first priority should be assigned the improvement of the fiscal condition of government and thereby strengthening government as a community institution. For the city this also required emphasis on industrial growth by means of annexation or merger which would be facilitated by extension of services to outlying areas. For the township industrial growth could be encouraged by developing as rapidly as possible the municipality's sanitary systems and by encircling the city with trunk-line sewerage and water mains. If, on the other hand, top priority were assigned to maintaining the institutional basis of political power, the importance of industrial growth and development of sanitary facilities would be downgraded. Improvements in these facilities could be delayed, and developments in the neighboring municipality could be ignored.

Each municipality's decision-making pattern arranged these various objectives in order of priority. Woodruff's pattern stressed maintenance of the power of the groups that traditionally had been dominant. Officials and leaders of these groups accepted the fiscal difficulties arising from limited industrial tax base and overtaxed sanitary facilities. The township's decision-making pattern emphasized industrial growth and gave top priority to the acquisition of the utility facilities and to their development. The increase in the power of the Democratic party and in political conflict was to be expected.

Each municipality's decision-making pattern has been stable for many years.[46] Priorities for public officials did not vary by administration, by the party in power, or with the time—wartime or peacetime, boom or recession. They survived both normal and exceptional turnover of personnel in government positions. The specialization of city and township decision-making patterns also provided the basis of accommodation of each municipality with the other.

46. This mode of adaptation by city and by township to fulfilling multiple objectives simultaneously differs from the phase movement described by Bales in his small group research. Attention and effort was divided temporally between instrumental and expressive goals, with first one and then the other coming to the fore. Talcott Parsons, Robert F. Bales, and Edward A. Shils, *Working Papers in the Theory Of Action* (Glencoe, Ill.: The Free Press, 1953), Chs. IV, V. For additional discussion of phase movement as a strategy for performing multiple system functions see the following essays: Edward C. Devereux, Jr., "Parsons' Sociological Theory," and Chandler Morse, "The Functional Imperatives," in Max Black, ed., *The Social Theories of Talcott Parsons: A Critical Examination* (Englewood Cliffs, N.J.: Prentice-Hall, Inc., 1961), pp. 1–63, 100–52.

The pattern of phase movement describes in a general way those situations wherein the policies of a municipal administration vary from conservative to liberal, or from a stress on economy and thrift to one on growth and expansion, as one clique of leaders is replaced in office by a clique subscribing to different policies. In other communities the leadership consistently has followed certain policies over an extended time period. This distinction in community adaptation to multiple functional tasks between consistency and phase movements merits additional investigation. For comparative studies of leadership describing these differences in community policy see the following: Robert E. Agger, Daniel Goldrich, Bert E. Swanson, *The Rulers and the Ruled: Political Power and Impotence in American Communities* (New York: John Wiley and Sons, Inc., 1964); Robert Presthus, *Men at the Top: A Study in Community Power* (New York: Oxford University Press, 1964); Gladys M. Kammerer et al., *The Urban Political Community: Profiles in Town Politics* (Boston: Houghton Mifflin Company, 1963); Oliver P. Williams and Charles R. Adrian, *Four Cities: A Study in Comparative Policy Making* (Philadelphia: University of Pennsylvania Press, 1963).

Officials of Woodruff, from the thirties to the sixties, were insensitive to those developments in the township which signified declining prospects for solving internal fiscal problems through annexation or merger. City officials did not respond adaptively as the township became self-reliant for sanitary and related services, such as fire protection. The specific characteristics of city decision making included a number of practices related to the downgrading of sanitary facilities. These included scaling down and delaying implementation of recommendations of consulting engineers, negative decision making by refusing to provide either expanded service to the bomber factory or minimal service to Shady Lea Village, and inactivity. The last was manifest in reaction to the disposition of the utility plants in the township. Municipal officials were unconcerned over those changes in the township signifying a step-by-step elimination of annexation and merger as procedures for solving Woodruff's revenue needs. The agreement entered into during the first merger attempt symbolized this indifference. By purchasing water from the township, the Davenport administration delayed expansion of the utility systems and temporarily avoided a large bond issue. This agreement granted Nelson the time needed to plan and implement extension of trunk-line mains west of the city. It also signified the demise of the merger campaign.

Woodruff's emphasis on internal affairs was evidenced in the matter that became a principal issue at war's end: proposals for changing forms of government. While township officials planned for and negotiated purchase of the two utility plants, city leaders organized two election campaigns to adopt forms of government that helped the Republican party.

The orientation of Nelson and other township officials to the external environment, namely the city, was quite different. The former recognized the forces that sooner or later would impel city officials to resort to annexation and merger. They also recognized the vulnerability of inhabitants to such proposals if township government was unable to provide life-sustaining and protecting services. Township officials were not lulled into a feeling of security by city indifference to the township. This Woodruff reaction gave Nelson the opportunity to plan and to implement the pipeline encirclement of the city. Nelson and the township board from 1948 on took affirmative action to protect and strengthen the viability of township government.

The offer to sell water to the city was a brilliant maneuver to control Woodruff strategy. It offered Woodruff officials the excuse they wanted for not becoming concerned with territorial expansion.

Why did township officials respond to the manifold problems cited above by giving top priority to independence at the cost of changing the structure of power? Two factors seem pertinent here. First, in 1945 and 1946, township officials may have considered loss of leadership inevitable, either through annexation to the city or from the growth in power in an industrialized township of an urban middle and working class. The latter had the important advantage of maintaining the township as a viable political entity. Second, the township's commitment to Pacific Motors and the arguments put forth by Lockwood and Nelson influenced officials to acquire the federally owned utility plants.

The choice for city officials also can be attributed to a number of factors. First, many leaders misjudged the future economic role of the Woodruff area. They failed to appreciate the significance of the spacious airport and of the forty-minute drive by expressway to Metropolitan City. Belief in the restoration of the township to a rural province at war's end justified the emphasis on the city's internal problems. Second, existence of the decision-making pattern before 1941 simplified application to the circumstances originating with construction of the bomber plant. Third, certain elite groups committed to the restrictionist pattern, especially the bankers and the Chamber of Commerce, were highly influential. Their activities are considered in chapters that follow.

One type of spatial expansion would have eased some of Woodruff's fiscal problems while causing little if any change in the influence of various interest groups. Expansion westward would have provided some tax benefit to Woodruff, for middle-class housing areas and commercial territory would have more than paid for the services received from the city. At the same time most inhabitants of these areas were allied to the groups in the city's Republican party. City officials were no more aggressive in seeking annexation of these areas than of territory to the east. City policies also emphasized minimal investment of fiscal resources in city government.

Since innovative efforts, especially those concerning sanitary facilities, annexation, and merger, were likely to be costly, propensities for thrift also tended to close the door on the one alternative that could have improved the functioning of government in the Woodruff area. While township officials were hardly spendthrifts, investment in sanitary facilities was viewed as an investment in the future of the municipality.

Part II
Patterns of Community Influence

5. Banking and Leadership

Although the field of community studies reaches back to the beginning of this century, sociologists have neglected banks and bankers. The growth of interest in leadership and power inspired by Hunter's *Community Power Structure* has not notably advanced knowledge of the banker as a leader and of banks as community organizations.[1] Despite the paucity of information, several approaches to this subject have been employed. One approach treats the banker as an economic leader and seeks to determine his quota of power relevant to other economic and noneconomic influentials. Dahl and Wildavsky, for example, consider the banker to be less influential than certain political leaders.[2] A second approach seeks to relate the role of

1. The following studies of community leadership, which are considerably better than most investigations of this subject, have no items in the index on banks or bankers. Robert E. Agger, Daniel Goldrich, Bert E. Swanson, *The Rulers and the Ruled: Political Power and Impotence in American Communities* (New York: John Wiley and Sons, Inc., 1964); Robert Presthus, *Men at the Top: A Study in Community Power* (New York: Oxford University Press, 1964); Oliver P. Williams and Charles R. Adrian, *Four Cities: A Study in Comparative Policy Making* (Philadelphia: University of Pennsylvania Press, 1963).
2. Robert A. Dahl, *Who Governs? Democracy and Power in an American City* (New Haven: Yale University Press, 1961), pp. 115–40; Aaron Wildavsky, *Leadership in a Small Town* (Totowa, N.J.: Bedminster Press, 1964), pp. 52–71, 315–19.

the banker as a community leader to the activities of the bank. The Lynds in *Middletown In Transition* and Vidich and Bensman in *Small Town In Mass Society* attribute much of the influence of powerful men to their control over the community's credit facilities.[3] A third approach that also focuses on the bank emphasizes the network of relations between bank officials and the officers of companies with which the bank transacts business. The banker does not act singly as a leader but as a member of an informal clique of influentials.[4] A fourth approach, employed by Warner in Yankee City, sees the banking and manufacturing functions combined in particular "captains of industry." Influence is not attributed specifically to exercise of banking prerogatives but to a unique combination of economic activities. This status set is both cause and effect of the contributions the various leaders made to the economic development of the community and to the preservation of a variety of civic and cultural activities.[5] The study by Kammerer and her associates of seven Florida cities utilized a fifth approach, emphasizing both the "banking clique" and its policies on the "destiny of the town."[6] In several of the Florida communities one clique favoring and one opposing change were headquartered in different local banks. The authors fail to explain the precise reasons for the involvement of banks rather than other economic organizations in this type of community issue. Our data indicate that certain leaders, seeking financial support from the banks for their innovative ideas, bring this organization into the center of conflict over social change.

3. Robert S. Lynd and Helen Lynd, *Middletown in Transition: A Study in Cultural Conflicts* (New York: Harcourt, Brace and Company, 1937), Ch. III; Arthur J. Vidich and Joseph Bensman, *Small Town in Mass Society: Class, Power and Religion in a Rural Community* (Princeton, N.J.: Princeton University Press, 1958), pp. 146–47.

4. Floyd Hunter, *Community Power Structure* (Chapel Hill, N.C.: The University of North Carolina Press, 1953), pp. 77–80.

5. W. Lloyd Warner and J. O. Low, *The Social System of the Modern Factory: A Social Analysis* (New Haven: Yale University Press, 1947), pp. 134–39, 150–58.

6. Gladys M. Kammerer et al., *The Urban Political Community: Profiles in Town Politics* (Boston: Houghton Mifflin Company, 1963), pp. 33–44, 105–8, 145–48, 152, 162–63, 200–202. Agger and associates discussed one leadership clique in Petropolis in which three of four members were bankers. This clique was highly conservative and was opposed by other leadership cliques. Agger, Goldrich, and Swanson, *Rulers and the Ruled*, pp. 346–54.

The approach to the banks employed in this volume resembles the fifth viewpoint in emphasizing the policies of the bankers on the management of their enterprises and on participation in local activities. The influence of the banks and bank officials was transmitted through the agency of the decision-making pattern, which various bankers helped establish and to which the officers conformed when confronted with issues concerning the future of the Woodruff area. Our approach also emphasizes the importance of several historic events on the shaping of banking policies. These include the change in the economy from one dominated by locally owned concerns dependent upon the community's banks to one dominated by absentee-owned plants independent of local sources of credit. The circumstances attending bank reorganization during the depression also had important consequences for the community's leadership and policies on change and development. In one respect the approach used here differs from that of Kammerer and associates, who ignored the inactivity of bankers in local affairs. Inaction is regarded as having had important consequences for certain issues and campaigns.

Banking and Community Development

The importance of bankers to the social life of the community is a function of the role of banks in the local economy. Banks receive surplus wealth from the businesses and families of the community and allocate it to the units that need and can afford to borrow capital. By redistributing capital to borrowers, banks perform activities indispensable for the maintenance and growth of the economy. As a result of this distributive function, banks are connected to most institutions and organizations in a community. Any event or condition that sharply reduces or markedly increases the economic well-being of these structures has an immediate effect on the banks.

Ideally, the "interests" of bankers in increasing bank revenues and net profits should create a concern for all those segments of the community with which the bank is linked. Plant production, employment levels, retail sales, home construction and sale of homes, spending by the local government, and the economic and social activities of churches, schools, and many other organizations affect the volume of business of the local banks. On the assumption of a "one-to-one" relation of economic interest and human behavior, bankers would be disposed to develop and promote community action that would stimulate the development of the economy and total locality. They would have an interest in all components of the economy: social, educational, and political, along with manufacturing and commercial units. The nature of banking provides bankers and bank directors with a strong rationale for involvement in a variety of local activities, from industrial development to the improvement of minority group status.

The leaders of many organizations and institutions, social as well as economic, respect and value the judgments of bankers. Each organization has its fiscal activities, concerned with the collection or receiving of funds and the allocation to component parts and major operations. For assistance in increasing revenue or improving mechanisms of allocation, the judgments of bankers are valued. The interest of bankers in social structures with which the bank is linked and the assistance that the banker can provide permit key bank personnel to function as a reference group for the community on matters that may appear to be only remotely connected to the local economy. The banking team often has thrust upon it the responsibility of judging a wide variety of proposals for economic and social innovation. In Salem, Massachusetts, few plans involving the economic functioning of an organization were implemented without the approval of one of the bank presidents.[7]

Augmenting the influence of bankers as a reference group for the community on matters directly or indirectly affecting the local economy is the possession of extensive knowledge concerning different types of business organizations. Top bank officers and bank directors accumulated, during the course of normal banking activity, a vast amount of information on local business establishments and on the financial condition of many local residents. Much of this information is obtained from loan applications, which require disclosure of details of economic operations. Applicants may be called in by directors for further discussion of matters relevant to the processing of the application.

7. Ruth C. Schaffer, unpublished notes on Salem, Massachusetts (June, 1952-June, 1953).

Bankers, to be effective, should be sensitive to trends in the national, regional, and local economy which may affect the future of local business. Since few other residents have this perspective and access to relevant sources of information, bankers and bank directors possess a rare and vital expertise that leads citizens to view them as authorities on a variety of civic proposals and programs. They are the experts on how a given proposal or program will affect the local economy. A forthright statement of support by a banker may produce endorsement throughout the leadership hierarchy. Bankers are in a position to shape leadership and hence public opinion.

The lines of communication of key bank personnel to many of the economic and social organizations in the community, and to most of the business and civic leaders, is an important source of influence. Some of these leaders serve as directors of the bank or are among the banks most important customers. This interdependence facilitates continuous exchanges of information between the individuals and the units they represent. Bank personnel also participate in a variety of voluntary associations and organizations. In Woodruff, these men often served as treasurer of the school boards, Community Fund, Chamber of Commerce, Boy's Club, Family Service Society, and the churches. Bank officers can influence the basic policies of these organizations and align their activities with the views of the banks. Since bank officers advise a variety of individuals, those of modest means and the affluent, lines of communication extend to the lower and upper levels of the class structure.

Role Requirements of the Banker

The high prestige derived from the position of top bank officer and bank director contributes to the power that the incumbents may exercise in community affairs. The prestige depends on two factors, the importance of capital for the economy and the personal attributes that a bank official is presumed to possess. Role requirements, indicated above, stress knowledge and skills in the use of money for a variety of different community purposes. The importance of capital for the economy and as a basic support for high position in the stratification system invests the position of bank officer and bank director with high social prestige. This is augmented by the personal attributes deemed necessary in the incumbents of these positions—honesty, integrity, trustworthiness, and reliability.

Bank officers and directors epitomize many of the cardinal virtues of American society. In this sense they are above reproach. They have proven themselves capable of resisting the greatest of temptations, stealing other people's money. They can be trusted with confidential information concerning local business, the financial condition and spending habits of individual clients. The public reactions of these men to a civic problem or community project is widely regarded as the evaluation of a group of upright men concerned primarily with community welfare. A civic project can be more easily justified to the public if approved by bankers and bank directors. Possibly for this reason the mayor of New Haven took pains to find bankers to head two organizations essential for success of his urban renewal program.[8]

Apart from prestige, the influence of bankers is affected by several material considerations, the performance of the stock of the bank and the selection of persons as directors. In the case of the Woodruff banks, most of the shares were held by local residents. Profitable bank operations benefit the friends, colleagues, and associates of bank officials, the members of their social class, churches, and service clubs. The effects of good or poor stock performance may be translated into "peer group" evaluation of the "astuteness" of banker judgment on matters directly and indirectly pertaining to economic affairs. Where the investment in bank stock has paid off handsomely, the recipients, the members of the social class and voluntary associations to which the bankers belong, may feel some sense of appreciation for the gains that faith in their friends has brought. This may produce a sense of indebtedness among members of the higher classes which bankers, at critical times, could transform to acceptance of their suggestions.

Bank officials and directors also are in a position to influence the careers of community leaders. If selection as a director enhances the prestige and influence of local leaders, as we believe it does, then selection or rejection for these positions influences the amount of power a leader can amass. Men ambitious for a seat on the bank's board of directors may take pains to adopt opinions and act in a

8. Dahl, *Who Governs?* pp. 12–21.

manner that will gain approbation from top bank officials. The policies of the newspaper editor seem to have been affected by these considerations (see Chapter 7).

To the degree that bankers assert initiative in launching projects for development of the community or are called upon, overtly and covertly, to evaluate these and related plans, their judgments and reactions bear a close resemblance to the decision-making patterns that evolve. These men constantly review the budgets of economic and social organizations, evaluate the wisdom of expenditure increases or decreases, assess measures for increasing or decreasing revenues. In the process they communicate their conception of basic goals—of growth versus stability, risk versus certainty, change versus tradition, immediate versus long-range objectives. Gradually these preferences permeate the leadership structure and dominate the thinking of government officials. This is especially true where spokesmen for opposing viewpoints are weak or absent. A close correspondence exists between the fundamental policies of bank officials and the decision-making patterns of the community. The former are among the creators and sustainers of the decision-making pattern.

A History of Banking in Woodruff

Woodruff had two commercial banks, one a national and the other a state bank, during the course of the study. These were owned and managed by local citizens. Woodruff had two Savings and Loan Associations, one locally owned, the other a branch of an association in the Metropolitan City area. Several loan companies and credit unions also had offices in the community.

The commercial banks were of particular interest for their financial resources and lending powers far exceeded those of the other financial enterprises. While the two banks loaned money to business firms and individuals, the Savings and Loan Associations served persons interested in home construction and modernization; the finance companies and credit unions loaned small sums of money to individuals.

Each financial organization had a long history. The First National Bank was founded in 1863. A few years later M. A. Davenport became president and held the position until his death in 1912; he was succeeded by his son, M. A. Davenport, Jr. The latter Davenport served as president until early in 1933, when the comptroller of the currency denied the bank permission to continue operations. The bank reorganized as The National Bank of Woodruff. Until 1965, when the older son of Mike Davenport was named a director of the Savings Bank, no member of this family held a position in a local bank.

The Woodruff Savings Bank was established in 1887. Unlike its competitor, it had not been closely identified with any one family. The bank was reorganized in 1931.

The Building and Loan Association was founded in 1890. An attempt to move the organization some years later to County Seat City was prevented by several local men, including the head of the McDowell family. Since the association's inception, this family had at least one member and often two serving as officers. The McDowell furniture store served as the headquarters for the association until the early sixties, when it moved into an office in a nearby building. The association survived the depression of the thirties with little or no difficulty and prospered in the postwar era. In 1961, the association adopted the form and name of a savings and loan association.

The Savings and Loan Association maintained a close relationship with the National Bank. Three directors of the former, including Scheible and McDowell, were directors or officers of the latter, and the assets of the association were deposited with the National Bank. One director of the Savings Bank also served as a director of the association.

The number of shareholders in each of the three banks was small compared with a large industrial corporation.[9] To obtain shares in the two commercial banks a prospective buyer had to wait until an estate was sold and a block of stock became available. With few exceptions, large blocks of stock were owned by local people. A wealthy lawyer in Metropolitan City possessed 10 percent of the stock of the Woodruff Savings Bank and a few shares of the National Bank until the late sixties. His relatives owned an additional 20 percent of the Savings Bank stock. Although this family was the largest

9. The National Bank had approximately 460 shareholders in 1968 while the Savings Bank had several thousand.

stockholder of the Savings Bank, no member served on the board of directors or took part in policy deliberations.[10] No comparable situation existed at the National Bank; the largest stockholders were Woodruff residents. Members of one local family, the McDowells, owned the largest proportion of stock in the Savings and Loan Association.

Since Metropolitan City banks were forbidden by law to cross the county line, Woodruff banks had no competition within city and township. Competition was provided by branch units of both Metropolitan City and County Seat City banks, which were located but a few miles from downtown Woodruff. To consolidate their hold over the Woodruff trading area, the two Woodruff banks, in the late fifties and in the sixties, established branches east and west of the downtown business district.

Woodruff also had a credit bureau that was owned and operated by two members of a local family, the Endicotts, father and son. While the bureau performed important functions for each of the three fiscal units, along with and for local businesses, it was tied personally and organizationally to the National Bank. The Endicotts were close friends of the Lockwood family, whose head had been bank attorney for decades and became its president in 1963. Christian Endicott, who served as the manager for Lockwood's successful campaign as delegate to the state's constitutional convention, became director of the National Bank in the sixties. His cousin was named president in 1968 when Lockwood became chairman of the board of directors.

Bank Reorganization during the Depression

In the history of many nations and communities extraordinary events occur which alter basic patterns of social life. Understanding social organization is difficult unless one comprehends the nature of events that occurred during these periods. Two such events occurred in

10. Despite the stockholder's ownership of a large block of stock, he did not insist on a board position. He was reluctant to do so for several reasons: he was a nonresident member of a minority group, and the stock was purchased as an investment. If the directors had been willing to have him on the board, the stockholder would have been tempted to accept. His son served on the board of a bank in a Metropolitan City suburb.

Woodruff. In the early years of the depression the two banks were compelled to undergo reorganization. This created great hardship for Woodruff's institutions and citizens. The opposite change, prosperity, initiated by wartime industrialization and growing dependence of the local economy on absentee-owned factories, proved equally important. In both cases, forces in the national economy beyond the control of local citizens brought extensive changes to Woodruff. The nature and extent of the local changes were influenced by factors internal to Woodruff. The community was not inert in the grip of the larger society.

In the early years of the depression, the community's ruling family fell from its high pinnacle amid unhappy circumstances. The one family in Woodruff, the Davenports, who approximated the Choates and Weatherbys of Yankee City and the "X" family of Middletown, suffered a sharp reversal and never again held an equivalent position in the leadership hierarchy. The circumstances surrounding the family's decline in power and prestige had repercussions for leadership and for decision making.

Woodruff was gripped by the spirit of expansion and by the anticipation of wealth that pervaded the United States in the twenties. Fears raised by the Panic of 1907 for its banking institutions had been forgotten. To expand the local economy, a number of Woodruff leaders established an Industrial Association. This group sought to bring businesses to the city and with some success. A number of small manufacturing establishments came to Woodruff in the twenties, induced in part by commitments from several prominent citizens to invest sizable sums of capital. Midwest Motors purchased land in the city, and it was thought a plant soon would be built. The Chamber of Commerce, founded in 1920, constructed a hotel with eighty-five rooms and facilities for regular meetings of civic groups. Local citizens contributed more than $200,000 to establish the hotel and the corporation that managed it. Many leaders entertained the hope that Woodruff would become an important hub in the growing network of air-transport lanes. To further this dream, thirty businessmen each contributed $1,000 for the development of an airport.

The vision of an increasingly important city spread to the men on the school board and to the directors of the Country Club. The school board sold a $250,000 bond issue for the construction of a high school. The Country Club directors built a new club house with the proceeds from a $90,000 bond issue. Several local real estate speculators sought to capitalize on these changes, especially on the fact that Midwest Motors Company had purchased land for a factory in the city. Since it was expected that the demand for housing would expand rapidly once the factory was built, land was subdivided within and without the city. Prospective buyers, both far and near, were urged to buy before the boom took place.

The depression radically changed conditions of life for residents of Woodruff. Hopes for expansion were forgotten and survival became problematical. The school board and city council had difficulty making payments on their bonds. The Country Club declared bankruptcy and had to be reorganized. Hundreds of parcels of land were claimed by the state and sold at auction when owners were unable to pay tax bills. Several businesses went bankrupt and the number of Woodruff families on relief climbed steadily. The crisis intensified in 1931 when the Savings Bank closed in order to halt withdrawals and to acquire additional capital. Most citizens had confidence in the First National, the Davenport bank. It had more than twice the deposits of the Savings Bank and represented the foundation of the community's money market. If the First National withstood the crisis, and everyone believed it would, the depression would not be too severe. The community would endure without further intensification of the emergency.

Events shattered the hopes of Woodruff residents. The First National was denied permission to reopen by the comptroller of the currency, after the bank holiday in March, 1933. Hundreds of citizens, dozens of businesses, many organizations and institutions, and the local units of government could not obtain their funds. As the weeks passed and the bank remained closed, the local economy continued to suffer. Efforts to reorganize the bank were stymied for many weeks, and a number of local leaders questioned the need for two banks. After some time had passed, a new bank was organized to replace the First National. For the first time in over sixty years, the Davenports had no connection with a Woodruff bank.

The closing of the two banks had instantaneous and far-reaching effects on the local economy. At the time of the closing of the Savings

Bank in the summer of 1931, the city government had more than $155,000 on deposit, approximately the sum that had to be raised from property taxes for the municipal budget. The amount included the taxes collected for the school district. When the First National closed in March, 1933, the government had over $60,000 on deposit.[11] The situation had improved slightly by the end of the year for the government had regained over $40,000.

The councilmen heard grim news at the meeting of November 20, 1933. The city had fallen behind in its payment on bonds. It had been unable to meet an obligation of $13,500 that had come due on September 1. Councilmen discussed paying municipal employees with scrip. This had been done earlier in the year to enable the city council to meet a $9,000 payroll. The issue of scrip had since been redeemed.

Families and businesses were similarly affected. Payments from the First National to depositors were doled out over an eight-year period. Since the total payment was approximately 80 percent of the amount deposited in the bank, First National clients lost a fifth of their savings. Similar conditions prevailed at the Savings Bank. During the darkest days of the depression many of the economic problems of the citizenry and of community institutions were intensified by inability to obtain funds deposited in the two banks. Only the Building and Loan Association remained solvent during this period. Depositors were able to withdraw funds at any time.

The Banking Crisis and the Davenports

The significance of the failure of the First National Bank was more than economic. A pattern of leadership behavior was at stake which the Davenport family had maintained for over two generations. For seemingly valid reasons most citizens of Woodruff regarded the First National as a "pillar of strength." A bank director summed up community reaction to the banking situation: "People said it was the Davenport bank, that nothing would happen to it, not to the First National. Then came the bank holiday and people said it would reopen, that there could be no doubt of it as long as the Davenports were associated with it."

11. *The Woodruff Press,* December 19, 1933.

To the citizens familiar with the local banks and recent community history this faith seemed justified. The First National, founded more than two decades before the Savings Bank, was the senior bank in the community. Deposits of slightly less than $4 million were more than twice that of its competitor. By far the most significant fact of all was past performance. The First National had had little or no trouble withstanding the Panic of 1907. This accomplishment was attributed to the senior Davenport who was believed to have made the wealth of the family available to the bank, if needed. The Savings Bank, on the other hand, had a serious run that forced it to close for some time. The bank did not reopen until additional capital had been raised and changes had been made among the top officers.

There were additional indicators of the standing of the two local banks. In 1928, a relatively new and small bank seemed likely to fail. The federal examiner suggested to Davenport, in order to maintain public confidence in the local banks, that the First National acquire it. Davenport agreed. Officers of the Savings Bank were not approached as it was not in a position to purchase a "weak sister."

Another indication of the pre-eminence of the First National in Woodruff's monetary system was the unconfirmed and disputed explanation of the reorganization of the Savings Bank. Several knowledgeable persons, including officers of the latter, maintained that an informal agreement had been reached with Davenport and two County Seat City banks to provide capital in time of an emergency. The County Seat City banks, it was alleged, would not contribute unless the First National also assisted. Davenport's refusal to honor this agreement was said to have compelled the Savings Bank to be reorganized. Persons closely associated with the First National in the early thirties claimed that no such agreement existed. Whether or not this account is true, its significance for our purposes lies in the fact that economic leaders of Woodruff looked to the First National to maintain the community's fiscal organizations during the crisis period.

In many communities able bankers were trapped by investments that could not be liquified at a rate sufficient to meet client demand. This was partially true for the First National, which had invested a large amount of capital in municipal bonds whose value had plummeted. Other funds in a Metropolitan City bank could not be obtained. Nevertheless, the failure of the bank cannot be attributed solely to conditions that were more or less "normal" for the country in the early thirties.

Davenport violated the tradition established by his father in not announcing publicly that the family fortune would be available to the bank if needed.[12] In the opinion of a man who had been a director of the First National at that time, Davenport feared the loss of the family's wealth if such a commitment was made. While many in Woodruff might have excused the senior Davenport for not incurring this risk, other actions were more difficult to rationalize.

At some time before the bank holiday, Davenport apparently reached the conclusion that the First National was or could be in serious difficulty. For a number of months he withdrew the funds of the family and of two prominent families related by marriage and placed them in a New York City bank. Apparently none of the officers and directors knew that Davenport had made these transfers. Davenport reduced the risk of personal financial loss while allowing stockholders and depositors to assume that his confidence in the First National was undiminished. Davenport apparently had decided long before the bank holiday that, in the event of a panic, he would not stand behind the bank that the family had controlled for more than half a century.

One version of these events was provided by a long-term Woodruff resident with an interest in local history who, for years, held an important public office. In discussing the decline in civic pride which took place in Woodruff after the twenties, he said:

In 1933 when the First National Bank was in trouble, Davenport money was not in the bank. It was in a New York City bank. He had only a few hundred dollars in the bank. These are the facts as I was told them by the bank examiner. This is not hearsay.

It was a tragic event. I've often thought if, on the night when the people who had more than a thousand dollars in the bank met at the college auditorium to decide what should be done, Davenport had gone on the stage, and said, here is the two hundred thousand dollars I received from the sale of the farm to Midwest Motors, here are the deeds

12. By taking this step the X family increased its control over the city's banking organizations and strengthened its leadership position. Lynd and Lynd, *Middletown in Transition,* p. 78.

to the property I own, here is all I have, it stands behind the bank, that confidence would have been restored, and the bank would not have been in trouble. But Davenport did not even have enough money in his bank to be able to attend the meeting. It was tragic.

Among those who were close to the banking situation, Davenport's standing must also have suffered from comparison with the Savings Bank president. Upon assuming the office after reorganization, the president informed associates that the bank would have his assets if the occasion arose.

Davenport also made it difficult for some clients of the bank not to detest him. Before the bank holiday, the president of a small manufacturing firm came to the bank to withdraw the company's account. Having heard reports that the First National was in trouble, he wished to protect his firm. Davenport stopped him before he left the bank and gave assurances that the bank was sound. The manufacturer reopened the account. Several other depositors had similar experiences. One could excuse the president for seeking to instill confidence in his bank if he had not already done covertly what some depositors had the right to do overtly.

The reaction of these men to the disclosure that the Davenports had removed the family fortune from the bank needs little elaboration. To many local residents Davenport ceased to be a leader. Some people refused to speak to the former president after the bank had closed. Davenport revealed the depth of community feeling when he told one researcher that he could not have been elected dog catcher.[13] Davenport retired from active participation in community affairs.

The Significance of the Bank Failures

The depression marked a turning point in Woodruff as it did throughout the nation. The depression signified the end of one era and the beginning of another. The period during which local leaders and businessmen, by imagination, energy, and capital helped develop the community's economy was over. In the future, the decisions of executives in corporate headquarters thirty miles away, in

13. Robert O. Schulze, "The Bifurcation of Power in a Satellite City," in Morris Janowitz, ed., *Community Political Systems* (Glencoe, Ill.: The Free Press, 1961), p. 77, n. 33.

New York, and in government bureaus in Washington, D. C., would have a far greater impact on the economic growth of the Woodruff area. This change more or less coincided with the fall of the Davenports. Both changes reshaped the decision-making pattern and modified the local leadership structure.

In the nineteenth century the enterprise and capital of local leaders developed the Woodruff economy. Costs of organizing a new enterprise and moving into the market were relatively low, and the unspecialized nature of the economy encouraged a variety of activities. Davenport and other Woodruff businessmen launched an assortment of manufacturing firms—textiles, paper, steel, carriages, saw mills, etc. They engaged in real estate ventures and developed the business section of Woodruff. They took the initiative in bringing a Normal College to the community by assembling and donating a desirable tract of land. In Woodruff, the Davenports and families like them were "captains of industry."

The families that rose to prominence as leaders after 1930 could not match the contributions to the development of the community of families like the Davenports. The scope for local businessmen in the expansion of Woodruff's economy had declined drastically. The growth of the Woodruff economy became a function, not of local capital and initiative but of the wartime need for military aircraft and then of the postwar increase in consumer demand for automobiles. However extensive the abilities and know-how of Woodruff's leaders in the postwar decades, they could not acquire the record of community building activities which characterized the first two generations of Davenports.

Davenport's fall as bank president and as community leader symbolized the declining significance, as the economy became an appendage of national industries, of the once esteemed virtues of initiative, imagination, and enterprise. Risk taking, receptiveness to change, and acceptance of innovation did not bring major rewards. Since the appeal of chrome and horsepower had more to do with the prosperity of Woodruff, being on the right corner at the right time was far more consequential for business success. The creation of business opportunities was less essential for success than taking advantage of those generated by the operations of the automobile plants.

The traits and qualities valued highly in Woodruff were not those required for launching and establishing new ventures but those necessary for keeping a successful organization running smoothly. Charisma had been routinized; conformity to established procedures and goals was elevated to highest priority. This mood and attitude was transferred to the community as a whole. They were strengthened by the cultural shock following the migration of thousands of "hillbillies" into the area in 1942 and 1943. For community leaders preventing change and especially the loss of political power became the dominant considerations, just as keeping the existing business organizations operating had become the ultimate economic objective.

The Davenports represented one of Woodruff's last links to the "master builders" of the nineteenth century. While several men became very wealthy and successful during and after World War II, e.g., Sampson and Scheible, none could boast the community heritage that the Davenports possessed. None had ancestors in Woodruff who had built factories, office buildings, and railroads and had managed banks. An important resource of power, high prestige, was not available to Woodruff's leaders in the fifties and sixties in amounts equivalent to that possessed by leaders of previous generations. In this sense the fall of the Davenports in the banking crisis permanently weakened Woodruff's leadership structure.

While the elder Davenport's leadership position and that of the family suffered seriously, the family did not sink into obscurity. Davenport's influence as a cosmopolitan and local leader declined. He lost his position on the board of a Metropolitan City bank and his membership in at least one exclusive Metropolitan City social club. His counsel and judgment were not held on the high level of respect that they were formerly. He no longer supported two local organizations for the prominent families of Woodruff, the Country Club and an amateur theatrical group that he had founded at the turn of the century. The future position of the family in the leadership structure was impaired also by the fact that Davenport's older son, who had been assistant cashier of the First National, left the community after the bank failure. When he returned to Woodruff many years later, he took no part in civic and political affairs.

After the bank failure, the position of the family in the leadership structure depended heavily on the family paper mill. It provided a source of wealth and a degree of prestige which grew with the subsequent ascendancy of the automobile plants. The dominance of absentee-owned factories left the Davenports as Woodruff's only "industrialists." This classification made the Davenports useful to Woodruff's leaders in postwar years. Davenport's younger son Mike, who was associated with him in the paper factory, used this position as a local industrialist as the basis for a political career and a leadership comeback.

Woodruff's leaders in later years were able to turn to members of the Davenport family for overt leadership roles as a result of their silence concerning the circumstances of the bank failure. Only a few "insiders" knew that the elder Davenport had placed the financial position of the family ahead of the depositors and stockholders. During the weeks when the fate of the First National was obscure and subsequently when efforts were underway to raise new capital, nothing was said publicly or in the newspapers concerning the reasons for Davenport's nonparticipation. On the contrary, some leaders publicly sought to place responsibility on the comptroller of the currency for imposing unreasonable conditions for operation of a "sound bank." When Davenport was not named to the board of the new bank, the average First National depositor assumed that he, along with other directors, had lost interest in banking.

The silence was motivated by the desire to quickly restore public confidence in Woodruff's banks, which was even more necessary in the weeks and months following the bank holiday. Public disclosure of Davenport's role in the failure of the First National might only have persuaded depositors that bankers were untrustworthy and that their money was safer in a secret hiding place or in a County Seat City bank. The leaders and bankers maintained silence to protect themselves, the banks, and the community's institutions. This silence also prevented an even greater loss of prestige and influence for the Davenports. It preserved for future years a measure of the charisma that the family had accumulated by its contribution to the development of Woodruff. The silence made it possible for Mike Davenport, in the forties and fifties, to regain some of the family's influence. This action allowed the community to retain in the leadership structure a family that had links to the "golden days" of another era. The prestige that this gave all the leaders was used again and again in the decisive days of the forties and fifties.

Bank Policies[14]

The men who have managed Woodruff's banks since reorganization have been cautious, deliberate, unobtrusive, and skeptical of innovation. They have made no effort to capture the imagination of local citizens or to make headlines in *The Woodruff Press*. They have sought to blend into the organizational structure of the community and to conduct the affairs of the banks in a routine, orderly, and successful manner. They have applied these preferences both to the conduct of banking and to participation in local affairs.

Similarities in the policies of the two commercial banks have been more important than the differences. Two guidelines have been heavily stressed: a preference for the certainty of short-run advantages to the uncertainties of long-run benefits and a desire to minimize, as much as possible, the risks of banking policies. Taken together these policies represent a "play-it-safe" approach to everyday banking decisions and to the problems of the Woodruff area. They strengthen adherence to customary ways of doing business. The longevity of these preferences can be attributed to weak banking competition within the Woodruff area and to the dependence of the local economy on absentee-owned plants. In the long run, daring and imaginative banking policies contribute less to the overall growth of the Woodruff economy than the expansion of operations in the automotive plants. Nevertheless, it would be erroneous to conclude that banking leaders could make little or no contribution to various sectors of the community. Much could be done to improve, for example, the downtown business district, merchandising practices, old buildings, and city and township relationships. Much could be done to improve the industrial tax base of the city

14. While the authors did not make a systematic study of banking practices, a considerable amount of information was obtained during the course of interviewing many different respondents. Although some of the data, especially those concerning rejection of loan applications, are difficult to evaluate because of the fragmentary nature of the reports, the over-all situation conforms closely with patterns of participation in local affairs and in the merger campaigns.

to make it possible for Woodruff taxpayers to have slightly more money available for consumer purchases or for savings, hopefully in Woodruff establishments. The need for a variety of internal adjustments increases as industrial and population growth occurs.

The two banks compete with each other for Woodruff accounts, and each tries to outdo the other. Over the years, the Savings Bank has been slightly more adventurous than the National Bank. The Savings Bank first entered the automobile financing market in 1943. It also preceded the National Bank in remodeling the interior of its downtown office and in opening a branch office. Reversing this state of affairs became one of Lockwood's objectives when, in 1963, he assumed the presidency of the National Bank. The exterior of the National Bank was refurbished ahead of that of the Savings Bank. The former opened branches in other sections, such as the University, before its competitor.

Despite the competition between the two banks, basic policies were similar. In lending money the bankers preferred many small loans to one large loan. Any request for a loan that came close to the limit stipulated by law, about $40,000 for the National Bank and $60,000 for the Savings Bank, made the officers extremely nervous. The bankers preferred to spread out the risk among many small loans rather than to concentrate it in a few large loans. The banks tended not to lend money to men who wished to open a new business or to expand an established one, where a sizeable amount of capital was required. The applicants generally were referred to banks in Metropolitan City. The local banks preferred to invest capital in consumer loans, such as home improvement and automobile loans. They abhorred F.H.A. and V.A. housing loans and much preferred conventional home mortgage arrangements. Many college professors failed to obtain a mortgage from a local bank and were compelled to obtain one from a bank in a nearby city. Both banks, especially the National Bank, had a strong preference for investing assets in high-grade, tax-free municipal bonds.

Procedures for examining and approving loan requests also were highly circumspect. The Savings Bank centralized lending authority by establishing low limits on the amount that a bank officer could lend without obtaining approval of the directors. For senior officers, loan applications in excess of five hundred dollars had to be referred to a committee of directors and the two top officers. The necessity for a unanimous vote of the committee assured careful if not prolonged deliberation. Requests to open or increase a line of credit also had to be approved by the committee.

The suspicion of bank directors toward innovation is illustrated by the decision to open a branch office. Despite the rapid growth of the township, and especially the eastern half, since the Second World War, the banks did not open any branches until 1959, seventeen years after the construction of the bomber plant. The banks did not recognize the township as an important source of accounts until its population exceeded that of the city by several thousand, nor was the process of decision making in this instance either easy or quick. The proposal to open a branch in the eastern half of the township was considered for three years by directors of the Savings Bank. Initially the advocates of the change were completely in the minority, with all opposed or uncertain with the exception of two directors. When approval finally was granted, it was considered to be a "big step." Directors of the National Bank were even more reluctant, granting approval shortly thereafter in order to keep up with the competition rather than by choice. The fact that this move could have been taken several years earlier is indicated by the fact that the cost of opening a branch for both banks was repaid substantially ahead of schedule. This led to the building of several branch offices within the next few years.

The emphasis on immediate as opposed to longer-run gains is indicated by a conflict between the Savings Bank and Midwest Motors. Not all of the absentee-owned businesses had accounts with the two local banks. Some, especially the supermarkets, preferred to transfer funds daily by Brinks truck to depository banks in Metropolitan City. By contrast, both Midwest Motors and Universal Motors maintained a cash balance in the local banks. In the late fifties the manager of the Midwest Motors plant in the city became dissatisfied with arrangements concerning the cashing of employee checks. It had been the custom of the banks to charge a small fee for this service. The plant manager, desirous of improving relations with employees and with the union, sought to modify this practice. He offered to maintain a large cash balance in the bank if employee checks were cashed without charge. When bank officials rejected the offer, the manager transferred company funds to banks in other communities.

Universal Motors had reached a different agreement with the two banks. The company paid the cost for cashing employee checks and also kept a balance in each bank. The company had a balance in the Savings Bank of $50,000. Each year Universal Motors asked for and received a line of credit. Although the directors of the Savings Bank approved a large amount, $175,000, Universal Motors never had used it.

The extent to which business transactions with the plants of absentee-owned companies contributed to the profits of the two banks is not known. Certainly the large bank balances kept by the automobile companies, large by Woodruff standards, and the profit from cashing employee checks were important to local bankers. Officials of the Savings Bank were negotiating at the time of the study for the restoration of the funds of Midwest Motors. The bankers may also have had some hope, no matter how small, that someday Universal Motors might take advantage of its line of credit. It is possibly for this reason that the company made such a request.

Bank Policies and Community Issues

The conservativeness of bankers in operating their organizations extended to policies on participation in community action. The basic objectives were not growth or development of the Woodruff area or the strengthening of some segment of the local economy but to avoid wherever possible the loss of accounts. Since each bank served interest groups whose goals were in conflict, this objective could not be realized if it became associated with a particular approach to a local problem. Each bank had customers in the city and in the township, including both units of government. Each bank had clients among downtown and suburban businesses, among locally owned and absentee-owned establishments. Under these circumstances, the most favored strategy emphasized delay in making a decision. Banking officials procrastinated in the hope that a consensus would emerge which they could support. If this did not occur, officials remained neutral and inactive. Wherever possible, bank officers translated innovative proposals, e.g., the downtown mall, into standard banking problems, such as the eligibility of a specific business for a loan. They preferred not to see the plan in terms of community problems and community development. The operation of these rules and their consequences are illustrated in several projects of some importance for the Woodruff area.

A Downtown Shopping Center

Early in the sixties a short-lived civic group, supported by a few of the town's leaders, became the nominal sponsor of a proposed shopping center to be built, not in an outlying area but in downtown Woodruff, by a national supermarket chain. The plans for the proposed center, several blocks east of the main business district, included a department store of approximately 40,000 square feet, a supermarket of 20,000 square feet, and parking for 500 cars. The cost, including land acquisition and razing buildings, was estimated at a million dollars. While a modest development, the project would increase the value of property in a community whose tax base had remained virtually unchanged since 1957. Anticipation of increased payrolls and retail activity and the improvement of land values in the area might have interested the banking community. Although the vice-president of one bank served on the executive committee of the civic group, neither he nor any other person affiliated with the banks promoted the effort to establish the shopping center in Woodruff. Success must be attributed to the efforts of the developers, several Metropolitan City businessmen, a local architect, and especially to the desire of the councilmen to improve the city's tax base.

For many years, the supermarket chain had been seeking land adequate for a larger store with ample parking. Officers of the Savings Bank easily could have assisted the firm since the largest single bank stockholder also served as director of the supermarket company. A conference with their stockholder, whom the officers knew personally, could have been arranged. Lending an element of urgency to such a discussion was the fact that the supermarket firm was about to purchase a parcel of land in the township west of Woodruff, which could be used for the proposed shopping center.

The initiative was taken not by bank officers but by a County Seat City resident who was a member of the civic group and who owned a Woodruff department store. He persuaded the attorney to meet in Woodruff with interested committee members. This conference stimulated the interest of the director of the supermarket firm in a shopping center a few blocks from the downtown retail district and provided impetus for the project.

The establishment of the shopping center had to overcome one major obstacle. City-owned land including a small public park fronting on Midstate Avenue was needed for an adequate parking facility. Previous proposals to modify this land usage had provoked strong objections from residents of the area and from officials of the elementary school located across the street. To avoid a referendum on the sale of the land, councilmen arranged a land transfer with the developers. Not a single bank officer aided the negotiations although one bank director vigorously supported the swap at the public hearing. A store building that he owned, which had been vacant off and on for years, was located close to the proposed center.

Soon after the councilmen approved the exchange of land, the bankers discarded the cloak of disinterest. An officer of each bank phoned the local agent of the developers requesting the name of the executive who had authority to place the firm's Woodruff bank account.

Since the bankers recognized the value of new commercial accounts, their failure to assist the development of the downtown shopping center requires explanation. Apart from the new accounts one or both banks would obtain, land values in the area would increase, and the center might possibly stimulate the expansion of the entire retail district. Expressions of approval to councilmen, offers of assistance to the developers, meetings with the city manager to facilitate the land swap, and persuading downtown merchants not to oppose the project were logical actions.

Since four of the bankers were downtown businessmen and at least an additional fourth owned downtown commercial interests, they either accepted or acquiesced to the views of the downtown businessmen. The latter believed that the projected shopping center would not attract new business to the downtown area. They felt it would increase competition, already keen, for the discretionary dollar in Woodruff. The "economic interests" of the banks were restricted to preserving harmonious relations with old and established customers regardless of the direct economic gains and possible long-run benefits the shopping center would bring to both the banks and the community.

Downtown Mall

Since both banks were closely tied to downtown property owners and merchants and downtown businesses were customers for loans and for credit arrangements, the banks could be expected to assist efforts to improve the main retail area. Early in the sixties, several younger men, including the son of the executive secretary of the Chamber of Commerce and the architect who was active in the shopping center development, began to explore ways of strengthening the downtown stores. Since a mall had been highly successful in a neighboring city, a similar arrangement for Woodruff was given serious consideration. The architect prepared a tentative design, and a group of local businessmen examined the mall in the sister city. One major stumbling block appeared to be the cost per business for improving the fronts of their establishments. A number of merchants considered the expense to be excessive.

While the idea of a mall was taking hold among some of the downtown businessmen and its success in other cities was under consideration, banking officials watched, listened, and did nothing. Their position avoided the central question of whether a two-block mall that ran across Midstate Avenue would strengthen the downtown shopping area in the growing competition with outlying stores and shopping centers. Bank officials reduced the problem to the orthodox question of whether a specific request for a loan to improve a business along the proposed mall should be approved. Inevitably, if the mall had been adopted, this question would have been important. In the early stages of the program, delineation of alternatives and evaluation of the merits of each were imperative. Once attention focused on the mall and difficulties were encountered, support from the major business and financial interests were indispensable for success. The lack of consensus on the desirability of the proposal, especially because of opposition from older merchants and downtown property owners, some of whom were directors of the two banks, prevented any forceful supportive actions.

Repertory Theater

From these examples the reader may gain the impression that inactivity was a way of life for the banking community on proposals for local change. The financial support each bank gave to the efforts to establish a repertory theater in Woodruff indicates some of the circumstances in which more than minimal help will be given. In 1963 and 1964 a group of college people and civic leaders developed plans for creating a repertory theater in Woodruff, with a cast headed by nationally known actors and actresses, as a permanent addition to the cultural life of the area. It was suggested that the theater specialize in Greek drama. The leaders of the movement may have been inspired by the success of the repertory theater in County Seat City.

A successful project would have considerable economic impact on the community. Since performances were to be given throughout the summer, thousands of tourists would visit the community, spend several nights in local motels and hotel, eat in restaurants, shop in downtown stores, and buy gasoline at service stations. The plan had an additional advantage. The influx in the local population, unlike the influx caused by industrial expansion, would be temporary. The distribution of political influence in the city would remain unchanged. After a few days the visitors would return home, leaving behind valuable sums of money.

Many different groups gave the proposal its support, local and absentee-owned industry, the university and university people, professional people and merchants. To strengthen the attractiveness of the community to tourists, which was a major weakness in the plan, consideration was given to restoration of some of the city's nineteenth-century mansions, some of them examples of Greek revival architecture. A sum of money was raised sufficient to employ several top-ranking performers, a noted director, assemble a cast, and make other necessary arrangements. Two Greek plays were selected for the first summer's program, and these received good notices in nationally prominent newspapers. Unfortunately, the repertory theater did not survive beyond the first year.

Each of the two banks contributed $7,500 to the theater project, an amount greater than the budget for the first merger campaign. The major reason for contributing to this project that was at least as, if not more, questionable than the mall proposal was the broad consensus in favor of the plan that had developed among many influential segments of the local population and the absence of organized opposition. The bankers would make friends with this contribution while a lesser donation, or none at all, would have alienated influential people.

Shady Lea Village Housing Development
Another revealing incident occurred in the mid-fifties. In 1954, Woodruff Township acquired the land and buildings of Shady Lea Village from the federal government. The township board solicited plans from area builders for a housing development in the village. The firm that presented the most suitable plan would be selected to redevelop the village.

Soon after the township board had disclosed its intentions concerning Shady Lea Village, an attorney from a New York law firm visited Lockwood, the attorney and a director of the National Bank. He urged the latter to form a group of responsible, local businessmen to acquire and develop Shady Lea Village. The experience, know-how, and resources of a national real estate corporation would be available to them. In a sense the business group would be the local agent of the larger corporation. The latter would be the "silent partner."

The bank director suspected that this offer did not originate with the realty corporation but with Universal Motors, who had acquired the former bomber plant from Pacific Motors. The company could have been motivated by concern over the impact of inferior housing on the morale of its Woodruff employees. Since the firm could not openly enter the housing field without inviting demands for housing assistance from all communities in which its plants were located, a more discreet and covert method could be used. When the National Bank attorney asked the representative whether the offer originated with Universal Motors, a strong, negative answer was given. Nevertheless, Lockwood was not convinced.

Directors of the National Bank were the least likely group to spearhead the formation of a business group for the redevelopment of Shady Lea Village. Business and civic interests in the community had fought the location of the housing project in the Woodruff area in 1942. Since the project consisted of temporary wartime housing, and was inhabited by a substantial number of migrants from the rural South, the housing area was considered a slum. Because they felt that "dirty, illiterate, immoral people" resided there, Woodruff leaders rejected the opportunity to annex the area early in the fifties.

Several financial aspects of the housing project appeared to be disadvantageous to the banks. Both organizations had a long-standing policy of refusing F.H.A. and G.I. mortgages. Apart from the paper work, which the bankers disliked, they considered persons who needed federally insured mortgages as poor risks. Since these persons were in the lower-income brackets, they might be unable to meet payments in the event of a financial setback.

Despite these considerations, a local group was established which included four or five directors of the National Bank and several local businessmen. Plans were prepared and submitted to the township board. As the group had no previous experience in the housing field, its plans were rejected.

The willingness of some directors of the National Bank to be involved in this undertaking appears to contradict the emphasis on restricted, immediate economic goals.

Actually, the risk of loss was slight and the prospect for financial gain excellent since a reliable and experienced corporation had guaranteed the success of the venture. If the realty corporation had not pledged its assistance, the local business groups would not have considered the housing program.

Participation in Merger Campaigns
The involvement of bank officials and directors in the two election campaigns to unite city and township conformed closely to traditional policies. With the exception of the 1963–64 campaign, no bank officials played an active role in the election controversy.

Since the two campaigns are analyzed in detail in Part III, it suffices to review briefly certain phases, especially fund raising. The budget for the first election campaign had been set at the modest sum of $6,000; Mike Davenport had accepted responsibility for raising this amount. During the planning phase of the campaign, bank officials and directors took no active part and made no contribution in ideas or effort. Their lack of interest also was shown by the fact that neither bank was represented at the first meeting devoted exclusively to financing the campaign. In discussing the assignment of persons and groups to be solicited, Davenport and his advisors recognized and verbalized the hopelessness of approaching bank officials. The fear of losing township accounts would prevent these men from contributing. Employees of the two banks gave token contributions, a few hundred dollars, at the most. The possibility was not considered that the bankers were being overly cautious since the names of donors would be kept secret.

Although Lockwood accepted the leadership of the second election campaign, the bank directors and officials did not change their policy on participating in a controversial election issue. Since Lockwood, as president of the National Bank, failed to obtain tangible assistance from his colleagues, he had no chance of persuading officials of Universal Motors and Midwest Motors to contribute funds. This was one of several factors that forced Lockwood to surrender the leadership of the campaign. His retreat wrecked the plans that he had formulated and the leadership group he had assembled. Defeat was inevitable.

Over the years the leaders of the two banks were remarkably consistent in the management of their enterprises and in regulating participation in community affairs. In both spheres of activity these men have emphasized the risks of losing current accounts and not the goal of strengthening present or of attracting new accounts. They believed that whatever advantages would accrue from efforts to improve a sector of the community, whether the downtown retail district or area political structure, would be more than offset by the loss of angry clients. Vigorous action, as in the Shady Lea housing project, was taken only on those rare occasions in which the normal risks were offset by an extraordinary promise of gain or by a total community commitment to the venture. Bankers therefore refused to allocate valuable resources for the accomplishment of social change. Some of the reasons for this refusal are examined below.

Banking Performance, 1935–1968

Woodruff bankers were not compelled by economic necessity to participate actively in efforts to change various features of the community. While some of the alterations, especially those improving the downtown business district, retailing functions, and the efficiency of governmental operations, would have benefited the banks, the amount of gain may have seemed minor compared with the increments resulting from growth of the local university and expansion of operations in the absentee-owned plants. Since the profitability of banking operations would improve appreciably by application of sound and traditional management procedures, embroilment in local controversies of uncertain merit appeared to be too costly.

The data on the growth of deposits for each bank since 1935 support this view of community expansion. Bank deposits in the sixties increased by about 140 percent (see Table 2). From 1950 to 1968 the increase was approximately 274 percent. Both banks participated in this growth, with the National Bank in the sixties enjoying a slight percentage advantage over its rival institution.

The importance for the local economy of trends in the national economy and of automobile production also may be seen in Table 2. The five year-periods with the highest rates of increase in bank deposits for both banks occurred when the absentee-owned factories were operating at peak capacities. These high growth rates took place during World War II, the Korean conflict when the former bomber plant produced cargo planes for the air force, and in the sixties when the automobile industry had several consecutive banner years. During this latter period the local university also experienced a marked increase in enrollment, from about 6,000 in 1962 to about 17,000 in the fall of 1969. Plans to enroll 25,000 students by 1975 gave the Woodruff economy another important source of growth.

The pattern of stock splits reflects the influence of absentee-owned factories. Both the Savings Bank and National Bank declared stock splits and stock dividends in years when the largest factories were running at high levels. The Savings Bank had a 100 percent stock dividend in 1947, during the era of postwar expansion. Both banks had stock dividends during or immediately after the Korean conflict. The Savings Bank declared a 60 percent stock dividend in 1951, and the National Bank a 100 percent split in 1953. In the early sixties, automobile manufacturing exceeded eight million cars per year for several consecutive years. The National Bank had another 100 percent split in 1963; the Savings Bank had a 25 percent stock dividend in 1962 and a ten-for-one split in 1967.

The rewards that bank officials distributed to stockholders were evident from cash dividends paid and changes in the value of the stock. When the Savings Bank first paid dividends in 1941, the year that the bomber plant was built, a dividend of $4.00 per share was

Table 2. *Total Deposits and Percent Change in Woodruff National Bank and Savings Bank, 1935–1968*[a]

Year	Total Deposits			Percent Change		
	National Bank	Savings Bank	Total	National Bank	Savings Bank	Total
1968	29,256,000	37,717,000	66,973,000	39.1	36.9	37.8
1965	21,026,499	27,555,094	48,581,593	84.7	65.1	73.0
1960	11,386,000	16,694,000	28,080,000	−0.2	5.8	3.3
1955	11,404,000	15,783,000	27,187,000	63.7	44.2	51.8
1950	6,964,410	10,946,000	17,910,410	24.7	31.1	28.6
1945	5,582,363	8,347,000	13,929,363	269.2	195.9	219.8
1940	1,539,181	2,820,000	4,359,181	69.5	62.4	64.7
1935	908,000[b]	1,736,812	2,644,812			

a. The data are from *Moody's Bank and Finance Manual* (New York: Moody's Investor's Service, Inc, 1936, 1941, 1946, 1951, 1956, 1961, 1969). The data for 1965 are from bank statements published in *The Woodruff Press*, January 15, 1966, for the Savings Bank and National Bank, respectively.

b. Estimated amount of deposits for year specified.

distributed. Dividend rates increased and in 1964 the bank paid $10.00 per share. This rate was maintained after the ten-for-one stock split. While the per share amounts paid by the National Bank were much smaller, the percentage gain compared favorably with that of the Savings Bank. In 1943, the National Bank paid $.50 per share, in 1959, $1.20, and in 1968, $1.00 per share. The value of a share of Savings Bank stock more than doubled from $175 in 1950 to $375 in 1964. The per share value of National Bank stock increased from $25 in 1957 to about $40 in 1964, before a stock split.[15]

The prosperity that Woodruff and the banks enjoyed during and after World War II is evident from the program of physical expansion. In the late fifties both banks remodeled the main offices. In 1959, the Savings Bank opened a branch east of Woodruff; the National Bank did likewise the following year. In 1963, the National Bank expanded the east branch bank at a cost of $25,000, renovated the exterior of the main office at a cost of $50,000, and, in 1964, announced construction of two new branches west of the city, with one adjacent to the college campus. A short time later the National Bank renovated the interior of the main office. Not to be outdone the Savings Bank constructed a $150,000 branch office on the west side. In 1969, it opened a second branch in the eastern section of the township. In the sixties, a period that coincided with an upsurge in university enrollment and automobile manufacturing, both banks carried out ambitious programs of expansion. These facts indicate some of the important reasons for the satisfaction of bank executives with the local economy and, in general, with community affairs.

Demographic Characteristics of Top Bank Personnel[16]

The basic outlines of the decision-making pattern, established and crystallized during the travail of the depression years, held Woodruff in its grip for at least three decades. The persistence of this

15. The financial information was obtained from Moody's *Bank and Finance Manual* (New York: Moody's Investor Service, Inc., 1936, 1941, 1946, 1951, 1956, 1961, 1969). Data for 1965 were obtained from bank statements published in *The Woodruff Press*, January 15, 1966.

16. The data on bank directors and top bank officers, i.e., president and

pattern could be attributed to the fact that, down through the years, the bearers or carriers of this leadership tradition, the key bank executives and directors, were homogeneous in social characteristics. Similarity of social background strengthened consensus on decision making.

The bank directors and top bank executives were white, males, married, almost exclusively Protestant, and Republican. Except for several attorneys they were either large property owners or business-men, long time residents of the Woodruff area and, for the most part, of the city. They had worked with one another in the Chamber of Commerce, Community Fund, and service clubs, had labored to-gether on committees and drives. They knew how each of their associates felt on important issues. The similarity in background and in interaction patterns strengthened the similarity in outlook toward Woodruff, its problems, and its future.

Older men do not readily change basic beliefs held for a lifetime. Woodruff's bankers had followed certain decision-making patterns during their adult years. Resistance to change was suggested by the fact that the directors were older than the total group of forty-six city leaders (see Chapter 3). Over 63 percent of the bank directors as compared with 22 percent of the forty-six leaders were sixty-one years of age and over.

The directors over sixty came to maturity before World War II. They were young when Woodruff experienced the boom of the twenties; they reached maturity during the depression and war years. Since they were fully aware of the rapid changes that the community and its economy experienced, they could compare the assets of the banks, the dividends, and the value of the bank stock in the fifties and sixties with levels in the thirties. Utilizing this frame of refer-ence, the banks and their personal holdings were doing well. Ambi-tious programs of social and political action were not needed.

The preference for directors whose families resided in Woodruff for many decades reinforced the decision-making pattern. Approxi-mately 59 percent of the bank directors as compared with less than

vice-presidents, were obtained in 1962 by use of a one-page mail question-naire. The use of follow-up letters in several instances resulted in a complete return of the questionnaires. The data on directors pertain to the early six-ties.

3 percent of city leaders belonged to families that had arrived in Woodruff before 1900, whereas 31 percent of the forty-six city leaders arrived in Woodruff after 1941. At the time of study, no bank director had come after 1941.[17] The majority of directors were raised in families that had associated with each other for generations, whose members shared memories of Woodruff as a small, farm trade center and college community. These associations, traditions, and recollections reinforced consensus on the community and its condition.

The occupational background of the directors did not require many years of higher education. A fourth of the bank directors were merchants and more than a fifth were manufacturers.[18] Another fifth were full-time officers of the banks. These three categories accounted for two-thirds of the bank directors. The remaining directors included two attorneys, a politician, and a contractor. With very few exceptions, the directors owned land, or buildings, or enterprises, or all three in Woodruff. Woodruff property ownership was considered an important attribute in the director selection process.

Policies on recruiting directors excluded automobile industry executives despite the presence in Woodruff of the administrative staffs of two divisions and the staffs of the several plants.[19] College administrators, distinguished educators, and other professional men, notably physicians and architects, were not given serious consideration.[20] The directors of the two banks seemed less concerned with inviting the most able and successful men in the area to serve on the board than with excluding those, who, by industry, professional,

17. Each bank appointed a top administrator of the local university to its Board of Directors in the fall of 1965 to replace a director who had died. The National Bank chose the man who had recently moved to Woodruff to assume the office of university president. The Savings Bank selected a university vice-president. Conflict of interest difficulties led to their resignations as directors a few years later.

18. Three directors were retired from the business world but were classified by the occupation held before retirement.

19. Universal Motors prohibited plant executives from serving as directors of a bank in the community in which the plant was located. Since Woodruff bank officials never mentioned this rule to explain the absence of automobile executives from the Board of Directors, it was assumed that they were unaware of its existence.

20. See footnote 17.

or educational experience might advocate "unorthodox" courses of action. Homogeneity in occupational background strengthened consensus on key objectives and policy-making procedures.

The preferences for homogeneity extended to religion. While the predilection of the forty-six city leaders toward membership in the Congregational and Methodist churches was greater than for any other church, the proportion was still larger for directors of the banks. Whereas 42 percent of the city leaders were members of the Congregational and Methodist churches, 60 percent of the bank directors were so affiliated. The proportion of persons who were Catholic was about the same for leaders and for directors. No director was a member of the Baptist church, and only one city leader was Baptist. Surprisingly, no bank directors were members of the two churches usually associated nationally with the upper stratum, the Presbyterian and Episcopal churches. The fact that two directors were not members of any church was a departure from the expected pattern of church membership.

The exclusion of persons who lived outside Woodruff, regardless of occupation and industry position, and the preference for businessmen whose families had been in the community for fifty years or more preserved the homogeneity of board members. The directors of the local fiscal organizations, through the selection of successors, preserved the influence of the small, hereditary group of local businessmen and strengthened conformity of decision making in certain areas.[21]

Conclusion

Woodruff's banking leaders were exponents of a variety of decision making that prized the continuity of basic social and cultural pat-

21. The process of succession, which could be postponed but not prevented, began with the appointment of two additional directors to the National Bank in 1964 and the replacement of a Savings Bank director in 1965. While, in each instance, the replacement was under forty, kinship relations and family position influenced the selections. In the case of the National Bank, one director, Harding's younger brother, was the son-in-law of the bank's chairman. The other appointee, Endicott, a member of a Woodruff family that had resided in the community for three generations, if not more, was a very close friend of the bank president, Lockwood, and a cousin of the bank's cashier. An important departure from the rules of selecting directors occur-

terns. They were not innovators, nor did they encourage others in this direction. Not since the thirties had any Woodruff bank officer or director, except for Lockwood in the 1964 campaign, served in a capacity that legitimized or tangibly supported annexation, merger, or other plans for modifying area political structure.

Bank officers and directors followed certain decision-making patterns when participating in local projects and community affairs. Projects and plans that were likely to result in controversy and conflict in the short-run or that might alienate bank clients were avoided regardless of the prospects for strengthening the local economy and improving the community. Bankers counted on the expansion of the university and of automobile plant activity to provide improved earnings and profits for their organizations. By "playing it safe," the bankers did not offend old customers—their friends and colleagues—and did not alter social and political patterns while enjoying expanded and expanding bank activity.

---

red in 1965. The new president of the local university was named a director to replace one who had died. Selection of a newcomer to Woodruff as director, albeit one who had served elsewhere as a bank director, was a striking innovation.

The Savings Bank named Mike Davenport's older son to its Board of Directors. After more than thirty years, a Davenport held a position in a Woodruff bank. The appointment was not solely the result of the long-term placement of the Davenport factory account in the Savings Bank. The selection was intended to strengthen management of the bank after the sudden loss of two young vice-presidents. One became president of a bank in another city, and the other died after a brief illness. The prestige of the Davenport name in Woodruff would assist the bank during the transition brought on by turnover of key personnel and the expansion problems of the sixties.

6. The Woodruff Chamber of Commerce

In contrast with the leaders of Woodruff's banking community, whose way of life was noninvolvement in local controversies and social issues, the Chamber of Commerce was committed to action. Its leaders and executive secretary were involved in many different spheres of local affairs, commercial, industrial, and political. The Chamber always seemed to have a highly publicized project underway: a study of downtown parking facilities or parking meters, a committee report on some phase of local government or on a school bond issue, an appreciation day for absentee-owned plants, or a sales promotion for downtown merchants. Chamber activities generated newspaper reports, which in turn created an image of the organization as a "steering committee" for the community.

A number of factors discussed in previous chapters suggest that the influence of the Chamber went beyond "busy work." It appeared that leadership in Woodruff was provided more by certain organizations than by individuals. Woodruff's leadership had been weakened by the decline of an important family and the inability to find successors. The city's leaders lacked the stature of the X family of Middletown, the Choates and Weatherby's of Yankee City, or the economic elite of Regional City (see Chapter 3). Many of the wealthier and more prestigious leaders withheld basic resources from the groups working for and against some proposal (see Chapter 5). The leaders of the banks strengthen the inertial tendencies that existed in Woodruff as in every community. The executives of the absentee-owned plants lived outside of Woodruff and tended not to be concerned with its problems. The Chamber's influence derived not only from the community's need for leadership but from the pattern of involvement in problem situations that the association developed from its inception in 1920.[1]

History and Functions

The Woodruff Chamber of Commerce, a member of the national organization, was founded in 1920 during a period in which the

1. Students of community leadership and action have paid little attention to the Chamber of Commerce. Where the researchers take note of the organization, they usually mention in passing that it or one of its officers took a particular position or action in reference to some issue, without examining the reasons, the influence of this action, or the organization's traditions. The neglect is somewhat surprising since the Lynds referred to this organization in their two studies of Middletown with a frequency that suggested that its role was of some importance. The Lynds viewed the Chamber as an instrument of business-class control of the community and as an expression of its values and objectives. They wrote: "Operating under such a set of traditional assumptions and backed financially by the owners and managers of the city's productive resources, the Chamber of Commerce and its business-class members have thrown their weight increasingly on the side of more organization among management and less organization among labor . . . ." Robert S. Lynd and Helen M. Lynd, *Middletown in Transition: A Study in Cultural Conflicts* (New York: Harcourt, Brace and Company, 1937), pp. 34–35.

Among those researchers who pay even scant attention to the Chamber, opinion on its influence is divided. One reason for its lack of influence in some communities appears to be the lack of consensus on objectives and programs. Cf. Aaron Wildavsky, *Leadership in a Small Town* (Totowa, N.J.: Bedminster Press, 1964), pp. 278–79. Although Banfield does not report on the actions of the Chamber in the issues analyzed in his case study (he mentions briefly the Association of Commerce and Industry), his remarks on the role of civic associations seem applicable. The membership of such associations generally divide on basic issues, thereby forcing the leaders to choose between involvement in a local action situation and the preservation of the association. The latter objective generally is preferred, forcing the organization to adopt a "hands off" policy. Edward C. Banfield, *Political Influence* (Glencoe, Ill.: The Free Press, 1961), pp. 294–303.

An example of division within the Chamber which had an important impact on a major conflict occurred during the shoe strike in Yankee City. The small businessmen in the Chamber supported the workers, and the manufacturers supported the management of the shoe factories. This division apparently

rural aspects of the township fostered a city-centered Chamber membership. By the 1960's, with area development and a decrease in rural living patterns in the township, the Chamber had taken on a somewhat fallacious area title, Woodruff *Area* Chamber of Commerce, and an increased number of township business memberships.

The structure of the local group consisted of a president, a twenty-one member executive policy-making board—five elected by the membership annually for three year terms, five elected by the board for one year, and the past president—and a paid executive secretary. During the forty-nine years it had existed, only four secretaries had been employed.

---

contributed to community support for the strikers, a factor that favored the success of the strike. While Warner states that the Chamber played an influential role in the strike, he failed to provide supporting evidence. These observations on the Chamber, written more than twenty years ago, also should have created some interest in the role of the Chamber in local affairs. W. Lloyd Warner and J. O. Low, *The Social System of the Modern Factory: A Social Analysis* (New Haven: Yale University Press, 1947), p. 35.

A recent comparative study of leadership found the Chamber to be influential in two of the four communities studied. The authors regarded the Chamber as "Probably the most powerful political force in Gamma . . . but it usually worked in combination with other groups or through the citizens' committees." In Delta, the Chamber reflected the community consensus against a variety of proposals for change. Despite these and other tidbits, the authors also fail to elaborate on the structure and function of the Chamber in relation to other features of local leadership. Oliver P. Williams and Charles R. Adrian, *Four Cities: A Study in Comparative Policy Making* (Philadelphia: University of Pennsylvania Press, 1963), pp. 192–97, 303–5, 312–15.

Kammerer and associates reported that the division between leaders favoring and those opposing the development of the community which embroiled the local banks also were manifest in the Chamber of Commerce. Gladys M. Kammerer et al., *The Urban Political Community: Profiles in Town Politics* (Boston: Houghton Mifflin Company, 1963), pp. 28–29, 86–89, 97.

Two hypotheses on the influence of the Chamber is suggested by this brief review of the literature of community leadership studies. The first of these is that the Chamber tends to be more influential in smaller than in larger cities. The various elites in the latter are more diverse and exercise influence through arrangements other than formal associations. The studies in this category are: Roscoe C. Martin et al., *Decisions in Syracuse* (Bloomington, Ind.: Indiana University Press, 1961); Banfield, *Political Influence;* and Floyd Hunter, *Community Power Structure* (Chapel Hill, N.C.: The University of North Carolina Press, 1953). Second, among smaller cities, the influence of the Chamber varies inversely with the degree of influence of both the community's informal leaders and the political leaders. The Woodruff data appear to support this hypothesis.

Functionally the local organization advocated the promotion and development of commercial, industrial, and civic affairs. In addition, the organization publicly proclaimed a *status quo* position throughout its history: "It is not only the things which we help make happen, but those things which we prevent from happening that really count. This process is the real measure of our 'production,' not the occasional spectacular accomplishment."[2] This action/inaction commitment of the Chamber contributed to the development and maintenance of Woodruff's decision-making patterns. By formally embracing a policy of prevention, the Chamber fostered the firming up of the definitions for acceptable and unacceptable community development.

Whenever township leaders or dissident city residents expressed feelings of antipathy toward Woodruff City, entwined in their discourse were usually charges against the Woodruff Chamber of Commerce. Accusations were of two varieties: the Chamber controlled and had controlled Woodruff city government for years, and the Chamber had prevented and retarded the development of outside business and the investment of outside capital that would compete with the interests of its members. These statements combined with preliminary observations gleaned from perusing the pages of local newspapers, Chamber minutes, and official records of the Woodruff city government drew attention to the role of the Chamber in community decision making.

For over forty years the Woodruff Chamber of Commerce, a city-oriented organization, had a close and influential association with the local body politic. Evidence of its city-directiveness was the fact that it never, to our knowledge, officially proposed action or made similar recommendations to the township board. At first blush, it seemed as if active leadership in Woodruff might be described as a form of collective rule, with considerable influence vested in a voluntary association representing the business and property interests of the city. Further study indicated that this organization, rather than any other in Woodruff, had more members who assisted in the development, stabilizing, and maintenance of Woodruff's patterns of decision making. This chapter reviews several techniques used by the Chamber of Commerce over the past

2. Woodruff Chamber of Commerce, *Flier* (1959).

forty-nine years to minimize policy-making changes directly related
to the latter:
1. Selectivity of action and interest areas.
2. Lengthy tenure of its executive professional.
3. Restricted participation of economic "outsiders."

City Government
In its many years of activity the Woodruff Chamber of Commerce
developed some important features. When Woodruff residents
wished to refer to a dominant clique and power group they used
such terms as "the city fathers," "the downtown boys," "the important leaders." When the informant was pressed to explain exactly to whom he referred, he responded in one of two ways: either he
named one or two men and concluded "you know, the Chamber of
Commerce," or he immediately mentioned the Chamber of Commerce.

The homogeneity of the men elected to the city council and the
membership of the Chamber of Commerce during the latter's first
thirty years of existence encouraged a very close working relationship between the two. Under the mayor-council form of city government, when the mayor does not devote full time to the position, the
council and mayor must depend on individuals and groups to guide
the development of governmental policy. The most successful advisory service the councils and mayors possessed, until the city
manager form took its place in 1947, was the Woodruff Chamber
of Commerce and the services of its executive secretary. Until the
retirement of its second executive secretary in the spring of 1962,
the Chamber still played an important if somewhat more tenuous
part in the framing of fiscal policy.

Facilitating the alignment of the two structures was the frequency
by which presidents and directors of the Chamber held key positions
in city government. Since the founding of the Chamber in 1920, at
least five presidents served as mayor. Mike Davenport, for example,
served for five years with an additional three years on the city council. Another held the post of mayor for four years, and the post of
councilman for several years. Between 1947 and 1963, three Chamber presidents served as mayor for a total of ten years.

Other important posts in local government have been held by

Chamber presidents for long terms. The post of city attorney was held by two men consecutively for a total of more than forty years. One served for at least thirty years, and another held the post for twelve. One Chamber president held the office of assessor and treasurer for a short period. Erickson served as president of the planning commission for several years, and Wasmund, the Chamber's executive secretary, held a seat on that body for about ten years. His Chamber successor was named to the planning commission in 1964.

Two Chamber presidents held other important government posts. Sampson was appointed to the County Board of Supervisors representing Woodruff from 1943 to 1965. The other president was elected to the State House of Representatives from 1956 to 1964; his father had occupied that seat for more than thirty years.

The Junior Chamber of Commerce also has been an important source of manpower for city government. The credit that the organization received for adoption of the city manager, nonpartisan form of government did much to establish the tradition of the Jaycees as training ground for future community leaders. Many of the young men who were active in that controversy subsequently held positions in city government. The Jaycees who took charge of the consolidation campaign of 1957–58 saw themselves as following the tradition established by their predecessors (see Chapter 8). This tradition was maintained in later years, e.g., the mayor pro-tem of the 1969–70 city council was a former Jaycee president. The tradition also has influenced the township members of the Jaycees, several of whom ran successfully for office in township government.

A number of factors contribute to a union of governmental and Chamber decision making. The various city organizations have interchanged key personnel for many years. The similarity in socioeconomic characteristics of these men combined with past association on a variety of committees and local projects enhances an identity of outlook. The dependence of city government on the Chamber and the expectation of many city officials to resume participation in its activities once their term of office has expired also strengthens the union of the two organizations.[3]

3. For a discussion of the factors influencing the degree of influence that private organizations have over government agencies, cf. Henry W. Ehrmann,

The Chamber of Commerce functioned as an almost semi-official arm of local government. Communication flowed in two directions. The Chamber called to the attention of councilmen conditions with which it was concerned and suggested remedial programs. The council publicly referred a variety of community problems to the Chamber of Commerce for study, later acting favorably on the latter's recommendations. A partial record[4] speaks for itself:

1924 The Chamber of Commerce developed annexation plans for city expansion of two areas west of the city for city council.

1929 Chamber of Commerce and City Council work together to secure a favorable decision on the location of a State Hospital.
Chamber of Commerce executive secretary interpreted meaning and cost of annexation to the city before groups on east side living in effected area for the Chamber of Commerce and city council.

1933 Chamber of Commerce assisted city by setting up central registration system for unemployment relief.

1943 Chamber of Commerce launched City Charter Revision Study. The Charter Revision Committee elected in 1945 consisted of three Chamber of Commerce Directors as members. Chamber of Commerce encouraged the Junior Chamber to organize a successful campaign for charter acceptance.

1955 Chamber of Commerce helped negotiate an agreement between the city and a major industrial company making available city owned land for plant expansion —resulting in the employment of 550.

1956 Study requested of Chamber of Commerce by city council of long range parking program. Study made and submitted to the city council.

1960– City Manager, U.S. Postal officials, place decision on
61 location of new city post office in the hands of the Chamber of Commerce.

"Interest Groups and the Bureaucracy in Western Democracies," in Reinhard Bendix, ed., *State and Society: A Reader in Comparative Political Sociology* (Boston: Little, Brown and Company, 1968), pp. 257–76.
4. Woodruff Chamber of Commerce, *Flier,* 1959.

Many items in the newspapers reported formal city council action requesting Chamber of Commerce response to a program, a course of action, or even the submission of a program in certain areas. It is the public formality and overtness with which the business of the Chamber and council were entwined through the years that was surprising. Certainly local Chambers throughout the United States have made little pretense about their lobbyist functions. Doubtless the record of the successful pressures their members and professionals have brought to bear upon local public officials would be lengthy. Chambers flourish or falter on the success of these efforts; their professional executives move on to larger Chambers on the basis of these achievements. Most of the functions, however, are carried on behind the scenes.

Until the late sixties the Woodruff City Council functioned administratively while in most important matters the Chamber of Commerce exercised the legislative role. The councils may have felt that without Chamber approval a program would fail, or they may have used the Chamber as a sounding board for community leader reaction. In any case, the Chamber and its leadership, more than any other Woodruff organization, supported certain decision-making patterns and had steadfastly, over the years, in its policies, action, and inaction on community development refused to tolerate conflicting approaches. Through its board and committees, the Chamber became the one Woodruff organization performing overtly and publicly for or against community-wide programs after they had been evaluated. The assumption of this role by the Chamber made it possible for various levels of Woodruff leadership to control the course of community development from behind the scenes.

In 1943, the Chamber initiated a study of the city charter which led to the establishment of a charter revision committee by the voters in 1945. The committee included three directors of the Chamber. In 1956, the Local Affairs Committee reviewed the operation of the new form of government. It recommended establishment of a number of standing citizens advisory committees to increase citizen participation and interest in local government. Committee members may have considered this a means for increasing Chamber influence over local government. The councilmen ignored these recommendations. In 1958, a Chamber committee again studied the operation of local government. The desirability of a return to the ward system was considered, but no action was taken.

On occasion, the Chamber functioned as a "trouble-shooter" for municipal government by analyzing some phase of public administration. In the mid-fifties the Local Affairs Committee studied the operations of the police department. Criticisms of the department had been aired publicly and the Chamber sought to discover the sources of dissatisfaction.

Exercise of Public Influence
Throughout its history the Chamber sought to influence the electors on selective issues. Generally the Chamber acted in two ways: public statements in the press on the official position of the Chamber, while similar statements appeared in the organization's bulletin that members received, and the solicitation of funds to publicize favored positions. The public endorsement by the directors of the Chamber for specific proposals was sought by many interest groups. Millage proposals for the schools, municipal bond issues, annexation plans, fluoridation of water, urban renewal, liquor by the glass, and revisions of the city charter are examples of issues on which the Chamber publicly expressed its position. In many instances the city council refused to take action until it was assured of wholehearted support from the Chamber. This function was usually performed when the city council wished to obtain citizen approval for an "extraordinary" expenditure of public funds. To avoid major criticism and to gain assurances that public opinion favored the allocation of funds, the issue was placed on the ballot—even when the city council had authority to take action without a vote of the citizens. Relying on the Chamber to mobilize public opinion on behalf of a course of action that all or a majority of councilmen favor but that was opposed by some group or faction in the community increased the influence of the Chamber. It gave the organization a veto power over these matters. If the Chamber refused to support the proposal, the city council was unable, or at best handicapped, in efforts to obtain voter consent. It was not customary for the mayor to dramatize issues for the electorate or "to go to the people." On these types of issues, the city council proposed and the Chamber, in fact, disposed of the matter.

While examples have not been numerous in the past four decades, two that occurred were important. In 1938, the city council feared opposition to a proposal to include water softening facilities, at a cost of $7,000, in the plans for the water-treatment plant. It was placed on the ballot, and the Chamber took the initiative in organizing a campaign for a favorable vote. A Chamber committee prepared information on the advantages of water softening and circulated it throughout the community. Selected Chamber members wrote letters to the editor backing the improvement, and the Chamber purchased space in the newspaper to emphasize its advantages. The election drive succeeded.

In the mid-fifties, when the city manager recognized that expansion of the city's water treatment and sewage disposal plants could no longer be delayed, he discussed the financial arrangements, a $1,700,000 bond issue, with the directors of the Chamber first. After assurances of Chamber support for the bond proposals had been given, the manager presented the details to councilmen. During the course of city council deliberations the city manager kept the president and directors of the Chamber well informed. The manager sent a copy of the analysis of the bond issue prepared by Woodruff's bond consultant in March, 1955, to the president and members of the Chamber, as well as to the mayor, councilmen, and members of the planning commission.

The discussion of the relationships between the Chamber and municipal government leads to the conclusion that durable patterns of interdependence developed during the fifty-year history of the organization. Neither this association nor the government body were likely to stray too far from the interests and wishes of the other.

Economic Functions

The "governmental" role played by the Chamber of Commerce was equalled if not surpassed by its role in the economic life of the community. Between 1920 and 1939, the Chamber assisted seven industries, five minor and two major, to locate in the community. After that date it gave lip service to its attempts to attract industry while accomplishing nothing. The lack of city industrial land and poor township-city relations were factors in its failure. In 1924, the

Chamber assisted in the establishment of a credit bureau; in 1930, it took over the Community Fund Campaign and continued as the Community Fund headquarters until 1965; and in 1931, it was selected as the organization with the appropriate manpower and money to reorganize the Woodruff Savings Bank and, in 1933, the National Bank. It organized the Junior Chamber of Commerce in 1938, became headquarters of the Local War Council in 1942, sponsored Junior Achievement in 1952, organized a committee for the development of the downtown mall and the redevelopment of the downtown area in 1959, and in 1962 organized a committee for industrial development.

The above record is one of overt accomplishments. In addition, the Chamber and its executive secretary performed other functions that prevented action or change of various kinds. New city-located, small-scale industry or large-scale businesses that might have changed the residential and political complexion of the city and possibly its patterns of decision making were covertly prohibited. To protect its commercial membership the Chamber attempted to prevent the location of outside competitive stores within the community. During the war period, when overnight war expansion brought thousands to the community who were hungry for the basic goods of life and who lacked the time and transportation to travel in search of them, the Chamber successfully killed a million dollar merchandise mart that had been planned to be located adjacent to the industrial plant site. The Chamber listed this accomplishment in its 1959 flier addressed to its membership.

Among the many economic activities of the Chamber were those which pertained to the establishments in the central business district. The relationship among the men who owned the property and buildings, those who operated the stores, and the Chamber was especially important. The Chamber sought to strengthen the c.b.d. (central business district—major downtown commercial and retail district) in its competition with the outlying shopping centers. Its committees studied traffic flows, parking facilities, and renovation of buildings, and they also made recommendations to the city council and planning commission, e.g., a thoroughfare plan for the c.b.d. and changes in the use of parking meters.

The efforts over a long period of time to protect and strengthen the c.b.d., coupled with the seasonal promotions to boost the sales of the stores in that area conveyed to the citizenry the belief that the Chamber was used by the "city fathers" with equity in the c.b.d. The public recognized or believed in the existence of a direct and material connection between the Chamber and downtown businessmen. This association limited the influence of the Chamber as a molder of public opinion on certain election issues. On the other hand, many felt that what the Chamber and its leaders considered unfavorable to their special interests would be inimical with planned, orderly community growth. The legion of Woodruff residents who believed this tended to enhance the importance of the Chamber's public position on community-wide issues. It enabled the Chamber to play a valuable role in the maintenance of that variety of change supported by the patterns of decision making which had emerged.

Meeting Crises

The importance of the Chamber to the community as a whole and for economic stability in particular was revealed by its activities in situations in which disruptive changes were threatened or occurred. Under these circumstances the Chamber sought to maintain the effectiveness of an organization or sector of the community, to prevent a "harmful" innovation, or to provide an important community service hitherto unavailable.

As an example of the first function, the Chamber played an important role in the reorganization of the National Bank in 1933, bringing together the various persons and groups interested in such an endeavor and providing the organization required for raising new capital.

There are many examples of attempts by the Chamber to prevent changes that appeared harmful to some segment of the community, especially the local economy. In 1933, the Chamber expressed its opposition to a bill pending in the legislature which could have curtailed drastically the operations of Woodruff University. During the depression years the Chamber registered and found jobs for the unemployed in order to keep relief costs down. In 1942, Chamber officials joined with other groups in the county to protest government plans to establish a permanent housing project for defense workers adjacent to Woodruff. In the early fifties, at the request of officials of Pacific Motors, Chamber directors contacted public officials in Washington in an effort to prevent cancellation of the firm's military plane contract. Most of these Chamber programs were aimed at keeping the organizations and economy of the community functioning in a normal manner.

The Chamber Executive

The man responsible for the operation and development of a large portion of local Chamber program is the professional employed for that purpose. The executive secretary or director is a community organization man whose future mobility depends upon how well he does his job. Usually he is employed by a small Chamber and climbs the ladder to larger Chambers or more important community organizational opportunities. The average length of employment for Chamber executives in the United States is approximately four years.

In its fifty years of existence the Woodruff Chamber of Commerce has had four executives. The first held the position for eight years, the second for almost thirty-three years, the third from March, 1962, until 1967, and the fourth from 1967. The tenure of the second secretary is subject to analysis in terms of the relationship between executive succession and organizational change.

Richard Wasmund, the second executive secretary, performed the duties of the office to the satisfaction of those men who held the organization's reins of power and influence. Throughout his thirty-three years of service, men like Scheible, McDowell, Davenport, Sampson, etc., had an important influence on the functions of the Chamber of Commerce and of Woodruff. Their leadership gave continuity to the aims, interests, and concepts of what the community should be and should do and offered this continuity in the character of the same set of leaders. Even in 1969, many of the leaders of the thirties were still active; some had launched sons into board and organizational positions they once held. From the early years of his employment, Wasmund spoke the same language, held the same views, and was willing to function professionally within the confines of the framework of "community" and decision making which these men had conceived. Except for a major observable threat to his position in 1959, he remained comparatively unchallenged.

The satisfaction with Wasmund's professional services rested on more than the continuity of leadership. In addition to his work for the Chamber of Commerce he undertook other activities as secretary which were needed and for which he did not receive adequate financial compensation. Besides the World War II activities that he assumed for the Chamber and the Automobile License Bureau that for a number of years was housed at the Chamber, the assumption in 1930 of the Community Fund campaign was a staggering burden. Wasmund continued to direct the campaign for twenty-eight years, until 1958, when another professional assumed this responsibility. It is noteworthy that Wasmund's first significant challenge came in 1959, a year after he gave up the direction of the Community Fund.

Once the community and Chamber leadership had made a commitment to the employment of specialized personnel to fill some of Wasmund's functions, his value decreased. Previously it would have been exceedingly difficult to find a man to replace him who would be willing to bear the weighty and diverse load he had carried for years. The redistribution of Wasmund's work altered the picture. Dissatisfactions and complaints against Wasmund could not be buffeted by the claims of irreplaceability.

Why Wasmund was interested in remaining in Woodruff for thirty years at a small salary is not an easy question to answer. Certainly he was satisfied and happy with the work and his unique accomplishments. He was active in his church. His home was in a good housing area immediately adjacent to one of the few prestigious housing areas in Woodruff. He was allowed to undertake an interpretor-"leg-man" role for the community on state and national levels. Many plane flights in connection with the above, particularly in the forties, were recorded in Chamber of Commerce records and in the newspaper. This type of responsibility gives an individual a feeling of personal value, unrealistic as its limits may actually be. In addition, the fact that rich, but not affluent, commercial interests dominated in Woodruff after the twenties allowed Wasmund to assume a higher personal status position than a professional community organization man usually affects. We might categorize him as an almost-but-not-quite leader. By the mid-fifties new "professionals" began to staff other organizations in Woodruff, a city manager, professional city planners, male executive director of the Family Service Society, and the director of the Community Fund. It is likely that Wasmund, as the lone community organization professional, may have received special status considerations, particularly since he was employed by a high status organization in a community that boasted no other top salary professionals until after World War II. Wasmund's retirement came in the spring of 1962 at the age of sixty-one.

A lengthy secretaryship has an effect on an organization and a community. While organizations and communities need the continuity and stability certain types of leaders give to them, most professionals in community organizations ought not to be included in that group. In general these professionals are mobile in their younger years. This mobility allows them to assume more challenging and remunerative positions and allows a community to relieve itself of unacceptable and unproductive employees within an acceptable framework of change. Moreover, new candidates bring to these positions new ideas, more advanced training, new ways of getting things done and of solving problems, and perhaps new contacts with other geographical areas. Certainly each executive must operate to some degree within the acceptable action and decision-making patterns that have evolved in their community. The most important single characteristic resulting from the mobility of the professional community organization man is that, with the change from one man to another and during the period of adjustment, scrutiny, and evaluation that follows, the organization or elected community representatives must assume control and direction.

Regular turnover among executive officers makes it more difficult for the membership of an organization to shift the responsibility and initiative for program, projects, interest, etc., to that professional. Certainly in the change of position from one professional to another, some members must be able to convey the purposes, programs, and expectations of the membership to the newcomer. When an executive continues to assume the same position year after year it is natural that the membership would allow him to take over their functions. Over the years, Wasmund undertook more and more of the organizational and program aspects of the Chamber which are usually assumed by board members. As long as these functions were performed within bounds, the leaders seemed to have accepted this change, even favored it. Wasmund's public protective function allowed Chamber leaders to assume a less public, more behind-the-scenes role in periods of heated community conflict and change than would have been possible had the secretarial occupant changed every few years. In essence, by minimizing the role of top Chamber leaders and relieving them of much public responsibility, he absorbed the brunt of criticism of township and city residents who felt Woodruff's policies were dysfunctional to community development or to their own interests. While much criticism of Wasmund's methods were recorded, few attempts were made to remove him. Perhaps some of Wasmund's success could be attributed to his willingness to undertake many member responsibilities.

Ultimately this tendency may weaken an organization. It becomes the membership's organization in name only. More important, the assumption of member functions severely limits the development of the new leadership every group depends upon. This was the conclusion concerning much of the activities of the Woodruff Chamber of Commerce: Wasmund eventually assumed many of the low—and middle-level organizational tasks. This limited low-level leadership service opportunities while maintaining and relegating top-level leadership positions to those who had proven their allegiance to the types of economic and social change that the Chamber was organized informally to support. It is questionable whether new members would have been attracted to the Chamber if it had not represented "prestige" in the eyes of many newcomers and up-and-comers.

In addition to the assumption of members duties, which is a dual responsibility, a professional ultimately learns the accepted patterns for change or prevention of change and falls into the rut of seldom diverging from them.

Chamber Membership

The interests of the Chamber of Commerce centered primarily on the city of Woodruff. When the organization took action or adopted positions with area implications it was the result of a recognition of the importance of the matter to the city. This concern was symbolized by a proposal early in 1958 to change the name of the organization to the Woodruff Area Chamber, sixteen years after the building of the bomber plant. By 1958, the population of the township almost equalled that of the city, and its rate of growth indicated it would move ahead in the very near future. The value of the tax base of the township had far surpassed that of the city. If the directors of the Chamber had been alert to the changes beyond the borders of the city and wished to improve co-operation with township government, the change in name, which was not a structural change, should have occurred a decade before. Nevertheless, in a retaliatory act against township citizens which symbolized the myopia of Chamber leadership, the directors dropped the proposal for a name change immediately after the defeat of consolidation. Four more years elapsed before the change in name was approved.

The limited horizons of the Chamber can be illustrated, if only in part, by the membership composition and by the difficulties experienced in placing executives of absentee-owned plants on the Board of Directors. The men elected as president, as directors, and as chairmen of committees almost always had an economic interest in the city, either business or professional, although many resided in the township. These township citizens were city oriented: they were not members of organizations that were concerned primarily with township affairs such as the two township political parties, they did not run for political office or serve on governmental bodies in the township, and they were not part of the informal cliques that met to discuss and to decide township issues. With few exceptions, they were not recognized as township leaders.

The inability to encourage township leader participation in the Chamber can be attributed to the identification of the organization with the interests of the city. Many township leaders would hesitate to belong to and participate in the Chamber lest they appear compromised in the eyes of their supporters.

Strong sentiments of exclusiveness operated against industrial plant executives. In 1952, the manager of an automobile plant, one of the largest sources of Chamber revenue,[5] was nominated for the

5. From *The Woodruff Press* and unpublished minutes of the Woodruff Chamber of Commerce.

office of a director of the Chamber and was not elected. To prevent a repetition that might prove embarrassing, the by-laws were revised and approved the following year to expand the number of directors from fifteen to eighteen, allowing the directors to select three board members for a one-year term. Bypassing the general membership permitted one or two executives of absentee-owned plants to be named as directors of the Chamber of Commerce.

Plant executives who have been named directors remained second-class members of the Chamber: they served for one year instead of three and chaired committees whose work areas did not pertain to local interests, e.g., national and state affairs. The facts suggest a strong feeling on the part of the majority of members that positions of importance in the Chamber, positions that influence community policy, should be limited to men who lived and who had an economic interest in the area. The leaders and members wished to confine the direction of the Chamber to the local elite; they had little desire to share power with "outsiders." This had an important influence on perpetuating the parochial interests of the Chamber.

These arrangements satisfied the executives of the automobile plants, permitting them to maintain a proper balance between demonstrating an interest in Woodruff and taking part in the Chamber without threatening the influence of local leaders. It provided sources of information on local matters that affected the plants, especially considerations of governmental changes. Undoubtedly attendance at Chamber meetings gave automobile executives the opportunity to assess the progress of annexation or merger campaigns, e.g., the degree to which the proposals had the support of the top leaders, thus facilitating the formation of adaptive policies. The barrier between the leadership of the auto factories and the leadership of the Chamber was maintained by mutual consent.

The major contribution of auto executives who served as Chamber directors consisted of suggestions for improving the efficiency of the organization and of the Chamber-sponsored Community Fund. Industrial officials took the initiative in recommending the separation of the two organizations in terms of executive leadership and in office arrangements. In this sense the executives made policy, although in areas unrelated to basic economic and political issues. By sharing low-level policy making, Chamber directors gained substantial revenues from company memberships and gratuitous services of company officials and public relations men for the community fund.

The Chamber and Territorial Expansion of Woodruff

With one exception, the organization's position on the spatial growth of Woodruff coincided with that of the city council. The Chamber, as well as the local leadership, newspaper, and banks, the major sources of influence in the community, had been a potent force for preserving the city-township division.

The history of the utility systems and policies of the city and the township indicates the high level of agreement that existed between the city council and the Chamber (see Chapter 3). Leaders of the Chamber did nothing in 1941 to encourage city officials to plan for the provision of services to the bomber plant. They did nothing at the end of the war to encourage municipal officials to seek the acquisition of the two utility plants in the township. On the contrary, they assisted the township to purchase the plants by sending their executive secretary to Washington to express the city's satisfaction with the arrangement. Chamber leaders agreed with councilmen in 1953 that water service should not be made available to residents of the Country Club area until the section had been annexed to Woodruff. The leaders of the Chamber agreed with the councilmen, over a thirty-year period, that utility services should not be used as a means for furthering the territorial growth of the city.

Some of these experiences should have demonstrated the importance, as a prerequisite for change, of educating township and city citizens on the benefits of governmental reorganization, which, in turn, would require a plethora of facts on tax rates, municipal finance, duplication of services, and forms of government. The reaction of Chamber directors on three occasions over a five-year period to the possibility of a study by "experts" from outside the community indicated satisfaction with the present governmental pattern. The thwarting of such studies was consistent with two other facets of the structure of the Chamber: the retention of the executive secretary for three decades and the membership policies that limited the influence of township leaders and executives of the automobile factories. These two policies minimized the likelihood that persons would be placed in policy-making positions whose views might differ basically from those of the leaders of the Chamber. The fear that outside experts might recommend, on the basis of incontrovertible evidence, courses of action deemed undesirable by Chamber leaders generated no enthusiasm for such studies. Chamber officials never took advantage of an offer made by Universal Motors officials in early 1958, in the midst of the merger campaign, to assist in a study of community problems. When requests for such aid finally were made in 1963, the Chamber did not initiate them, but rather, they came from the sponsors of annexation.

The citizens' committee sympathetic to a new annexation proposal recommended a study by one of the nation's most reputable firms of consultants in public administration (see Chapter 10). Strong opposition to this study was voiced at a meeting of the executive committee by the new Chamber secretary and a director. They argued that all the necessary facts were available and the firm of consultants was overrated. When an attempt was made to call for the question, the Chamber secretary urged postponement of the vote. Although the committee voted for the study, the members of the Chamber refused to contribute the necessary funds. This refusal made it impossible to carry out the study.

Opposition to the Chamber

Intricate and close relationships tied the Chamber to city government and other institutions of the community. If it appears that the Chamber was Woodruff's substitute for a "ruling elite," the explanation lies partly with the absence of countervailing power. Union leaders took very little interest in civic affairs apart from the selection of persons to run for elective office with the covert support of the Democratic party. The leadership of the Negro community was split into several factions. Leaders of the southern white minority were concerned with township politics. As a consequence the business and professional men who dominated the Chamber provided the councilmen and city manager with the opinions and sentiments that most closely approximated that of the articulate citizens of the city. The influence of the Chamber in the city for four decades resulted in part from the inability of opposition groups to exert influence with municipal officials.

The influence of the Chamber in the community must also be attributed to the absence of groups of business and professional men who believed that the policies of the organization—those concerning the township and the problems of expansion, some phase of economic development, or any other local issue—had been detrimental to Woodruff. During the lifetime of the Chamber, more than five decades, no major attempt ever was made to modify the organization and its policies from within or to replace it with another organization. Certainly there was no well-defined belief that the Chamber's policies on utilities and spatial expansion helped to place the city in its present political straitjacket. Much of the dissatisfaction with the Chamber during the study period centered on the person of the executive secretary who was accused of not permitting the younger members sufficient latitude in directing the organization. These critics failed to voice discontent with Chamber policies on community issues. The conflict was personal and political rather than ideological. The dissatisfaction in the winter of 1959 of Sampson and Davenport with the Chamber, which led to the establishment of a short-lived civic group (see Chapter 5), resulted largely from their feeling that the organization had not given proper support to some of their pet interests. It is difficult to avoid the conclusion that for four decades the Chamber had translated the decision-making pattern of the city into specific proposals and worked for their enactment through the city council. There is little or no evidence suggesting that the opposition to the Chamber, if any existed, could be attributed to a basic and strong discontent with its policies. The Chamber's actions were consistent with those of the top echelons of the leadership structure, the economic notables, and of the newspaper.

There was little reason for believing that Chamber influence was waning. Several developments in the mid-sixties signified continued vitality. In October, 1963, despite the explicit editorial objections of the editor of *The Woodruff Press,* the new executive secretary was appointed to the Planning Commission, a post once held by Wasmund. To the objection voiced by the editor that the executive secretary represented the downtown businessmen, the councilmen replied that such representation was needed. The councilmen apparently did not believe that a downtown merchant might provide equally adequate if more obvious representation. Second, the state highway department dropped its plan to expand a street skirting the new downtown shopping center as the major link between the expressway east to Metropolitan City and a state highway west to County Seat City. Instead a thoroughfare running through the downtown business district was to be utilized for the north-south connection. Third, by 1965, business and professional leaders had organized and financially supported a massive program for a Greek theatre. The Woodruff Industrial Development Committee, organized in 1962 as a semi-official though separately incorporated arm of the Chamber of Commerce to stimulate area industrial growth, had become, by 1964, more concerned with the city's central business district and the development of the Greek theatre. With national and international encouragement, local leaders proceeded to develop this city-oriented project which, if it had been successful, could have represented a tremendous business stimulus without altering the leadership and governmental structure of the area.

For fifty years the Chamber of Commerce represented and acted in behalf of the commercial and propertied interests of the city of Woodruff. By mutual consent the executives of absentee-owned plants avoided efforts to shape Chamber policy on local issues although the automobile companies represented the largest single source of revenue for the organization. The influence of the Chamber in municipal affairs and with the city council was augmented by the vacuum created by the absence of strong organizations representing the interests of several minority groups and a nucleus of local "big-money" leaders. As long as the executive secretary was closely attuned to their desires and the city council was not pressured by dissenting interest groups, the upper-level citizens and economic leaders could enjoy life with the knowledge that events in Woodruff would follow the preferred course. For the most part the Chamber and municipal government remained in harmonious relationship.

The Chamber of Commerce was undoubtedly the most influential community organization in Woodruff. It shaped and molded decisions on a variety of community concerns from bond issues to police administration. In time of community crisis, such as the bank closings and large-scale unemployment, the Chamber planned and directed action. It performed major and minor service functions, e.g., Community Fund and Automobile License Bureau. It formulated a system for joint decision making with city government and shaped leadership attitudes toward city-township relationships and cooperation that remained operative for many decades.

Conclusion

The influence that the Chamber has exercised over the years derives in large part from the functions it has performed. These include: legitimization of the exceptional spending programs of city government; sustaining of a variety of social services through its sponsorship and support of the Community Fund; recruitment and training of young men for public office; establishing a fund-raising agency for various drives and campaigns for which other organizations or institutions have no responsibility; the formation of certain organizations for which there is a recognized need; and the preservation of certain essential organizations in a crisis situation.

Some of these functions, such as the support given the Community Fund and the banks, benefited the community, many of its institutions, and residents. Others, such as a personnel office for local government, also serve the goals of special interests. The ability of the Chamber, at various times, to take action that benefited the entire community undoubtedly enabled it to better serve its major constituents, the downtown business interests, and the larger property owners.

Over the years the Chamber exercised its considerable influence to prevent the political reorganization of the area. A principal strategy has been in the selection of situational features for treatment as public issues. Generally the Chamber has neglected those which were crucial for territorial and industrial growth and has focused on those that tended to protect the major loci of power in Woodruff. The Chamber has been in tune with and a principal advocate of the restrictionist pattern. While Chamber officials led the fight in the thirties for adding water-softener facilities to the plans for the new water-treatment plant it accepted city council reduction of the recommended capacity (see Chapter 3). The Chamber defined certain features of city government as a problem and worked for adoption of certain modifications while taking no affirmative action on the acquisition of the utility plants in the township. The need for expansion of the city's utility facilities to assist the west side of the township and keep alive hopes of westward expansion was ignored to keep municipal expenditures at a low level. By the time the Chamber approved plans for the bond issue in the mid-fifties, hopes for annexation had been virtually exhausted.

In subsequent years, when the township had ringed the city with utility mains and each municipality was developing its own governmental bureaucracy, Chamber officials refused to support in principle and financially the plan to acquire systematic and comprehensive information on the consequences of this political structure and on the relative merits of various alternatives. This refusal had especially serious consequences for the 1963–64 unification campaign (see Chapter 10).

The Chamber has protected the social and political structure of the city against the powerful forces for social change emanating from the larger society—from absentee-owned industry, from the community's position in two metropolitan communities, from Woodruff's accessibility to one of the nation's most important manufacturing centers, and from the forces of growth originating outside but operating within the city.

7. The Newspaper

Despite the growing concern of social scientists with mass communication and the refinement of the methodology of polling public opinion, students of community have neglected the role of the newspaper and of journalists.[1] After reviewing the community literature on the newspaper John C. Sim concluded: "The vague, almost shadowy, role assigned to the community newspaper editor and publisher

1. As soon as the authors began to study the consolidation movement, a clipping file of all pertinent community items was started. Two papers, *The Woodruff Press* and *The County Seat News* covered local events. In addition to clipping items for the entire period of study and writing, approximately sixty years of back issues of *The Woodruff Press* were examined.

Notes were taken at meetings of the town board and other organized groups. In a short time one of *The County Seat News* reporters began to sit with the authors. In addition to her reporting duties, she was completing her master's degree in political science, and this mutual academic interest created a bond. A year after the study began she moved to another state. Before her departure she was interviewed and much was learned that assisted the evaluations of the researchers. Her replacement, who later became a permanent staff member of *The Woodruff Press* in 1962, was also interviewed. The owner-editor, Amdur, of *The Press* in 1957–62 and the new editor who followed were interviewed and observed. Throughout the study the authors felt that their contact with and opportunity to observe members of the press on the two newspapers, both reporter and executive, was fortunate. The relationships were personal, friendly, and also on a first-name basis.

167

in almost all studies of community leadership or community power structure has been puzzling to those who have accepted the historic evaluation of the 'power of the press' . . . but in the main these press-oriented investigations have only thrown into sharper relief the manner in which sociologists have tended to ignore the community press in case studies."[2]

The few studies that provided information on the local press or on the newspaper editor as leader present conflicting findings. Several researchers found that certain local leaders, especially elected officials, often are sensitive to the views of the editor expressed either in the paper or in private conversation. New Haven's Republican mayors were reported to have met weekly with the wealthy editor of the city's two newspapers. The editor's influence declined with election of Lee, who was returned to office repeatedly despite the editor's outspoken opposition. Nevertheless, Lee sought to avoid a newspaper campaign against high taxes by implementing his program in a manner that did not necessitate tax increases.[3] Elected officials in Toledo were sensitive to the position on governmental actions stated in the editorial page of the local paper. Their view of the power of the newspaper publisher seemed to have substantial basis in fact, for he had broken several politicians who had been his political adversaries.[4] Another example of the power of the press is provided by Meyerson and Banfield in their study of public housing in Chicago. *The Chicago Sun Times* had endorsed the position of the Chicago Housing Authority that several public housing projects be built on vacant land in white neighborhoods. When the paper lost interest in the program, the city council voted to build most of

2. John Cameron Sim, "Community Newspaper Leadership: More Real than Apparent?" *Journalism Quarterly,* Vol. 44, No. 36 (Summer, 1967), 276–80. See also Alvin J. Remmenga, "Has The Press Lost Its Influence in Local Affairs?" in Edward C. Banfield, ed., *Urban Government:* (New York: The Free Press of Glencoe, 1961), pp. 378–89. An analysis of the use of the community newspaper as a source of systematic comparative data on community structure is found in Robert W. Janes, "A Technique for Describing Community Structure through Newspaper Analyses," *Social Forces,* Vol. 37, No. 2 (December, 1958), 102–9.

3. Robert A. Dahl, *Who Governs? Democracy and Power in an American City* (New Haven, Conn.: Yale University Press, 1961), pp. 259–60.

4. The authors are indebted to the incisive work of Reo M. Christenson, "The Power of the Press: The Case of 'The Toledo Blade,' " *Midwest Journal of Political Science,* Vol. III, No. 3 (August, 1959), 227–40.

the new housing units in the black ghetto.[5] This outcome resulted partly from the belief of the Housing Authority's chairman that the loss of newspaper support made continued opposition to the city council a losing proposition.[6]

There are indications that newspapers educate those citizens who already are well-informed on local issues but fail to reach the majority of readers. In a survey of registered voters' knowledge of an election campaign to revise a city charter, only a third of the respondents correctly identified the newspaper's position on this issue.[7] Additional evidence of the ignorance of voters on matters well publicized in the local press led Dahl to state: "Political indifference surrounds a great many citizens like impenetrable armor plate and makes them difficult targets for propaganda."[8] Greer reported similar findings on the knowledgeability of citizens concerning an effort to establish a metropolitan government despite intensive newspaper coverage.[9]

To determine the influence of the local press one must attempt to distinguish between the impact on public opinion of news stories and editorials and the relationship that the editors and publishers have with community leaders. It was not possible for the researchers to conduct surveys to measure the influence of the press on public opinion. Attention focused on the pattern of news handling, editorial policy, and interaction of the editors and owners with community leaders. The role of *The Woodruff Press* in presenting and/or interpreting to the citizenry the nature of the changes taking place during the critical war and postwar years and the consequences for maintaining and modifying decision-making patterns were the central problems.

A good local newspaper is assumed to be one of the most effective of city and area builders and boosters. Its function is the gathering and transmission of news. The very concept of a "good" local news-

5. Martin Meyerson and Edward C. Banfield, *Politics, Planning and the Public Interest: The Case of Public Housing in Chicago* (Glencoe, Ill.: The Free Press of Glencoe, 1964), pp. 215–18.
6. *Ibid.*, pp. 216–17.
7. Dahl, *Who Governs?* p. 266.
8. *Ibid.*, p. 265.
9. Scott Greer, *Metropolitics: A Study of Political Culture* (New York: John Wiley and Sons, Inc., 1963), p. 113.

paper projects an imagined or stereotyped picture, developed and expanded from the interpreted records of successful and unsuccessful newspapers, embraced in literature, and popularized through various media. Added to the idealization is the general public's reinterpretation of the role and the perpetration and embellishment of varieties of this view taught in schools of journalism. The attitudes toward the role of the newspaper held by the community leader, the general public, and even the editor himself is a composite of the relationship between the idealized journalistic norms and the functional relationships that a business enterprise must develop in order to survive within that complex of power we call the American community.[10] Within this idealistic-realistic framework the scope of the field and the vagueness of its limits are apparent. Since Woodruff had supported a newspaper for almost a hundred years, it was possible to derive some understanding of community-wide problems and issues that the area had faced and the individuals and groups who became publicly involved. Of particular concern was whether editors, in the context of an idealistic-realistic continuum, had reacted to, subscribed to, supported, ignored, or opposed the decision-making patterns of the community in the presentation of news and the use of the editorial page over the last forty years.

Since 1908, Woodruff's population had maintained one locally printed newspaper, *The Woodruff Press,* managed and later purchased by James Amdur. In 1946, Amdur's son, Donald, joined his father in business. After his father's death in 1957, Amdur assumed the position of publisher-editor. In 1962, *The Woodruff Press,* after fifty-eight years of Amdur control, was sold to the Kent Newspaper Group.[11] In 1968, the Kent Group sold *The Press* to the Clark Corporation.[12]

10. For studies of the differences between leader and public views of a newspaper's role, see Alex S. Edelstein and J. Blaine Schulz, "The Weekly Newspaper's Leadership Role as Seen by Community Leaders," *Journalism Quarterly,* Vol. 40, No. 4 (Autumn, 1963), 564–74; Alex S. Edelstein and Joseph J. Contris, "The Public View of the Weekly Newspaper's Leadership Role," *Journalism Quarterly,* Vol. 43, No. 1 (Spring, 1966), 17–24.

11. A group differs from a chain or syndicate. The former grants each newspaper autonomous decision-making powers while the latter plays an authoritative role in the decision-making process.

12. The Clark Corporation was also a group. It was a recently organized corporation that purchased a sizable number of weekly and daily newspapers in the midwest.

The observation of patterns of decision making in Woodruff focused attention on the contribution of local newspapers to the development of community consensus. Of particular concern was the position of *The Woodruff Press* and *The County Seat News,* a group-owned paper, on issues such as the distribution of public services, annexation and consolidation, local political candidates, and controversial programs on which the community was divided. Closely related was the role of the publisher-editor and editor, as economic or social leader, as participant in community organizations. The analysis and conclusions are based on observation and reconstruction, structured and unstructured interviews with community leaders, observations of group participation between 1957 and 1963, study of sixty years of *The Woodruff Press,* and a comparison of issue coverage during the past twenty years in the latter and *The County Seat News.*

Frame of Reference[13]

Whether one concludes that a particular newspaper has been and is a functional or dysfunctional community institution depends upon the standards or criteria used in the process of evaluation. We concluded that, in addition to exhibiting a slow, steady growth in circulation and financial solvency, an effective newspaper ought to, on occasion,

1. exert potent political power; wield influence; make, break, criticize a politician; push through or block a public policy;
2. act as referee on a community issue; through the editorial page become the arbiter of community affairs;
3. lead as well as reflect community thought;
4. exercise its power judiciously. A newspaper has influence because it has won community respect. In order to maintain this relationship its power must be used in a responsible manner;
5. give its readers depth information on local issues;
6. have some knowledge of the decision-making pattern and the power structure in the community and area of location and must utilize that knowledge.

13. Christenson, "Power of the Press," pp. 227–40.

We concluded that an editor ought:[14]

1. To be insightful—have keen discernment and understanding on at least one level of news, e.g., local, state, national, international, etc.;

2. not to be unduly and recognizably influenced by individuals or groups;

3. to reflect a concern for minorities and underprivileged individuals and groups;

4. to maintain social distance from individuals and groups who might be assumed to have influenced him, e.g., the social circle he is in may be thought to condition his interpretation of community events;

5. to identify with the over-all improvement and prosperity of the community.

It is recognized that an important community function of an effective newspaper, as defined above, is as an agent of social control. Periodic examination of the conduct of a community organization or institution may encourage it to operate in a more responsible manner.

The County Seat News and The Woodruff Press

Between 1957 and 1962, *The County Seat News,* published in County Seat City and part of a major newspaper group that purchased *The Woodruff Press* in 1962, sold subscriptions to a large segment of evening newspaper readers in the Woodruff area. A Woodruff page appeared five days a week. *The News* maintained an office in downtown Woodruff which housed several reporters, one assigned to city and one to township news.

The city news reporter, Bill James, the senior *News* man in Woodruff, lived in Woodruff, and was a member of the Junior Chamber of Commerce Area Improvement Committee, which spearheaded the consolidation attempt. When *The Woodruff Press* was purchased by the Kent Group, which owned *The County Seat News* in 1962,

14. For studies that suggest both the public's and editor's conception of the role of editor, see Sim, "Community Newspaper Leadership"; Edelstein and Schulz, "Weekly Newspaper Leadership"; and Edward C. Banfield, *Political Influence* (Glencoe, Ill.: The Free Press, 1961), p. 275.

James became city editor of the former. A short time after the paper was again sold in 1968, James succeeded to the position of editor.

The level of reporting on Woodruff affairs by *The County Seat News* before 1962 was excellent compared to the stories that appeared in *The Woodruff Press*. *News* personnel policies demanded qualified reporters working for higher salaries than the Woodruff paper. The combination of these two factors gave greater stability and continuity to the *News* staff.

The Amdurs had initiated a low salary-scale policy for all *Woodruff Press* employees, typesetter and reporter alike. During their ownership, scab labor, men working for lower wages and under conditions contrary to those prescribed by the trade union, were used. On a number of occasions city and township leaders commented negatively on the Amdur low-wage policy and its effect on the attitudes of *Press* employees as reflected in the level of the paper. "Amdur gets what he pays for: a cheap product. A quality product costs money!" The name "Woodruff Gyp" was frequently substituted for *Woodruff Press* by its city and township critics. During the five years of investigation before the 1962 purchase, *The News* had two Woodruff township reporters while as many as six or eight *Press* reporters took a turn at township meetings. *The Press* reporters who "filled in" at township hall had regular assignments in other sections of the county.

The Press gave greater coverage to Woodruff society and club news than did *The County Seat News*. Reports of social affairs in Woodruff appeared once or twice a week in *The News,* usually in the form of a sentence or a brief paragraph. *The Woodruff Press* staff printed verbatim the lengthy stories prepared by club secretaries or wrote an equally detailed report of an affair.

The two newspapers differed in several other important aspects. *The County Seat News* was located in County Seat City, a more prestigious community than Woodruff in terms of income, occupation, housing levels, educational institutions, and formal and informal associations. *The News* catered to and identified with the interests of County Seat residents. It was one of a large group of newspapers; as such it could be classified as absentee-owned. *The Woodruff Press* had been managed by a member of the Amdur family since 1908 and owned by the family since the 1910's. Besides community and ownership differences, *The County Seat News* maintained an active, locally written editorial page concerned with national, state, and local issues. On several occasions between 1957 and 1962, editorials focused attention on Woodruff problems. During the identical time period, *The Woodruff Press* selected the few editorials published on national and state level issues from wire services and printed a few innocuous editorial statements on local affairs. *The County Seat News* as an absentee-owned area paper, lacking economic dependence on Woodruff business advertisers, was less restrained in the publication of criticisms of the basics of Woodruff City and Woodruff Township decision making. *The Woodruff Press,* locally owned and economically supported by local business advertisers and solicitous of every township subscription, was subject to more control over possible critiques of either political unit's decision-making pattern.[15]

Circulation

Circulation and circulation trends are measures by which advertisers, potential advertisers, publishers, stockholders, and often the public can rate and judge a newspaper. Circulation statistics are compiled and maintained by the Audit Bureau of Circulations (ABC). ABC is a co-operative association of advertisers, advertising agencies, and publishers for the verification of the circulations of newspapers and periodicals. Between 1950 and 1960, *The County Seat News* and three metropolitan city newspapers, *The Metropolitan City Press, The Metropolitan City News,* and *The Metropolitan City Times* were members of ABC. *The Woodruff Press* was not a member until 1962. Comparable figures, therefore, were not available. By 1962, *The Metropolitan Times* had been purchased by *The Metropolitan News.* Statistics for *The County Seat News* are from audit reports for the twelve-month period ending September 30 of each year indicated. A figure for *The Woodruff Press* was estimated for 1960 and another is for the six-month period ending De-

15. Banfield suggests that a newspaper, like any other business enterprise, desires favors from local government. It cannot afford to make an "irreparable break with a political head who can give or withhold assistance in matters of great importance to the newspaper." Banfield, *Political Influence,* pp. 95, 255.

cember 31, 1962. The other figures are for the twelve-month periods ending March 31.

Table 3 shows the approximate number of copies of each paper distributed in the Woodruff area for selected years between 1950 and 1968. It appears that the three papers that maintained the largest circulation within the Woodruff community between 1955 and 1962 were *The Woodruff Press, The County Seat News,* and *The Metropolitan City Press,* respectively. While circulation increased for each of the latter between 1960 and 1962, *The Metropolitan City Press* with an increase of 51 percent and *The Woodruff Press* with an increase of 44 percent significantly outdistanced their competitors.

The phenomenal increase in Woodruff's *County Seat News* subscriptions between 1950 and 1960 was an indication of the extension of dominance of County Seat City over Woodruff. The trend was more significant than it might appear on the surface. During the twenties, *The News* had attempted, without success, to set up a Woodruff office and to expand its Woodruff circulation. A new attempt in the fifties thrived until the purchase and expansion of *The Woodruff Press* by the Kent Group. In 1963, *The County Seat News* closed its Woodruff office and eliminated its Woodruff page. The reason given was a sizable drop in circulation.

From 1963 through 1968 *The Woodruff Press* increased circulation to a high of 51.3 percent of distribution. The 1968 summary figures show a slight percentage drop to 49.6 percent. *The County Seat News,* which took a substantial drop in circulation after *The Woodruff Press* was added to its group, 30.0 percent in 1960 to a low of 9.3 percent in 1965, showed an increased in circulation after *The Woodruff Press* was sold to the Clark Corporation in 1968.[16] By the late sixties, *The Woodruff Press* published approximately 50 percent of the newspapers circulated in the Woodruff Community followed by *The Metropolitan City Press,* 26 percent, and *The County Seat News* and *The Metropolitan News* tied for third place with 12 percent of the circulation (see Table 3).

The decline in circulation of *The Woodruff Press* in the fifties was a result of dissatisfaction in Woodruff with inadequate news cover-

16. *The County Seat News* discontinued all newspaper distribution to the Woodruff Community in 1965, resulting in the large circulation loss.

Table 3. *Approximate Number and Percent of Area Newspapers Received for Distribution in and Redistribution on Rural and Urban Woodruff Routes for 1950, 1955, 1960, 1962, 1965, 1968[a]*

	1950		1955		1960		1962		1965		1968	
Newspapers	No.	Percent	No.	Percent	No.	Percent	No.	Percent	No.	Percent	No.	Percent
Woodruff Press	—	—	—	—	5,500[b]	31.0	7,331	35.0	9,814	51.3	11,212	49.6
County Seat News	1,203	11.4	2,710	24.2	4,928	30.0	5,334	26.0	1,775	9.3	2,711	11.9
Metropolitan City Press	3,561	33.8	3,805	33.9	3,114	19.0	4,714	22.0	5,191	27.1	5,830	25.8
Metropolitan Times[c]	3,949	37.5	3,374	30.1	1,571	9.0	—	—	—	—	—	—
Metropolitan News[c]	1,820	17.3	1,321	11.8	1,797	11.0	3,471	17.0	2,357	12.3	2,873	12.7
TOTAL	10,533	100.0	11,210	100.0	16,510	100.0	20,850	100.0	19,137	100.0	22,626	100.0

a. Letters and reports from the Audit Bureau of Circulations, Chicago, Illinois, 1961, 1963, 1969.
b. This is an estimate by the purchaser. *The Woodruff Press* was not a member of the Audit Bureau of Circulations until 1962.
c. *The Metropolitan Times* was purchased by *The Metropolitan News*, resulting in the increased Woodruff copy distribution by the *News*.

age on all levels and the lack of any recognizable editorial policy. News coverage and editorial statement, controversial or otherwise, sell newspapers and in turn sell advertising space.

The Kent Group and Clark Corporation were able to develop an editorial and news policy that satisfied and maintained a substantial reading public.

The Editorial

We have assumed above that the difference between an effective and an ineffective newspaper depends upon the assertive, positive role it takes as a source and user of power in community decision making. The most efficacious tool that a paper has at its disposal is the editorial through which the editor expresses his views. During five years of this study, Donald Amdur was publisher of *The Woodruff Press*. His father had been an active community leader during the World War I period, the era of prosperity of the twenties, the depression of the thirties, World War II, and the population and industrial growth that followed. In other words, the Amdurs had been participant observers during historical periods of change and as newspapermen had been in a position to publicly comment and to judge aspects of these developments.

Over the forty-year period during which the Amdur family owned *The Woodruff Press,* a number of important community issues and programs developed on which one might expect some editorial comment. First, in 1915, an attempt was made to write a new city charter. Second, in 1926 and 1929, city efforts to annex township land on both the east and west side were initiated. Third, during the thirties and forties, Woodruff growth was reflected in sewer and water extension programs. Fourth, in 1946, a new city charter was proposed incorporating a change in city government from strong mayor to city manager. Fifth, in 1958, an attempt was made to consolidate Woodruff City and Woodruff Township. Each issue represented change and possibly a reorganization of political power. In the case of numbers two and five, there was a basic conflict with both the city and township decision-making patterns advocating separate political and social identification. The third would have embraced a public financial commitment previously unknown in the city. Only in the tens and twenties was there evidenced a vigorous editorial policy with minimum regard for opposing area culture patterns.[17]

The 1915 Charter Proposal

At the 1914 spring election, nine charter commissioners were elected to revise the 1877 Woodruff city charter. On March 3, 1915, a charter that proposed a three-man commission elected at large and a city manager was defeated by 77 votes, 698 to 621. The campaign over the document was bitter. Opponents argued that the commissioner-manager form was a step toward monarchy, that the proposed charter would (1) centralize government, (2) allow all the commissioners to be elected from one area, and (3) place government and power in the hands of men, including the University faculty, who had no sympathy toward the working man. The mayor and the city attorney, the latter a director and later president of the Woodruff Savings Bank, presented the above arguments at meeting after meeting. In addition they maintained that charter acceptance would "drive colored out of the community."[18]

James Amdur wrote a number of editorials on the issue in which he answered the charges of the vocal opponents and urged the acceptance of the document. The editor maintained that the rights of Woodruff residents were safeguarded through charter provisions for initiative, referendum, and recall. He criticized the old form that placed government control in the hands of a large, ten-man council and a part-time mayor rather than a small body assisted by a full-time "Business Manager."[19]

The editor published both sides of the issue in news columns. Editorially he attempted to exert influence over the electorate in favor of the document. By taking this overt position he criticized the mayor and the city attorney, at least one of whom possessed considerable status and prestige.

---

17. Breed indicates that the sociocultural structure of a community does affect what newspapers print or omit. Warren Breed, "Mass Communication and Socio-Cultural Integration," *Social Forces*, Vol. 37, No. 2 (December, 1958), 109–16. See also Edelstein and Schulz, "Weekly Newspaper Leadership," p. 573.

18. *The Woodruff Press*, February 26, 1915.

19. *Ibid.*, March 1, 1915.

The 1926 Annexation Attempt

In the spring of 1926 an attempt was made to annex several parcels of land on the city's western border. James Amdur wrote a number of editorials in support of the proposal. After the proposal failed, Amdur wrote the following energetic editorial of reproach on April 6, 1926.

THE PRICE OF A BLUNDER

The striking example of carelessness and poor judgment in city planning and the consequences is emphasized in the annexation vote recorded here Monday. Less than a dozen residents live in this area on Iroquois Avenue, enjoy advantages of the city, but remain a part of the township. City property has extended beyond them on every side, yet these few are rural residents and pay only rural taxes . . . .

While the situation is quite miserable, some good may yet come of it if present city officials will apply the teaching. Even now plans are under way for extension of several connections to property not in the city limits. It may be that the property owners and residents in this section will arrange to become a part of the city after they have city conveniences but the incentive to become part of the city is much stronger before city conveniences are extended than afterward. It is much better business to *know* that property served is to be taxable than to provide it with city services and trust to luck for the revenue.[20]

Again, Amdur attempted to exert political influence through this editorial. He criticized Woodruff politicians and he attempted to alter what had evolved into a policy. Publicly he supported the spatial growth of the city at the expense of the township. By reviewing the situation he provided the reader with information, emphasized the importance of geographical expansion through annexation, and tried to lead them in thought toward a course of action that he felt would be more compatible with future community growth. During the twenties, Amdur wrote several other editorials on annexation and several on the important trends in community development in which he expounded the philosophy of "no annexation, no city services." Although the extension of sewer connections mentioned in the editorial quoted above were made, Amdur's forecast proved correct. The property involved was not annexed to the city until the late fifties. Combined with the unpopularity of increased public financial commitments, Amdur's editorial doubtless influenced future policy: further services without annexation were denied.

20. *Ibid.*, April 6, 1926.

Sewer and Water Plant Expansion

Amdur wrote very few editorials after 1930, and during the crucial war and postwar eras, he published few news stories on the critical problems of basic utilities, city territorial expansion, and industrial expansion. Two factors appear to have played an important part in this change of policy in managing the newspaper, the lack of success of several campaigns waged in the twenties and a strong interest in business ventures. Perhaps these two factors were related, with business acumen and involvement in real estate ventures developing in the wake of journalistic failures. With the exception of the annexation of one small College Hill parcel, remarkably few of Amdur's editorial campaigns succeeded. Inability to gain the coveted position of bank director may have led Amdur to believe that a high price had been paid for publicly differing with the views of many leaders (see Chapter 5). Certainly editorial silence on controversial issues allowed the Amdurs, as a family, to associate more closely with Woodruff's leaders and prestigeful social groupings. Amdur essentially modified his policies to fit the decision-making pattern developed by Woodruff's leadership.[21]

21. The change in Amdur's editorial policy from one of outspoken support for expansion in the early decades of this century and neglect of these matters in subsequent decades has a recent parallel. The three editors who succeeded Bowes at *The Woodruff Press* in 1966 took a more restrained approach to problems of city expansion. (See the section on the new editor later in this chapter.) James, the one with the longest tenure, did not advocate programs of this nature as frequently or openly as had Bowes. Editorials on the subject generally were limited to the day before a vote on annexation was to be held. However, his position on the necessity and advantages of growth did not deviate from those set by Bowes.

This change could be explained by the editor's unfamiliarity with the community. He might consider it prudent, in light of this circumstance, not to be too outspoken on complex and controversial issues. However, Bowes, in exactly the same situation four years earlier, declared his position on intermunicipal affairs from the day he took office and, in the years that followed, found opportunities for restating this position. The new editor would have had to recognize that frequent exposition of the advantages of Woodruff's territorial and industrial expansion had not had any pronounced favorable effect on the voting tendencies of township citizens. Under these circumstances the third editor, James, might have felt that his paper should concentrate on programs that had leadership support and better chances for success. Shaw and Irwin, in a series of intensive interviews with 117 weekly newspaper publishers in Washington, found that the editors who were most knowledgeable concerning the community power structure worked with community leaders *before* initiating a community project. Robert McGregor

Those editorials that Amdur did write after 1930 lacked fire and filled few of the functions for community growth suggested by his earlier work. In the thirties and forties, periods marked by depression, war, and recovery, utility expansion both within and outside city limits was an important community problem (see Chapter 4). In 1937 and 1938, when the city electorate was asked to approve bond issues for construction of the sewerage disposal and water-treatment plants, Amdur wrote a few editorials urging voter approval. While he did not put forth the vigorous effort that he had made in earlier years, he stated his position clearly.

After the outbreak of World War II the federal government constructed a large bomber plant and complementary utilities in Woodruff Township. With the consummation of the war, the township industrial plant, its housing, and the utilities were marked for public disposal. Not once between 1942 and 1947 did Amdur comment editorially on the significance of the township utility plants for future area development, although he had shown earlier a recognition of the relationship between utility services and annexation. A news story in 1946 describing the technical features of the utility plants was one of the few reports on the utility facilities in the township published in *The Woodruff Press*. An advertisement placed by the U.S. War Assets Administration which specified the availability of the utilities for purchase was run in *The Woodruff Press* in July, 1946.

It is easy to sit in judgment on inaction or sins of omission viewed in the perspective of time and shrouded in the limitations of reconstructed history. In Amdur's case, criticism is valid. During the twenties he pointed time and time again to the significance of city services as forces, even bribes, in efforts to expand the community. He strongly advocated and seemingly won support for a public policy of no city services unless an area were annexed to the city. Utility services were weapons, one of the few available by which the city could acquire the township land needed for the industrial and population expansion of the fifties and sixties which Amdur predicted again and again in the twenties. Overlooking its significant conformity to the city's decision-making pattern, we may criticize

---

Shaw and P. Lee Irwin, "Comprehensive Survey of Washington Weeklies," *Report #6* (June, 1960), mimeo.

the lack of exhibited insight of Woodruff city leaders in allowing and, on occasion, assisting the township in acquiring the government utility plants. They may, in turn, rejoin that they failed to recognize or comprehend the relationship between the acquisition of the plants and boundary expansion. In Amdur's case the criticism is not a shot in the dark. He stated his position irrefutably and never expressed a change in that position. Men who dined with him regularly for years before his death in 1957 reiterated his continued dynamic interest in the expansion of the city's boundaries. Amdur, it seems, was willing to make a private verbal but not a public written commitment concerning city expansion.

The City Charter, 1946

In the spring and fall of 1946, the voters of the city of Woodruff had placed before them a new city charter that proposed a city-manager, weak-mayor, council-at-large, nonpartisan form of government. The leadership of the city split on the values of the proposed charter. The charter was defeated in the spring election but was carried in the fall election. Between February, 1946, and November, 1946, there were twenty-nine articles, sixteen advertisements, and five editorials in *The Woodruff Press*. Seventeen articles, eleven advertisements, and two editorials appeared before the spring election and twelve articles, five advertisements, and three editorials appeared before the November election. Fifteen out of seventeen of the spring articles and eleven out of twelve of the fall articles were favorable; seven out of eleven spring advertisements and all the fall advertisements were favorable. More than half of the articles and twice as many advertisements appeared before the spring election, while one more editorial appeared before the fall than before the spring election.

Amdur neither took a position favoring the proposal nor did he attempt editorially to bring the two groups together before or after the elections. Many leaders and residents who were active during the charter controversy believed the charter passed on the second attempt in November, 1946, because the Woodruff Junior Chamber of Commerce took over the campaign after its first defeat at the polls. The Jaycees held several community meetings, wrote informative letters to the newspaper, and rallied the support of a number of important community leaders. It is questionable whether the Jaycees represented the "yeast," the success-giving ingredient, or whether their meetings and the added time period fostered a more informed public. If the latter contention is correct or falls close to the truth, it suggests that had the newspaper fulfilled its function of educating and disseminating information, or had it simply called community attention to the proposition through a series of stories, it might have saved the city the cost of a second election and eliminated a continuous ten-month conflict situation, with repercussions in terms of leadership disagreement that was still evident in the late fifties and sixties.

The Consolidation
During the consolidation campaign discussed in Part III, the local and out-of-town newspapers constituted the major organs for informing and influencing the electorate. Since the democratic process provided the legal procedures for resolving the consolidation controversy, each side had to sway the voters. Both pro- and anticonsolidation workers sought to influence the newspapers in support of their positions.

The proconsolidation forces had a number of advantages over their protagonists. The owner-editor of *The Woodruff Press* had overt reasons for favoring consolidation. Unification of the city and township conceivably might have brought gains to *The Woodruff Press*. If identification with the larger community were legally strengthened, if commercial and industrial development occurred, and if population growth were stimulated, the newspaper might increase circulation and the volume of advertising and consequently profits would increase. Also, as a member of at least one leadership group that tacitly supported the proposal, it might be assumed that the owner-editor, Donald Amdur, might back the proposal.

During the campaign, several middle-level leaders of the consolidation movement and Mike Davenport expressed displeasure over the treatment of the issue in *The Woodruff Press*. Amdur found himself in the crossfire. He sought to resolve the conflict by maintaining a semblance of objectivity and impartiality. He never editorialized for or against "unification," and he published a legion of correspondence heavily weighted in favor of the anticonsolidation

Save the Township Committee. To pacify some of his friends, he published a series of front-page informative editorial-like articles written by the Jaycee public relations man. The public was allowed to assume that Amdur or a reporter was the researcher and the writer.

On several occasions the leaders of the proconsolidation drive pressured the editor to take a forthright and public position in favor of consolidation. Apart from publishing the Jaycee public relations man's articles, covering consolidation events, and contributing financially to the drive, Amdur provided minimal co-operation.

As a man of wealth and social prominence, Donald Amdur, in all likelihood, considered himself immune to any retribution that Davenport or the other lower- and middle-level active leaders could impose. Amdur may have assumed that Davenport would not apply strong pressure on a social equal. Davenport may have likewise have assumed that strong measures might have been damaging to their personal relationship without gaining major or important campaign concessions from the editor. Amdur filled his position as editor and played his role within the "no position" confines that had represented *The Woodruff Press* policy since the early thirties. The community and its leadership had learned to live, accept, and function within this framework for thirty years. Undoubtedly it satisfied many leaders.

The Save the Township Committee may have weighed heavily in Amdur's assessment of the situation. Before the development of the consolidation issue, *The Woodruff Press* had been struck by members of a typographical union that the editor refused to recognize. Local unions and area union members supported the strikers with a boycott resulting in a loss of circulation. Amdur was wary of any action that would alienate additional subscribers and strengthen the serious inroad in circulation *The County Seat News* had made by 1957–58. In March, 1958, several members of the Save the Township Committee met with Amdur and threatened to initiate a township boycott of *The Press* unless the anticonsolidation drive received adequate coverage and the paper remained neutral. History, the decision-making patterns, and economic considerations were on the side of the Save the Townshippers.

The lack of a firm editorial policy on consolidation was detrimental to the issue. *The Woodruff Press,* as the *one* and only locally controlled medium of mass communication should have defined community needs, should have directed the attention of the reader to the functional requirements of the total locality. By refusing to write editorials on any subject, by utilizing statements written by a national press service, the owner and editor deprived the community of an influential spokesman. This function could not be met as effectively by a newspaper published outside the community. *The County Seat News* and the Metropolitan City papers rarely or never editorialized on Woodruff matters.

Over the forty years of Amdur newspaper control, a shift occurred from an editorial policy opposed to salient features of Woodruff decision making to one that was little or no editorial writing at all. *The Woodruff Press* failed also to inform and educate the public during and immediately following World War II concerning the irreversible changes occurring in the area and their significance for relationships between city and township. The presence of modern utility plants and industrial facilities would lead inevitably to continued industrial and population growth in the township and would threaten to perpetuate the status of Woodruff as a small enclave. Amdur made few, if any, efforts to enlighten the public concerning the difficult choices that would confront Woodruff when the war ended. This failure strengthened and encouraged the recurrent use of the decision-making pattern by municipal leaders.

In a one, locally published newspaper community, the image or picture that residents get of the community is generally supplied by the newspaper. An effective editorial policy on important community issues may often mobilize public opinion for or against an issue.[22]

New Ownership and the New Editor

In March, 1962, the Amdur family sold *The Woodruff Press* to the Kent Group. At the time of acquisition, *The Woodruff Press* had an

22. Presthus found many of the same practices in both the Edgewood paper and that of Riverview. He concluded that Edgewood's attitude toward "self help" versus "outside" government aid was responsible for the lack of editorial responsiveness. This was not true in Woodruff. *The Press's* deficiencies were not based on negative attitudes toward government support but rather on the desire of leaders to make decisions concerning federal or state support in private where the pros and cons and their respective strings could be weighed. Robert Presthus, *Men at the Top: A Study in Community Power* (New York: Oxford University Press, 1964), p. 222.

estimated circulation of 5,500 subscriptions. A year later the number increased to more than 8,500, up 54 percent; by 1965 circulation had doubled.

The new editor was William Bowes, a forty-year-old Texas-born newspaperman with considerable experience. Upon assumption of the position he initiated, stated, and continued to maintain an aggressive editorial policy until his departure in the fall of 1966. On March 12, 1962, he wrote:

> . . . a newspaper holds a very special place in any town.
> At its greatest it can be a tremendously vital force for civic good and community growth.
> At its worst it remains the most effective means yet devised for transmitting information of, for and about a specific city.
> But even this doesn't begin to tell the full story, for, unlike any other type of business enterprise, a newspaper is in a very real sense owned by the people it serves.
> . . . by you!

Bowes followed this with editorials on a variety of local, state, and national issues. During the course of the first year under the new ownership, he took positions on a number of controversial issues, attempted to initiate action on several others, and advocated a union of city and township under one government. These editorials evoked a number of negative responses from both township and city readers.

Unlike his predecessor, Bowes created an impressive record of editorial opinion. In the three months preceding the major city council and township board elections of April 1, 1963, he wrote ninety-five editorials. Two were expressions on more than one topic. Of the ninety-seven topics in the ninety-five editorials, forty-one were concerned with Woodruff, twenty-six were of state-wide interest, thirteen were national in scope, five were general topics, and twelve were Saturday samplings from other newspapers.

During the week before the April, 1963, elections, *closed* meetings were held by a number of middle- and lower-level community leaders and city officials to determine the feasibility of a large-scale annexation of township land to the city of Woodruff. Bowes was invited to attend. His position at the meeting was one of interested observer and not of active participant. Nevertheless, when a small-scale annexation of a section of the eastern part of the township including the two largest industrial plants was proposed, Bowes's statement that he could not go along with a land grab succeeded in altering the plans of the spearheading group. A "package" that was unacceptable to Bowes and that he considered to be incompatible with the best interests of the entire area his paper served would not receive editorial support from *The Press*.

The editor was invited to attend the closed planning sessions for a number of reasons. First, his editorials early in 1962 suggested a favorable opinion on the matter. Second, it was evident to *Woodruff Press* readers that Bowes was willing to take positions on controversial community issues. Third, the organizing group understood that the newspaper, willing to take a favorable stand editorially, might be the deciding factor in a recognizably difficult campaign. And fourth, Bowes had proven to be a man of integrity. His willingness to say "yes" or "no" supported by what he considered to be reasonable proof, to stand up and be counted regardless of the wishes of special interest groups, and, on several occasions, to the position taken by the power groupings in Woodruff lent a value to his opinions, judicious or not, because they presumably were not influenced by local favors or spoils.

On April 5, 1963, annexation petitions were filed with the Iroquois County clerk. The next day Bowes published the following front-page editorial.[23]

We doubt if anyone has much question as to how *The Press* stands on the annexation proposal filed yesterday by the City. We're in favor of it, for here lies the answer to this area's future.

Further, we doubt, if even the bitterest opponents would deny that together a united city and township can find the best answers to problems that directly affect every one of us . . . .

But that will not be the issue upon which the campaign will be waged. It's going to be a bread-and-butter fight, revolving around such traditional questions of similar contest in the past as—

"What will I get out of it? When will I get it? How much is it going to cost me?" . . .

If, as Supervisor Gary Jones and Clerk Bill E. Strite have already stated, the township resident would receive little or nothing then he should vote no.

He also owes it to himself and his family, however, to make this decision on the basis of facts not emotional appeals. . . .

23. *The Woodruff Press*, April 6, 1963.

The following week several more editorials on the issue appeared. Between April 5, 1963, and May 5, 1964, when the issue came to a vote, over forty editorials were printed.

Sale to the Clark Group

The Kent Group sold *The Woodruff Press* in 1968 after the Supreme Court ruled that it was a violation of antitrust law for any company to own two newspapers in the same county. The Kent Group recognized, soon after purchasing *The Press*, that this action might have to be taken as a result of the pending Supreme Court case and local developments. In 1965, *The County Seat News* stopped all circulation in the Woodruff community. A sizable group of Woodruff City and Woodruff Township residents were incensed. Several Democratic leaders in both units attempted to fight the action. A professor at Woodruff University who was a long-time Democratic party leader consulted with the city attorney on possible courses of action. The township clerk filed a suit charging anti-trust violation. While federal investigators were called in no remedy was offered until the Supreme Court decision was reached. The sale to the Clark Corporation was imperative. The concern and action taken by Democratic party leaders in city and township were further indicators of the value they placed on a competing press and on the use of the newspaper for political campaigns. During the Amdur era, township politicians stated they could force *The Press* to publish stories and letters by threatening to offer these only to *The News* or by boycotting *The Press* in favor of *The News*. Even with the growth and development of a forceful press under Bowes they still wished to have available the tools of coercion and force—perhaps even the right to subscribe to the County Seat City paper! On the Kent Group side of the ledger was the fact that as long as there was a sizable circulation of *The News* in the Woodruff community, regardless of the circulation growth of *The Press*, large County Seat City advertisers would not duplicate ads in both papers. Without this revenue *The Press* could not survive.

Summary

A comparison of *The Woodruff Press* during the thirty years of Amdur family editorship with the first year or two under Bowes, using the criteria established for an effective newspaper and editor, placed the former at a distinct disadvantage. Although the Amdurs attempted to exert potent political power as a family, they did it through informal patterns of communication and not through the newspaper. They did not act as referee on community issues nor did they give the reader depth information on local issues. While Amdur and his son were knowledgeable concerning Woodruff's leaders, their utilization of that knowledge was limited by the boundary drawn by the city's decision-making patterns and their own personal advancement. The existence of the paper for over fifty years would lead one to assume that it reflected the interests and conception of what a community newspaper should be for many residents or for the community leadership. The pattern of its existence was functional to individuals and groups outside of the Amdur family. It had remained operational as a no-action paper for almost twenty-five years. Without local patronage, without advertising support, it could not have continued. The people who paid the bills were either satisfied or not unduly disturbed!

Amdur played his role as editor in such a manner that his money[24] and his type of social intercourse reflected an identity with the interests of the community's leaders rather than with the over-all improvement and prosperity of the community. This identification results in a downgrading of Amdur for at least three or four of the seven criteria. However, downgrading on any ideal standard of measure is just that. In the end a community organization's success or failure must be measured by its continuity and its ability to satiate the community it services. As a business enterprise, a newspaper, unlike a church, cannot continue to exist half-dead, half-alive for more than a very few years, certainly not for twenty-five. Pleasing the do-gooder, the social changer, or the nonconformer may be the least significant measures of its success.

During the first two years that the Kent Group owned *The Woodruff Press* the circulation increased substantially. Although the criteria of evaluation mentioned on pages 171–72 had been established before Bowes became active, *The Press*'s attempts to exert potent power by supporting or criticizing public officials in city and township, to act as referee on urban renewal, to lead and reflect some community thought by suggesting and urging a city capital improve-

24. Amdur invested heavily and successfully in local real estate.

ments fund, almost seemed insightful to our basis of measurement. In addition, local events received depth coverage.

As editor, Bowes's actions corresponded to the criteria of role performance listed above. On several occasions his earlier editorials contained statements that indicated a lack of total understanding of the community patterns that had evolved for getting work done in Woodruff. His insight and ability to interpret improved steadily and readers gained respect for both the paper and its editor. The power a paper has and its ability to exercise that power is dependent upon the community respect it has gained. In Christenson's analysis of *The Toledo Blade,* he states, "It often is not the power of the press as the responsibility to use it wisely. . . . It may be that no community group or no person—except a strong mayor, perhaps—can successfully contend with a newspaper which has won community respect, which *wants* to lead as well as mirror, which uses its power judiciously and is careful not to overplay its hand."[25]

Before the April, 1963, elections, Bowes editorially supported the fluoridation of city water, the proposed state constitution, and indirectly supported one city council candidate while evaluating the other contenders. In addition, he supported the Republican candidate for township supervisor, Gary Jones, who opposed Democrat Bill E. Strite. It is questionable as to whether Bowes's position could have affected voter returns. Certainly social scientists have recognized the complexity of measuring the impact of newspaper endorsement on election results.[26] Nevertheless, Bowes was severely criticized by the township Democratic party and a number of "old guard" city leaders for his support of Jones. As in the Blume and Lyons study of a monopoly newspaper in a local election and Banfield's findings in Chicago, regardless of ultimate value, candidates and party influentials placed considerable importance upon newspaper endorsement and the level of campaign coverage.[27]

25. Christenson, "Power of the Press," p. 227.
26. Norman Blume and Schley Lyons, "The Monopoly Newspaper in a local Election: The Toledo *Blade," Journalism Quarterly,* Vol. 45, No. 2 (Summer, 1968), 286–92; James E. Gregg, "Newspaper Editorial Endorsements and California Elections, 1948–1962," *Journalism Quarterly,* Vol. 42, No. 3 (Autumn, 1965), 532–38.
27. Blume and Lyons, "The Monopoly Newspaper," pp. 290–92; Banfield, *Political Influence,* p. 55.

Essentially, Bowes' contribution to Woodruff during his five years as editor outweighed the criticism. Absentee-ownership had improved *The Press* and made it a more potent community force than it had been under local ownership since the thirties. Woodruff, after living thirty years with a "no-editorial-policy" newspaper and dependency on whatever news and editorial space could be gleaned from *The County Seat News,* had a paper that gave every indication of developing into a consistent agent for community growth and development. *The Woodruff Press* under the Kent Group and Clark Corporation, in the sixties, was willing to report on men and organizations of power and influence and to pass judgment on them.

Despite its speculative character, it is useful to raise the question of whether the newspaper might have made a difference in the development of intermunicipal relations if the Amdurs, between the thirties and fifties, had pursued policies closer to those practiced by Bowes and James in the sixties. Could *The Woodruff Press* have been an effective spokesman for a few leaders, such as Harding and Erickson, who tried to modify Woodruff's decision-making pattern in the direction of favoring territorial and industrial expansion? Two factors suggest an affirmative answer. First, the voters of Woodruff have been aware of the need for and benefits of city expansion. Since the twenties, Woodruff voters endorsed every annexation and unification proposal placed on the ballot. This fact leads to the conclusion that considerable support would have existed in the city if Amdur had attempted to make an issue of some of the crucial decisions on utilities in the forties. Amdur, however, failed to inform the citizens of the refusal of city officials to consider the possibility of expanding the utility plant at government expense to meet the needs of the bomber plant and the refusal to provide water to Shady Lea Village. Also he did not criticize city officials in the years following the war for ignoring engineering recommendations to proceed with expansion of the two city utility plants. Amdur and his son share some of the responsibility for the inertia of public officials on these matters. Second, in recent years, citizens and officials of both city and township have shown an increased interest in municipal co-operation for performing certain governmental functions, notably the development of recreational facilities and garbage collection and disposal. In the late sixties, with the co-operation of

Midwest Motors, the two municipalities accepted responsibility for jointly developing the recreational potential of Midwest Lake, previously owned by Midwest Motors. The newspaper editor supported this move and other areas of co-operative endeavor. This recognition of area benefit from intermunicipal co-operation might have come ten or twenty years earlier had the paper, under the Amdurs, performed its educational function properly. Over the years, the newspaper could have been a potent force for slowing down the duplication of effort for vital services and for encouraging functional integration in important service areas, which sooner or later would have led to the territorial expansion of Woodruff.

Part III
Patterns of Action:
Consolidation and Annexation

8. Consolidation: Policy Formation and Campaign Organization

Woodruff faced many of the problems characteristic of large metropolitan centers. These problems included economic development and population mobility interlocked with outmoded political systems and constraining geographical boundaries. For many years city leaders had sought to maintain Woodruff's political and social systems through limitation of any area expansion that might alter the balance of power. Historically, those men who attempted to organize efforts to geographically enlarge Woodruff City or focus on area planning had to either alter their beliefs to align with the dominant culture pattern or were relegated to lower-level leadership positions. The attempts, the actors, the organizational structures that were created and abandoned in the search for area solutions to urban problems reflect the significance of Woodruff's decision-making patterns.

The Annexation Process

Efforts to annex township land to the city in the twenties, although not a complete failure, proved an embittering and disenchanting experience for some leaders in Woodruff. Three elections, in 1924, 1926, and 1929, resulted in the addition of only one westside parcel near the University. Twenty-one years elapsed before Woodruff attempted another large-scale annexation.

In 1950, a number of residents of Shady Lea Village—college students, businessmen, and professional men, believed that a permanent model housing area should be built to replace the temporary Shady Lea Village wartime housing. They concluded that this could best be accomplished if the area were part of Woodruff. In the forty-year period investigated, it was one of the few instances in which an organized group of township residents sought actively to become part of Woodruff.

City leaders regarded the plan with hesitation, fearing the cost of providing governmental services would be "excessive" and that the militant village leaders might "take over" city hall. To make the proposal more attractive, the township group included the former bomber plant and the utilities plants in the area to be annexed. Continued delays led the village leaders to issue an ultimatum: annex us or we will incorporate Shady Lea Village. Convinced that the residents would keep their pledge, the city manager persuaded city leaders to accept the lesser of two evils. Annexation petitions were filed. When Pacific Motors, fearful of tax increases, covertly financed a legal fight to prevent the election, an injunction was obtained which "temporarily" delayed the vote. City leaders and political officials breathed a sigh of relief. No city official pressed to remove the injunction, and it remained in force for three years. The annexation election never was held.[1]

The final annexation effort before the attempt at consolidation involved a 610-acre parcel west of the city which included Davenport's township-located paper factory. A successful election, its importance dimmed by merger efforts and an attempted recall of the township supervisor, occurred two months before the consolidation election.

First Steps

Over the years, the answer of some Woodruff leaders to future city development seemed to be geographic expansion. These men and

1. The city was so uncommitted to the annexation and so sure that the attempt would fail that during the early period of court action they negotiated to purchase water from the township.

women, usually young, idealistic, inexperienced aspirants to leadership positions, took stands that were in opposition to the community's decision-making patterns. By supporting the expansion of Woodruff's boundaries they threatened to considerably alter the city and township's leadership structure, political party hierarchy, and policies on future community development. Generally they felt the course they chose would benefit Woodruff. Most of them were not on a high enough leadership level to have had perceptive contact with top-level leadership from whom they could learn the avenues by which to effect acceptable community change. Each decade produced several of these dissenters. Time and experience either altered and discouraged their earlier visions, or they were spewed from the ranks of potential Woodruff leaders.

Each past attempt to annex township land had not developed in isolation, suddenly exploding like a roman candle full-blown. Each was preceded by extended talk between individuals and within community organizations, sometimes covering a period of years. Each possessed a type of rudimentary "research"—the pseudo digging out of "the facts" and "conclusions" by a citizen's group. The final reports seemed to summarize the original thinking of the group or one of its leaders. Final conclusions, with the addition of a few relevant statistics, could have been drawn and written at the first meeting.

The events that occurred between the 1950 annexation attempt and the 610-acres annexation and consolidation attempts of 1957–58 were, in a sense, a cumulative process. Three organizational steps were taken which focused on area problem solution between 1953 and 1958:

1. During this period the Civic Affairs Committee of the Woodruff Chamber of Commerce discussed repeatedly in formal meetings various aspects of community expansion.

2. In 1955, by joint action of the Woodruff Township Board and the Woodruff City Council, a Woodruff Area Planning Committee was appointed to study solutions to area problems.

3. In July, 1957, the Chamber of Commerce Civic Affairs Committee appointed an area planning committee that was to encourage joint participation of the senior and junior Chambers on a study of city expansion procedures.

Several of the same men who were personally committed to the expansion of Woodruff City boundaries were on more than one of the committees. One man, Gerald Harding, served on each of the above committees and played important roles in the 1958 consolidation and the 1964 annexation attempts.

Harding, during the seven years of study, was considered a lower-level leader. He was president of a Sand-Gravel Company and vice-president of a companion company that had prospered under his guidance. His introduction to community service was as a Jaycee; he had participated with Carl Erickson in the successful Jaycee charter fight in 1946. From his early tenure in community organizations he had advocated and had labored in behalf of geographic expansion of the city. Without this commitment to community expansion, his occupational and income level, combined with other favorable elements, e.g., class factors and personality attributes, should have elevated him to a higher leadership position.

The Filing of Petitions

On October 11, 1957, representatives of a 610-acre area lying northwest of Woodruff City filed petitions for annexation to the city with the county clerk. Four days later, spurred on by the county clerk, several members of the Woodruff Township Board proposed that the township push for incorporation into a separate city, surrounding the city of Woodruff. An incorporation committee was appointed with a township board trustee as chairman to study the matter and recommend a course of action. This move gave Harding, Erickson, and the Jaycee leaders their opportunity.

Opposition on nearly all fronts outside the township began to mount within forty-eight hours after the incorporation announcement. The county planning director cited the "lack of proper planning for future urban services, proper efficiency studies, etc." contained in such a proposal.[2]

The Woodruff city manager termed the township board's proposal "impractical—a very poor situation."

Between July 16 and August 8, 1957, representatives of the Chamber of Commerce, including Harding, discussed with officers

2. *The County Seat News,* October 17, 1957.

of the Jaycees the possibility of a co-operative effort at investigating three possibilities for the extension of city boundaries and development of services. After informal contacts on a number of occasions the Jaycee Area Improvement Committee decided to study and act on one of the suggestions—the consolidation of Woodruff and Woodruff Township. Originally the committee intended to follow a study course, secure "the facts," and then petition for a vote on the proposal.

Although Harding played the key role of innovator, encouraging and cajoling Jaycee leaders to direct their attention to area development, the timing of these activities was crucial. Harding's own Chamber of Commerce committee had discussed the problem for several years without result. It is questionable as to whether the Jaycee consolidation study would have evolved into action if the township board had not threatened separate incorporation.

The activities of both the senior and junior Chambers were not as circumspect as one might have wished. Both groups were comprised of city and township residents. Undoubtedly word of the Jaycee study and of a possible project to augment it reached the ears of the township board. The board, in turn, did not suddenly evolve its plan to incorporate the whole township. Ideas on incorporation had been entertained and threatened during the 1950 annexation attempt. The public move was given impetus by the filing of the 610-acre annexation petition and the rumors of a larger annexation attempt by the joint Chambers of Commerce. In turn, the renewed township board threat of October 15 was skillfully exploited by Harding, Erickson, and the Jaycee leaders. The Woodruff Junior Chamber of Commerce, literally forced by circumstances to give up plans for an academic study of the alternative approaches to city expansion, launched a full-scale offensive attack.

The organization's Area Improvement Committee, with the assistance of a lawyer member, drew up petitions, secured the necessary signatures, and filed consolidation petitions on October 29. On October 17, after the township had made its move, the city manager stated: "In recent months, study has been given by area groups and agencies to the possibility of consolidating or merging the city and township into a single unit of local government." The reporter noted, "The township board openly opposes such a proposal." On October

23, before the Jaycee petition had been filed, *The Woodruff Press* carried the following article:

JAYCEES HOPE FOR NEW CITY
At their regular meeting Tuesday night, the Area Improvement Committee of the Woodruff Junior Chamber of Commerce expressed hope that an entirely new city would arise through consolidation.

This new city would be based on some of the oldest American traditions, namely, that all the people would have the voice in the formation of their local government, it was pointed out.

The Jaycees feel that this issue should be placed on the ballot for the vote of the people. This vote would not establish a new city, but rather start the process whereby the people of the enlarged area select the government best suited for this area.

If this issue receives a favorable vote, then a charter commission would be set up and be composed of persons living in the entire area. It was pointed out this approach differs completely from annexation. Both the existing Woodruff City and Township governments would be dissolved and an entirely new form of government created.[3]

The township treasurer reported that since the news of the proposed incorporation was published, "my phone has been ringing— even at home. . . . Most of the comments are favorable to the proposed incorporation."

On October 17, 1957, the *County Seat News* published an editorial on the possibility of separate incorporation:

WOODRUFF TOWNSHIP'S PROPOSAL HAS STARTLING IMPLICATIONS
The consternation of Woodruff officials over the proposal of the Woodruff Township Board to incorporate the township into a city entirely surrounding Woodruff is understandable.

The implications of such a move are little short of fantastic. Woodruff, which has been trying to annex township land for needed expansion, would find itself, instead, with fixed boundaries. The city would be swallowed up, in a sense, by a larger community, which it appears might be known as Shady Lea. . . .

Two weeks after the formation of the township incorporation committee, on October 29, the Woodruff Junior Chamber of Commerce filed petitions with the county clerk for the consolidation of both units of government.

The triggering of this chronological course of events is interrelated.

3. *The Woodruff Press,* October 23, 1957.

Organizing the Campaign

The Woodruff Junior Chamber of Commerce was organized in 1938 with the assistance of the Woodruff Chamber of Commerce. It became recognized, over the years, as a training ground for future community leaders. As a young man's organization, it sometimes embarked on community projects of a seemingly controversial nature. In 1946, it successfully organized an attempt to change the form of Woodruff City government from a strong mayor and weak council to a city manager and council form. Several Jaycees, including Harding and Erickson, gained a measure of prominence in the late forties by providing the leadership that enabled the Junior Chamber to campaign effectively for political change. However, there was one significant difference between the attempt to change the form of government in 1946 and the 1957–58 consolidation campaign. The former was consistent with the basic aspects of the decision-making pattern, especially economy in government and the hope for more effective control over the city Democrats through nonpartisan, at-large elections. The consolidation attempt was in conflict with the decision-making pattern. The change would have necessitated large public expenditures for the extension of city services to undeveloped portions of the township. A unified Democratic party might have given Democratic leaders in the new city greater access to positions of political power.

Between October 22, 1957, and April 10, 1958, the Area Improvement Committee held many meetings. In addition, a selected panel of committee members met seven times between February and April, 1958, with a group of leaders who were expected to lend influence and financial support to the project.

A decisive division of these meetings into areas of concern is difficult. The meetings of October 22 and 23 focused on the petitions, securing signatures and filing the documents with the county clerk. After the filing on October 29, the meetings became a conglomeration of campaign planning and general gossip concerning the activities of the "enemy," interested groups, or individuals in and out of the city. Three November meetings were held to discuss fund raising, the employment of a public relations specialist, and the enlistment of support solicited through speeches before community organizations. One January meeting and four in February were concerned with an analysis of activities and gaining assistance from community leaders. Six meetings in February and March sought to enlist the public support of community organizations, to organize a publicity program, and to launch a get-out-the-vote campaign. The April 10 meeting, which took place after the vote, evaluated the entire campaign.

The Committee
The composition of a committee, in terms of the socioeconomic background and status of participants, forms a milieu by which to view and analyze roles played and decisions reached. The Area Improvement Committee of the Woodruff Junior Chamber of Commerce consisted of approximately seventeen men and an ex-officio member, the organization's president. All were local businessmen or professionals on the low managerial level. Some assisted their fathers or other family members in family businesses, several were in business for themselves, and the others consisted of a high school teacher, a lawyer, a newspaperman, a garage owner, an accountant, and a nurseryman. These young men hoped to work their way up the leadership and economic ladders of Woodruff. They pinched pennies, had limited clothing budgets, and were feeling their way in the occupational world. Not one of the committee members came from a prestigious or powerful Woodruff City family.

After the meetings of October 22 and 23, the work of the committee centered around five or six members until late in February 1958, when an attempt was made to expand the active membership. There were several factors that facilitated this pattern. First, the five or six men who carried the burden of responsibility for the campaign seemed to have a serious commitment to consolidation as the answer to area problems. They were willing to publicly announce the stand they had taken by speaking before any group in the community which would extend an invitation. Since various community organizations had to be approached in this manner, those who were not willing to express their views publicly or did not feel their natural abilities lay on the speaker's platform withdrew. Committee membership was confined to those who were willing to *publicly* commit themselves to consolidation of the city and township. Those Jaycees from both areas who were opposed to consolidation—and they predominated—were excluded and ignored.

The second limiting factor developed as the committee recognized that their group was financially hamstrung and needed to seek financial support from outside the group. As private contacts were made, the Jaycee president, who acted as liaison agent between his group and the Chamber of Commerce, recognized that financial assistance was available if the group allowed contributors to remain anonymous. The smaller the group of confidants, the easier this could be accomplished. The larger the group, the more questions would be asked concerning the contributors, why they were contributing, and whether this was truly a Jaycee project or a front for a more powerful group acting behind the scenes.

The Actors

The following men were most active on the committee. The Jaycee president, Philip Webb, was thirty-four years old and a certified public accountant. As president of the Jaycees he was on the Board of Directors of the Chamber of Commerce. Richard Wasmund, Jr., known as "Bud," in his late twenties, was the son of the executive secretary of the Chamber of Commerce, and assistant manager of Erickson Office Supplies. The owner, Carl Erickson, former president of the state Jaycee organization, had been active in the successful effort to change the form of Woodruff government and, with Gerald Harding, encouraged the Jaycees to embark on a study of consolidation in the summer of 1957. Donald Dunham, thirty-two years old, was an attorney in private practice, with an office next to Webb's. Charles Begley, thirty-two years old, was a horticulturist who owned a local garden supply center. Begley had been a member of the defunct Woodruff Area Planning Committee of 1955 and had taken undergraduate courses in city planning at the State University. Raymond Bates, thirty years old, was part owner of an area drycleaning firm. He was on the state Jaycee board and had chaired a number of successful Jaycee committees that had required energy, perseverance, and elbow grease. Thomas Thayer, thirty-one years of age, chairman of the Area Improvement Committee, owned a garage at the outset of the campaign. He sold his business later and worked temporarily as a route man for Raymond Bates's cleaning firm.

These six men were vice presidents of the Junior Chamber of Commerce during the consolidation campaign. Four had completed college; of the other two, Bates and Thayer, Bates had two years at the State Agricultural College. With the exception of Dunham, all were married.

Webb lived within the city of Woodruff, Dunham lived over the township line in a rural township and practiced law in Woodruff. Begley, Thayer, Wasmund, Jr., and Bates lived in Woodruff Township. Only one of the six key Jaycee leaders was a city resident. The challenge to the city's decision-making pattern came from township Jaycee members who were discontent with area development.

Why did these men actively work in behalf of such an ambitious program? It was not a game of marbles that might be played again and again to win back a favorite agate. It involved deep-seated emotions; new and old conflicts and disagreements; rural versus urban attitudes that had flared for decades past; the position of the southern migrant, his institutions and culture patterns, which were in opposition to the well-cleaved Woodruff status system with its supportive religious, civic, and political organizations. At meetings these men were called many derogatory names as they were individuals filling certain positions in Woodruff and representatives of the Jaycees. They were treated with disdain. Threats were publicly made on one occasion against the family and home of Thayer. Why did these men submit to the disparagement that resulted from the threat they posed to both city and township decision-making patterns?

Initially, as a group, they were following what they believed to be an established Woodruff procedure for personal leadership advancement. For twenty years, young men in Woodruff had served their apprenticeship, proving their leadership potential, by carrying out successful projects as members of the Jaycees. On enough occasions to give the matter prominence, the Jaycee organization had successfully sponsored issues of community change involving some difference of opinion within the city of Woodruff. The change issue was always located within the city of Woodruff and always attuned to the decision-making pattern that the key leaders supported. While it was considered an area organization, with a large percentage of its members living in the township, most of its major activities that embodied change were focused on and within the city.

A second consideration was the personal outlet and need for group activity. Bates, for example, stated that he crammed all his excess energy into Jaycee projects. For some it was an evening or several evenings away from home, sanctioned by the belief that valuable business contacts, leadership training, and occupational advancement were derived through these activities.

Third, no member of the committee, with the possible exception of Wasmund, Jr., had close informal ties with the top leadership group. A "new" city with expanded boundaries could develop new patterns and structure that might offer each of them a more fortuitous position of economic and leadership success than their present circumstances.

It is difficult to separate reasons for individual participation from those of the group. They are interrelated. Each committee member had something to gain from a successful election campaign. Philip Webb was interested in a political career. He had made an unsuccessful bid for a Woodruff City Council seat, supported by Erickson, just before the consolidation attempt. He saw his position of contact man with city leaders and as president of the Jaycees during a hopefully successful campaign as the answer to his political ascent.

At the first committee meeting the researchers attended, Charles Begley, with several other men, stated that the city planner would be replaced in the larger area by Begley if consolidation succeeded. Regardless of this "plum," it was apparent throughout the campaign that Begley believed in the consolidation concept.

Donald Dunham was building a law practice in the Woodruff area. Participating in a movement that might have considerable political and economic significance should make him more visible to businessmen and public officials.

"Bud" Wasmund, Jr., had been encouraged by his employer, Carl Erickson, and possibly by his father to work for consolidation. In his employer he had an example of a man who had gained some leadership position through past Jaycee activity. As the son of the executive secretary of the Chamber of Commerce, Wasmund knew the importance of Jaycee projects as a stepping stone to community positions of power and prestige. He did not, or refused to, recognize the importance of the relationship between the problem area and past decision making in Woodruff.

Thomas Thayer and Raymond Bates saw the Jaycee consolidation effort as a boost to their leadership positions. Thayer looked for a new employment opportunity during the last three months of the campaign. Bates was interested in advancement within the Jaycee organization, locally, state, or nationally. Harding's encouragement of an area expansion program and the timing of the township board's incorporation plan geared with the personal motives of the Jaycee leadership.

A Plan for Action

Before the consolidation petitions were filed, the Jaycee committee organized a speaker's bureau. Between November 27 and December 5, 1957, over fifty-four letters were sent to a list of community organizations compiled by the Chamber of Commerce. The list included all of the major service clubs, women's organizations, parent-teacher groups in the city and township, several of the civic associations, the fraternal organizations, and a number of social organizations. Out of the fifty-four, seventeen groups were addressed. In addition, twenty-two organizations not on the list secured a consolidation speaker from the group. Only four of the latter were city organizations. Most of the twenty-two were civic organizations or new groups organized because of the issue, such as the Woodruff Township Committee for Good Government and the Save the Township Committee. Only Webb, Dunham, Begley, Wasmund, and Thayer engaged in public speaking.

Besides the speaker's bureau, Webb felt that the Jaycees could not hope to initiate a successful campaign without the assistance of a professional public relations man. As a result, R. C. Leslie was brought into the group early in January. Leslie was a local Woodruff City resident of seven years duration whose public relations firm, officed in Metropolitan City, functioned in the Metropolitan City region of which Woodruff was a part. He had been active in the Westside City Civic Association and in the city Episcopal church. His initial contact with the Jaycees came through that organization's president. Leslie had supported morally and financially Webb's unsuccessful bid for public office a year before the consolidation attempt. Leslie could be classified as an "outside" specialist since much of his social and economic life were based outside the community. His attitudes and criticisms throughout the campaign were stated as an outsider looking with interest at an object from which he was partially and reluctantly separated. Leslie kept behind the scenes and never spoke publicly for the group.

As the movement approached its legal conclusion, the Jaycee committee would logically have been expanded to include most of the organization's active members. The exigencies of such a campaign seemed to demand a broadened leadership base and certainly an expansion in the number of workers. While the committeemen present at the early meetings came to several in March, the general increase did not occur. Three factors influenced this development. First, consolidation was a highly controversial issue. A large number of Jaycees were found to be in sympathy with retaining the *status quo*. These men felt that the Area Improvement Committee, influenced by a few leaders and by the desire for personal gain, acted without sufficient study of the problem and without the sympathy of the total membership. Second, the committee preferred limited membership to maintain secrecy during the prepetition filing stage and during the contacts with city leaders to secure financial assistance. Third, with the entry of the "official" public relations man, the work reins shifted to Leslie from the small overworked group. Rather than prepare their own material or suggest their own tactics, they allowed Leslie to assume the central planning and initiative role.

Although the group allowed Leslie considerable authority, the transfer did not transpire without criticism. On February 16, Bates asked the committee whether it represented the Jaycees or another group, saying that members of the Jaycee Area Improvement Committee should be notified of meetings and plans. This had not been done. Bates asked Begley and Dunham for an explanation. They passed the floor to Thayer, who described the group as a subcommittee of the total Area Improvement Committee. During the remainder of the February 16 meeting, Bates openly attacked any presentation of plans by Leslie and reiterated his belief in the undemocratic procedure of limiting the number of workers. His frank and creditable aggressiveness embarrassed the group. Bates, more than other members of the committee, recognized in the structure and functioning of the consolidation campaign an organizational departure from the democratic procedures of the other Jaycee committees he had worked on. Much of the decision-making process had become independent of the parent body; the committee functioned as a semiautonomous group. This eliminated for Bates the working-togetherness, buddy-to-buddy-sharing relationship that was, for him, the Jaycee organization. The behind-the-scenes use of power held little interest for him and offered few rewards.

Leslie's Activities

Leslie's role in the group entailed fund raising as well as over-all planning and publicity. With Webb he developed a series of meetings with a group of city leaders to raise the money necessary to wage the campaign. The campaign budget proposed by Webb, Dunham, and Leslie totaled $5,700. Dispersals were as follows:

$2,500 to Leslie for professional assistance
  500 brochure
  500 repayment of bank loan for petition filing fee
  500 to Dunham for legal fees
1,700 general expenses: posters, stickers, telephones, office space
_____
$5,700 TOTAL

Late in May, when the expenses were finally tallied, a total of $5,600 had been spent. Since over $5,800 was raised, the Jaycees met their commitments with a little to spare.

Leslie defined his campaign program as organizational and publicity. Publicity consisted of the writing, printing, and distribution of the consolidation brochure, preparing for publication in *The Woodruff Press* of twenty-three articles on the pros and cons of consolidation, a radio broadcast over an area station, with representatives of both sides, and letters to the editors of the two area newspapers by different Jaycee members written and approved or partially written by Leslie. He also purchased car stickers, buttons, and posters, compiled mailing and phone lists, and favored establishment of a consolidation office in both city and township.

In his organizational efforts, Leslie urged the Jaycees to form a committee of representatives from community groups favoring merger to secure a work force and to co-ordinate consolidation activities. Gerald Harding and a history professor from Woodruff State University were to represent the Chamber of Commerce and were added to the Jaycee's roster of speakers. Leslie also suggested that the Jaycees organize a non-Jaycee group in the township representing each geographical section to counteract the Save the Township Committee.

There were differences between Leslie's plans and his accomplishments. The brochure was printed and dispersed, the articles were written and printed, a radio broadcast over an area station took place, car stickers were purchased, phone lists and pre-election eve phoning were organized by one of Leslie's associates and accomplished by a paid group of women, and a city consolidation headquarters was set up in a vacant store although no attempt was made to establish similar quarters in the township. These accomplishments, creditable though they may be, were achieved by the efforts of relatively few individuals. The other plans, particularly those concerning organizational techniques, demanded group action. A committee of Jaycees, Chamber of Commerce, and American Legion representatives met. One unsuccessful attempt was made by a member of the Jaycees to develop a counter Save the Township group on the west side of the township. No attempt was made on the south or east sides. The last-minute telephone calling in the city Jaycee consolidation office was made by paid employees and not by volunteers.

Community Organizational Support
The work of the Jaycees and the efforts of the Chamber of Commerce for consolidation were never publicized as a joint effort. Only a handful of lower-level Woodruff leaders in the Chamber urged the Chamber to support the project publicly. Generally, Erickson and Harding were responsible for whatever Chamber activities transpired.

Throughout the first months of the consolidation drive, rumor had it that certain members of the Chamber of Commerce and its executive secretary wished to become actively involved in support of the issue. Webb and Leslie opposed this step. They believed that active involvement of the senior Chamber would strengthen the beliefs of some city and particularly township residents that the "City Fathers" were acting again for their own self-interest. According to Leslie's plan, after what seemed to be an adequate period of fact finding, various community organizations would publicly endorse merger. On February 27, the American Legion supported it; on March 26, the Chamber of Commerce; on March 27, Kiwanis; and on April 1, the West Woodruff (City) Civic Association.[4] Reflecting on the importance of the Chamber of Commerce in the history of the community, the level of its leadership, and its skillful manipulation of men and issues in the past, it is unlikely that the top Chamber leaders would have allowed the Jaycees generally, and a paid public relations man in particular, to dictate and control the public or private strategy of an issue, the success of which was considered vital to its members' interests. Leslie and the Jaycee leaders preferred to function with little interference from top leaders. This, in turn, played into the hands of most of the top leaders who did not wish to become involved or who were opposed to merger.

Both Webb and Leslie and presumably the other active committee members knew that the financial support necessary to wage the type of campaign Leslie visualized had to come from community leaders, leaders clustered in the Chamber of Commerce. The drive for votes favorable to consolidation could not have proceeded without requiring sizable amounts of money and without the utilization of men experienced in public affairs. If it had been possible, the Jaycee leaders and their advisors would have been completely independent of the men in the upper echelons of the Woodruff leadership hierarchy. The commitment to employ Leslie as public relations consultant and the law requiring payment of a $500 fee for filing of petitions compelled a quest for funds from the more affluent.

The Top Leaders

Organized activities of the men the Jaycees called and thought of as "top leaders" occurred during the final weeks of the campaign as

---

4. The prestigious Rotary Club, to which most of the top city leaders belonged, did not take a public position.

part of a series of seven meetings devoted primarily to fund raising. Early in the campaign Webb, as Jaycee president, asked Mike Davenport to accept responsibility for providing campaign funds. Although Davenport acquiesced, he did not attempt to fulfill his promise until two months before the election. By that time Leslie and the Jaycees had developed a campaign organization and implementation plans, with the former in a key policy-making position.

A paramount question for Leslie and the Jaycees in the spring of 1958 was whether Davenport and his associates would be satisfied to raise money or whether they would attempt to function as policy makers. Their concern might have been even greater had they recognized the problem that truly bothered the upper echelon leaders. The latter hoped to assure the defeat of consolidation *and* escape responsibility for the election outcome. For this stratagem to succeed, Leslie and the Jaycee leaders had to be unaware of the impediments to election victory which were created by the upper-level influentials. Accomplishing this feat was facilitated by permitting the Jaycees to have their way—granting them the opportunity to direct the merger campaign. If the Jaycees received the money they requested, it would be difficult if not impossible for them or the community to attribute defeat to the top leaders. A rift between the latter and the leaders who advocated government reorganization as the solution to many community problems would not develop. These men would continue to be motivated to participate in community affairs once the disappointment of the election defeat had abated.

The defeat of merger was given a high probability by the actions and inactions of previous years which led to the independence of many areas of the township (see Chapter 4) and to the township's industrial development. The city could not use its utility facilities as an inducement for merger; indeed, they were less adequate than those of the township. Moreover, township politicians would not permit the industrial tax base of the township, which was considerably greater than that of the city, to fall into the hands of city leaders. These conditions limited the possibility of merger success. The advocates of consolidation limped into the ring against a fast-moving opponent.

These factors left Davenport in a most precarious position. He sincerely believed that the spatial expansion of Woodruff was necessary for the area. Perhaps this conviction was a product of the requirements of his paper plant which, due to its location, could not be served in the near future by the township's utility facilities. Since Davenport's two sons recently had joined him in the company, assuring continuity for another generation, he was planning to expand facilities. Utility services would have to be obtained from the city. If the paper plant benefited from annexation, would not the entire township? These considerations led Davenport to look favorably on a change that other upper-level leaders did not regard as necessary. He may also have been influenced by the possibility of being elected the first mayor of the merged city.

As time passed, Davenport realized he faced a serious predicament. If he adhered to his convictions and energetically sought assistance from associates in the leadership structure, they might turn against him. If he confined his activities to fund raising and nothing more, the merger proposal would have little or no chance of success. If it were defeated, his reputation as a leader would not be enhanced. On the other hand, if he became deeply involved in the planning and managing of the campaign, defeat could be attributed directly to him and his standing would suffer an even greater setback. Under these circumstances, the most desirable course of action might have been complete withdrawal.

Davenport could or would not renege on his promise to aid the Jaycee leaders. In the final analysis Davenport had but one course of action: to fulfill his promise without becoming involved in the direction of the campaign. While conforming generally to this pattern of role playing, on a number of occasions Davenport went beyond the role of fund raiser. His efforts to gain specific forms of support from several persons gave an element of inconsistency to his role behavior and disclosed a sensitivity to pressuring from the men around him.

Meetings of the Top Leaders
The top leaders of Woodruff were not called together for fund-raising purposes until late in the campaign, two months before election day. This time schedule assisted Leslie and the Jaycees in their efforts to function as the campaign directors while enabling the

upper-echelon leaders to remain uninvolved. Before the first fund-raising meeting, no formal or organized policy-making machinery existed. There were few checks on the plans formulated by Leslie, Webb, Dunham, and their colleagues apart from informal discussions with Erickson, Harding, and Amdur. The campaign was organized along lines preferred by Leslie.

Since the fund-raising meetings involved several upper-level leaders and many lower-echelon influentials and were held over a two-month period, an organizational framework for policy making was available. Leaders would be receiving reports on campaign progress and problems from the Jaycees. In return for funds, responses, reactions, and suggestions could be offered by the leaders even if they were not requested by the Jaycees. The Jaycees could have been forced to hew to the line established by the leaders in exchange for needed monies. Before the first meeting, Leslie and some of the Jaycee leaders feared the possibility of a "takeover" by the top influentials.

For several reasons Leslie and the Jaycees had little cause for concern. The delay in arranging the meetings allowed Leslie to function as the principal policy maker, propagandist, and campaign manager. If Davenport and any of his associates seriously intended to use the meetings to modify campaign organization, they would be confronted with the task of rearranging one that already existed. This move would create the situation that most leaders wished to avoid, responsibility for the election outcome.

Thirty-five men attended at least one of the seven leader meetings. Only four—Davenport, Erickson, Amdur and Wasmund—attended a majority of the meetings. Only four other leaders attended more than three meetings.

The possibility of a top leader takeover was reduced by the unsuitability of the fund-raising meetings for policy making. Only eight men of the thirty-five attended a majority of meetings and could be considered to have a fund of information on the campaign sufficient for policy discussions. The majority came to only one or two meetings, were uninterested, and did not participate in discussion of policy matters on the few occasions when opportunities arose. These discussions terminated with most of the important problems unmentioned and unresolved.

Any doubts concerning the intentions of the men who assembled at the first meeting soon were dispelled. Both the opportunity and the justification for seizing control of the campaign became available. The major argument of the Save the Township Committee contended that merger would raise the taxes of township property owners. At the organizational meeting, before any discussion of fund raising took place, Davenport asked Webb what the Jaycees intended to tell the township voter about changes in tax rates. Webb initially tried to sidestep the question. When this failed, he admitted that, for the time being, he had no answer. The Jaycees had been unable to obtain the necessary information and Leslie had not yet prepared adequate statements on the issue.

The inability of the Jaycee leaders to cope with the opposition's most potent argument against merger so late in the campaign was a sign of incompetence. If fears of tax increases could not be eased or offset by prospects of important merger benefits, defeat would be inevitable. Certainly a strong case could be made for intervention by older, more experienced, and more powerful men. Why should the leaders contribute $6,000 for a campaign that could not succeed unless reorganization of the managing directorate first took place?

Davenport and his associates responded to Webb's performance with the admonition that the Jaycees furnish an adequate answer to the voters. Leslie and Webb were embarrassed but not dethroned. Uncertainty as to who was running the campaign was dispelled at a later meeting. Harding suggested an approach to the tax issue which Davenport approved: no specific reference was to be made to changes in the tax burden and emphasis was to be placed on the increase in governmental efficiency and reduction of duplication of effort, equipment, and services. Leslie disregarded this theme in his later newspaper articles, and there were no negative reactions or sanctions from the higher-level leaders. He wrote that merger would decrease city tax rates while hinting that those in the township would increase.

Selection of a Slate

Davenport and the leaders recognized the weakness of the Jaycee leaders and Leslie. This was revealed by the choices of candidates for the promerger slate. If a majority of voters approved merger of the two governments, a commission would be established to prepare a charter for the new municipality. On April 7, 1958, voters either would approve or disapprove merger and select candidates for the charter commission. The Save the Township Committee had the names of preferred candidates printed on cards and distributed them throughout the township. If many antimerger commissioners were elected, consolidation ultimately would be defeated even if the proposal were approved on April 7. To prevent this eventuality, a promerger slate was selected by Davenport and his colleagues at the final meeting of the fund raisers, a few days before the election.

Although several of the Jaycee leaders and Leslie had filed for the commission, none was chosen. The candidates selected were Davenport, Erickson, Harding, and two men who had served with the former mayor on the city council, neither of whom had participated in the merger campaign.

To offset the publicity given the antimerger slate, promerger candidates had to have vote-getting capabilities. The men had to be known throughout the area and to have demonstrated voter appeal. The Jaycee candidates and Leslie were untested in election races. If their ability to "sell themselves" to voters were in doubt, their effectiveness in presenting arguments for merger was even more uncertain.

Responsibility for negotiating with township commission members on the features of the proposed government and responsibility for writing the charter required men who were more knowledgeable and experienced than the Jaycee leaders. If these skills were required for preparing the charter, were they not equally vital for directing a winning election campaign? Davenport and his associates also sought to gain for themselves a large measure of credit in the event that a new municipality replaced the city and township. They sought to protect their leadership reputations in the event of an election miracle.

Raising Money

If many Woodruff leaders, with a few exceptions, preferred defeat of the merger, why would they contribute $6,000 to enable the Jaycees to conduct a creditable campaign? First, providing the funds requested by the Jaycees made it more difficult to attribute responsibility for an election defeat to the nonsupport of leaders. The blame, if there were any, could be assigned to the Jaycee leaders. Second, the procedure for fund raising placed little or no burden on the city leaders. It was acceptable to give token amounts; some influentials gave nothing. Third, the difficulties encountered in raising the $6,000 weakened the unity of the campaign directorate and further increased chances of merger defeat.

At the first leader meeting Davenport proposed a method for collecting funds which would require little time and effort: sixty men would each contribute a hundred dollars. Robert Sampson countered with the suggestion of soliciting contributions of ten and twenty dollars. This was quickly endorsed by the president of the Chamber of Commerce who pointed out that members recently had contributed to his organization's building fund. Davenport's recommendation would overburden some Chamber members.

Implementation of Sampson's proposal required a team of solicitors, an orderly distribution of solicitation assignments, time, and effort. If the amount collected fell short of the target, Davenport would be expected to meet the deficit, as he had accepted responsibility for raising the money. Sampson's opposition to the first suggestion created problems for the campaign and for Davenport. If Sampson had endorsed consolidation and pledged a hundred dollars, the other leaders would have felt obligated to follow.[5]

Davenport did not defend his proposal nor specify the disadvantages of Sampson's suggestion. Recognizing the futility of such a move, Davenport acquiesced. In the weeks that followed, Davenport and his associates struggled to raise $6,000. Not until a few days *after* the election did the fund raisers reach their goal.

The lagging fund drive gave Webb, Dunham, and the other Jaycee leaders one more worry. Expenses had been incurred, bills had to be paid, and the availability of sufficient funds was doubtful. While Webb and his associates believed the fund drive would succeed, the possibility of failure could not be discounted. From time to time the men considered what would be done if all the bills could not be met. Resentful of Leslie's takeover of their group, several Jaycee leaders hoped a shortage of funds would provide the excuse

5. An example of how this fund-raising procedure operated is provided by Floyd Hunter, *Community Power Structure* (Chapel Hill, N.C.: The University of North Carolina Press, 1953), pp. 173–74.

for not paying his fee. This not only intensified hostilities between these men and Leslie but put Webb in an awkward position. He had employed Leslie and had approved the fee. The desire of Webb's associates to renege on the fee implied criticism of Webb for this decision. In their opinion, Leslie either should have contributed his services or, if paid, he was their employee and subject to their orders. This situation made it difficult for Webb to maintain smooth working relations between Leslie and the men who were bearing the brunt of the campaign. The lengthy fund drive weakened the organization during the final weeks of the campaign, despite the unrelenting hostility of the Save the Township Committee and the township citizens. When the need for unity was greatest, the upper-level leaders, by their disinterest, had intensified internal conflict.

Role of Automotive Executives
The emphasis given to the campaign efforts of the Jaycees and several city leaders suggests that the executives of the local automobile plants played little or no part in the merger contest, that the outcome was decided by city and township residents. While it is conceivable that the absentee-owned companies gave valuable assistance covertly to one side or the other, evidence to support this view, with one exception, was not found. On the whole the auto executives followed the lead of most Woodruff influentials. They remained aloof from the contest.

If merger had taken place, the millage rate for the automobile factories would have risen and the tax bill would have increased. Although important, this financial consideration represented only a part of the concern of company officials. They were equally aware of the effect on local opinion of a public stand for or against merger. Since public opinion was divided, such an act might have angered a segment of the populace, possibly with unhappy consequences for local sales of their products and employee relationships. Furthermore, how could the companies contribute to merger when the proposal did not have the solid backing of most Woodruff leaders? Automobile company officials, by their neutrality, did nothing to mobilize public opinion in behalf of merger.

Some plant executives encouraged the lower- and middle-level executives, who were township residents, to openly oppose and work against consolidation. At first these men had expressed interest in or sympathy for merger. Within a few days of each other they publicly reversed their stand. In the weeks that followed, their executive superiors at the local plants communicated often with these men to gain information on the election campaign. During these conversations, the younger men were made aware of the anti-merger position of company officials.

Chamber of Commerce officers met twice with executives of Universal Motors to determine whether any assistance for merger might be forthcoming. However, top leaders did not request or initiate the meetings with officials of the automobile firm. The first meeting was requested by Chamber of Commerce officers, the second by executives of Universal Motors. Initially Chamber officials were told that the company would remain neutral and do nothing for or against either side. At the second meeting, a change of position was indicated. While the firm would not alter its public stand of neutrality, it now was opposed to merger. A tax expert from the company's main office contended that the cost of furnishing services to the undeveloped sections of the township would fall heavily on the automobile plants. The company preferred a program of gradual annexation to immediate merger of the two municipalities.

Company officials did make one positive offer; the firm was willing to assist local people in studying the governmental situation after the election. Whether or not this offer was sincere or an inexpensive way of expressing interest in Woodruff was not evident to the Chamber leaders. In any event, Universal Motors had made a suggestion and an offer that merited careful consideration. Subsequently Leslie, disappointed with the results of these meetings with officials of Universal Motors, attempted unsuccessfully to obtain their help.

Withholding public endorsement of merger was not without effect on the campaign despite the public stand of neutrality. The auto firm deprived merger forces of a major influential source of legitimation for their controversial plan. Since success depended on converting the township voter, merger forces were hurt by the position of neutrality. On the whole, except for the participation of young employees in the antimerger fight, the companies had not used their power to sway voters for or against consolidation.

This response to appeals for merger assistance characterized all of the absentee-owned enterprises in the Woodruff area. A direct request for money was turned down by the electric utility concern, by a railroad company, the airline, a supermarket, and several manufacturing companies. These enterprises refused to become identified with either the protagonists or the opponents of merger. The field of battle was left to local combatants.

Conclusion

The last weeks of the campaign were spent in a bevy of meetings. The active members of the Jaycee committee maintained a high level of participation until election day. They spoke at meetings, circulated literature, operated a city consolidation headquarters, and held committee meetings with their fellow Jaycees, with Leslie, with the leader committee, and with representatives of other interested community organizations. On election night, their cause, which had demanded months of work and had required a staggering number of hours sacrificed at the expense of their families, was defeated at the polls. By 1960, none of the active committee members were in positions of community-wide importance. They had either ceased to perform community leadership functions or were relegated to low positions in the Woodruff leadership hierarchy. Gerald Harding's brother Norman, who was a Jaycee worker on the edges of the campaign, was an exception.[6] He ran a successful race for the Woodruff City Council in 1963 and 1965, and Philip Webb, the president, served on the City Planning Commission in the mid-sixties.

Defeat of consolidation weakened the Jaycee organization. The membership had been badly split on the issue after the filing of the petitions. As a result the Jaycees, an organization known in Woodruff for its forthright positions and efforts on behalf of community betterment refused to take action or associate itself with controversial issues for at least seven years after the consolidation election. It attempted to regain the solidarity and strength of the past which had been built on successes in seemingly controversial areas through amicable programs, e.g., installation of auto seat belts, car inspec-

6. Norman Harding was a member of an economic dominant family who had strengthened his status position in the community when he married the daughter of bank president William Studer.

tions, and solicitation of library furniture. By the late sixties the organization had regained much of the original homogeneity of group but little of its former strength of leadership and community importance. It had, however, found a more acceptable place within the organizational structure in the city and township.

9. Saving the Township

Two groups, the Save the Township Committee and the Township Businessmen's Association, developed a well-organized, well-planned, well-executed, and successful program for defeating consolidation at the polls, including court action. Proponents of separate incorporation of the township as a city, loyal townshipians, and a few township farmers organized the Save the Township Committee or STTC. Unlike the Jaycee committee's proposal, which rejected the conservatism of the city's decision-making pattern, the STTC acted in accord with past township decision making. This enabled the committee to unite a variety of heterogeneous groups and individuals and to allocate the legion of campaign tasks to a large number of people in a manner that the Jaycees were never able to accomplish.

Unlike the Jaycee committee members and their relatively unemotional meetings tempered with behind-the-scenes planning by a small group of select city leaders, the STTC held fiery sessions in large smoke-filled halls before capacity crowds of men and women. Meetings were fraught with emotion and often ended with threats of violence; the Jaycee meetings were phlegmatic by comparison. The active participation of many southern whites influenced the color of expression. A number of the anticonsolidation campaign techniques had been tested and found effective in the southern communities from which these people had come. On several occasions when techniques were suggested and sharply criticized, comments were made concerning their effectiveness on "such and such" occasion in Kentucky, West Virginia, or Tennessee. Although several committee members frowned on the "background" and "emotionalism" of the "southern element," they were quick to prevent a possible split or conflict within the group. They recognized the inexhaustibleness of these people and their willingness to contribute unlimited time and talent to the campaign.

Women made an important contribution to the committee's work. They set the emotional temper at most of the meetings; much name calling and suggestions for punitive action against the proponents of consolidation came from women. Unlike the all-male confederates of the proconsolidation movement, the STTC afforded ample opportunity for feminine participation and leadership. The committee's position of secretary-treasurer and several committee chairmanships were filled by women. Throughout the month preceding the election, the STTC recruited several dozen women to actively assist their movement. The only female assistance secured by the Jaycees and city leaders interested in consolidation was the *employment* of a secretary for the Jaycee headquarter office and of women to telephone city voters on election day.

Save the Township Committee Meetings

Five public meetings of the committee were held between the last half of February and the last of March, 1958. The first meeting on February 20, 1958, was called by a Woodruff Township Board trustee. Two township trustees and two township officers, the township clerk and the treasurer, played major roles in the organization and activities of the committee. The direct involvement of township political leaders represented a further contrast with the proconsolidation campaign in which the mayor and city council made no public commitment in favor of the attempt. Leaders from the township's Democratic and Republican political parties, representatives from civic organizations, and aspirants for political, economic, and social leadership positions played superior and subordinate roles.

The tone of the first meeting, and of the other meetings that were to follow, was bizarre. From the striking incongruities of the charges against the city, the "city fathers," the Jaycees, the "down-town boys," the real estate "cliques," the Judas-like qualities of the township supervisor, the tax rates, and the differences in organizational techniques, the STTC provided an almost sensational contrast with the operations of the Jaycees and the city leaders. While both groups used their meetings to discuss rumors and actions of the opposition group, the tone differed dramatically. While the Jaycees considered ways of determining the facts, visited other communities that had previously faced similar situations of expansion, considered how to draw financial and public support from community leaders and organizations, the STTC considered and gloried in stories of higher city taxes, past city blunders, and the possible profit making that city fathers might derive from a consolidation success.

Years of smoldering hatred and of social discrimination of city leaders toward township residents were verbalized. Stories were told of city treatment of farmers in the twenties, of failure to provide sanitary services to township residents in time of crisis, of wartime exploitation of southern workers by city merchants, and of the negative attitudes of city leaders toward the 1950 attempt by Shady Lea residents to be annexed by the city. All of the bottled-up antagonism resulting from decades of city neglect, disinterest, and discrimination was verbalized again and again to eager, receptive audiences. The township's industrial, utility, and residential growth compared with the problems of the aging, declining city provided township residents with an enviable new position for "paying back the city."

Initially the early STTC meetings were attempts to expand the number of campaign workers. After the first two or three, the latent functions of the public gatherings became more evident. The same vocal group or groups were present; the same stories of city wrongdoings were told and retold; and the same tones bordering on hysteria were utilized. Doubtless the public displays united the various geographic groups into a unified whole and gave them the strength and the inspiration to devote many hours of hard, dedicated labor to the campaign. At each session self-styled specialists presented "facts and figures" on taxes, on problems of the extension of city services, on the glories of township government. A large proportion of the statistics were incorrect or misinterpreted. Misinterpreted or not, the anticonsolidation protagonists "had facts and figures" on the issue and against the city. By contrast, the Jaycees and their associates did not. While the city group asked questions of each other and attempted to contact the "people who would know," very little materialized. They contributed little at public meetings that could effectively refute the STTC figures. Citizens concerned over the inadequacies of township government were given few facts to win them to the consolidation band wagon.

Leaders

Since the STTC was organized to fight one issue, it recruited from other township groups. Approximately a dozen men and women were leaders of the movement. None of them, with the exception of Joseph Zeller, were comparable to those on the Jaycee financial-advisory committee. The organizational meeting had been called by members of the township board who were newly elected Democrats. No city government officer was connected with the Jaycee movement in any official capacity. Most of the STTC, including the township officials, consisted of rather ordinary men and women, with little training or experience in community organization and little education. These people organized and sustained an effective campaign.

A small group of young men who, late in 1957, held several meetings as a "Citizens' Group of Woodruff Township," gave additional strength to the STTC. Most of the members who were employed in area industry, e.g., Universal and Midwest Motors, seemed to favor consolidation. Several of the men expressed positive feelings for the new plan. By March, 1958, these men had become identified with the STTC movement. The "industry" men, encouraged by the interests of their plant superiors, had taken public positions, within days of each other, in opposition to consolidation. Gary Jones, a participant in this citizens group, became an important leader of the STTC. Although the two groups differed in terms of the class and status background of their participants, this early group formed a nucleus from which several Save the Township subcommittees were organized.

The most important leaders were Democratic party leader Ronald Parker, Republican leader Gary Jones, the township clerk, township treasurer, two township trustees. The others were not well-known civic leaders. If one wished, two dozen more could be added along with wives and husbands of those mentioned above. The ease of name naming is an indication of the broad middle- or lower-range "leadership" of the workers involved. Only Gary Jones and Ronald Parker were listed among the township's influential leaders.

Of the seventeen key leaders mentioned above, fifteen were Democrats and two Republicans. Jones, who served as township supervisor from 1959 to 1966, was the only active committee member with a college education. A third of the seventeen were northerners by birth and two-thirds were southern white migrants to the area.

Occupationally, the committee had two full-time township officers, three housewives, one farmer, and eleven blue-collar and clerical workers.

The age span was greater among the STTC than among the Jaycees. While the township treasurer was the only leader over fifty, half were beyond the Jaycee age limit of thirty-five.

STTC Attitudes toward Consolidation
The STTC leaders concluded that their opportunities and those of the residents they represented would be severely limited if the city and township were to become one. They felt that the old city leadership would take over and dictate the filling of offices, granting of favors, and making of decisions. Only recently had township minorities—Democrats, southern whites, Negroes—begun to fill influential and prestigious positions. Ascendancy to power, and with it mobility, had begun with election to the Shady Lea School Board in the late forties. Using the school positions as a springboard, Democrats made a clean sweep of the township board in April, 1957. Four of the seven board members were southern whites.

Township government and the two political parties had become a "place in the sun" for the southern whites and persons in the lower socioeconomic levels of township society. On a number of occasions committee members pointed out the secondary aspects of city as compared with township government, emphasizing the limited influence "poor folk" would have in the former. They wished to protect these political gains. What had begun to happen in Woodruff Township was precisely the same process that has been undergone when other cultural minorities have attempted to agitate for equal treatment, and these efforts were being made through exactly the same institution: government. The student of the assimilatory process of the immigrant Irish, Italian, Pole, and French Canadian would recognize the similarity between the former groups and the southern, hill-country white transplanted to the urban, industrial, Republican, religiously ecclesiastical class structure of the American Midwest.

Another component characterized the STTC movement and was reflected in township board and political party meetings: the emotional experience of functioning in and as a part of a dynamic, pulsating group. This was not a group attempting to operate within the finely drawn lines of a structured system for which proper forms have been derived covering most of the amenities of social intercourse. Rather it was one in which the spirit and motive—the kind of person involved (does he beat his wife, love his children)—were more important than the skill of execution. For example, during the 1960 presidential campaign several people from Woodruff Township volunteered to assist Democratic workers in County Seat City. One of the workers assisting in the office was reported to be a source of continual embarrassment to Woodruff City Democratic leaders because of her manner of expression: "Gimmy the phone!" "Gimmy that!" "Yeah!" They insisted that although she accomplished a tremendous amount of work County Seaters would look even further down their noses at Woodruff people with her as an example. In other words, County Seaters would not differentiate between Woodruff City and Woodruff Township residents. This type of consideration was relatively unimportant when the young woman functioned within the township party, at township board meetings, and on the STTC. Her faithfulness, her inexhaustibleness, her firm belief in the rightness of their cause, and her giving of what she had to give in the manner in which she was able to give it were all that was important.

Part and parcel of this component was the emotional release it afforded the participants. The shouting, the bitter accusations against the "City Fathers" whom, they felt, had discriminated against many of them during World War II and the postwar days, the work groups, and the feeling of accomplishment had real meaning for those involved. Often, as observers, we felt as if we were witnessing a fundamental revival meeting. At times, the emotional pitch became intolerable to the political moderate and to those whose organizational participation conformed to more traditional, undemonstrative forms of social intercourse.

The "Save the Township" Outsider

At the second public meeting of the STTC on March 5, the township clerk introduced Edward Sinelli, executive secretary of the Midstate Township Association. Woodruff Township was a member of this association whose primary purpose was the retention and maintenance of the township form of government and the defeat of any legislative proposal or local action aimed at the dissolution of the township. It was the executive secretary's function to implement this program. He could be called in, without charge, to assist an embattled township fight its opponent.

Sinelli spoke at five public meetings during the campaign. He made half a dozen additional trips for informal conferences with STTC leaders as well as a final evening appearance on the day of the election. Sinelli contributed the final sprinkling of spice to the work of the committee, allowing the latter to gain momentum and increase its working membership. He was an effective, dynamic, colorful speaker whose appearances had an evangelistic quality. In his first address Sinelli apprised township people that:

1. He was an expert on the defense of township rights.

2. He came bearing the good wishes of all the other Midstate townships who were watching Woodruff's progress and begging it to make a good fight for all their sakes.

3. He had carefully studied the issue between Woodruff and Woodruff Township and had reached the *expert* conclusion that the township must retain its independent status from "big government" in Woodruff.

4. He was able to quote example after example of what had happened to other misguided rural governments which had been swallowed up by their land-hungry urban neighbors. And,

5. He provided a number of key fight phrases around which the

work of the Committee was organized. In particular: "Always ask three questions: *What* am I going to get if I consolidate? *When* am I going to get it? How much will it *cost* me?"

Unlike Leslie, the Jaycee's advisor, Sinelli was in the forefront of activity and yet he did not attempt to direct every attack against consolidation. While he willingly spoke as an expert, he seemed to recognize that the STTC leaders could organize committees and get things done in ways that might be more culturally acceptable to their followers than those of an outsider. His important contribution was as an expert and as a master of the "fiery" word. The following are quotations taken from Sinelli's speeches of March 5 and 22.

> From what I see, from what I read in your papers, and from talking to people: *you have problems* [with the city]. In one city a man, a solid citizen, waited days before he was able to see the mayor. I want to open a door and be able to talk to the man governing me. . . .
> If the Jaycees had come up with a study it might be different. If they were sincere they should have gone to people in the township and the city, met together, formulated a study report, and presented it to the people. If annexation is orderly, and people want it, then it is OK. . . .
> There is a political science professor who said we should abolish most forms of local government. This is the kind of theoretical thinking which brings Hitlers, Tojos, and Mussolini's into being. I felt so strongly about this sort of thing I enlisted in the service on October 6, 1939, when Hitler marched into Poland!

Primarily, Sinelli focused the energy of the anticonsolidation forces on the economic unfeasibility of the movement, e.g., it would result in a substantial and burdensome increase in township taxes. Second, he lent an air of legitimacy to STTC action by filling the role of an outside expert who had studied the local problem and had the breadth of state and national experience to offer authoritative proposals. By contrast, Leslie was not an expert in the political area. He was experienced in the organization of public relations campaigns for commercial or industrial groups in which cultural differences and most especially cultural conflicts between individuals and groups are usually not the primary consideration.

Sinelli specified the committees the group would need. He emphasized the need for a door-to-door voter registration and information campaign, of literature and publications, of newspaper coverage, of a phoning committee, of public meetings. Before Sinelli became involved, the STTC was floundering about for a pattern of action. Participants reported time and time again that they "looked to him for the answers to questions we couldn't answer. He knew more about it than anyone else in the township." Approximately three weeks before the election, fatigued from weeks of campaigning, the work of the committee ebbed to its lowest point. With justified concern Sinelli was sent for. Again he was able to reinterpret the seriousness of the proposition; workers returned to the task at hand with a renewed spirit of dedication. Sinelli conveyed and instilled a strength of purpose and direction into the efforts of the STTC.

Sinelli had much to lose if merger won. Similar expansion attempts would be made by other Midstate township-locked urban centers. This could result in a serious loss of power and prestige for the Midstate Township Association. Sinelli's organization originated and thrived on one of the most important aspects of Woodruff Township's decision-making pattern—local political autonomy.

Save the Township Work

The efforts of the STTC were channeled into five subcommittees encompassing the work areas outlined by Sinelli as crucial for winning a sufficient number of "no" votes: Phone-Transportation Committee, Canvas or Registration Committee, Publicity Committee, Speaker's Committee, and Finance Committee.

The Phone-Transportation Committee called all township registrants who had not voted by forenoon election day, offered and arranged for rides to the polls, and continued calling prospective voters until the polls closed.

Operating on Sinelli's assumption that the consolidation issue would be won or lost at the polls, the Registration Committee, consisting of approximately fifty township women and men sworn in as temporary deputy registrars, developed a mass voter-registration drive. Final estimates revealed that every house in the township had been visited at least once and often two or three times, resulting in 998 new registrants.

A Publicity Committee, chaired by Ronald Parker, encouraged the membership to write letters to the local newspapers against the issue. Consecutively, the committee printed a card entitled *This is a breakdown of your tax by school districts,* a mimeographed page entitled *Consolidation?,* two printed newspapers, and a printed card that was distributed at each polling area on election day entitled *Vote No,* urging a vote for nine charter commissioners opposing consolidation followed by the list of names.

Although perhaps a hundred handmade posters and signs were produced, most of these were placed on cars to be used in motorcades. Two printed posters that appeared overnight on almost every tree and telegraph pole in the township were simple but obviously effective. They read, in large bold type, NO CITY TAXES and TAXES, TAXES, TAXES. Approximately five thousand of these were distributed.

In order to assure equal coverage of the anticonsolidation side by the "city paper," a subcommittee of the publicity committee consisting of Ronald Parker, Gary Jones, and Joseph Zeller met with Donald Amdur, the owner of *The Woodruff Press,* in March, 1958. Mr. Amdur agreed to publish material submitted by the STTC provided it had news value and was not submitted to the *County Seat News.* A similar restriction was placed on Jaycee material. In order to secure the meeting with Amdur, Parker threatened to organize a mass boycott of *The Woodruff Press* if anticonsolidation interests were not treated fairly.

Between March 1 and April 5, approximately thirty-nine anticonsolidation and twenty-one proconsolidation letters appeared in *The Woodruff Press.* Twenty of the anticonsolidation letters were directly attributed to STTC members or friends, and nineteen were written by interested but unaffiliated citizens. Seven of the proconsolidation letters were directly attributed to the Jaycee members, and fourteen were written by unaffiliated citizens. While only a little over sixty letters were published in this one-month period, twice this number were submitted. Below is the text of one of the letters written by the chairman of the STTC publicity subcommittee:

The Jaycee proposal presented to the people of Woodruff and Woodruff Township should be called by exactly what it is, "Tax land grab." The city in a recent annexation of 610 acres has increased its land area by 25 percent, not counting the 100 acres annexed of the Paster property.

The Jaycee proposes to take in the entire township regardless of the need for development of city property.

Most serious aspects of this land grab is the ruling of the county prosecutor, regardless what anyone may say there is no precedent in the state of Midstate for the ruling that the voters of each autonomous unit of government be counted as one. This is in my opinion in conflict with the state statutes and in violation with the American concept of good government.

The township supervisor violated the confidence of the people of the township by giving his endorsement to this plan at the County Board of Supervisors level.

I urge the people of the township to study this proposal carefully prior to April 7 election.

RONALD PARKER
Planning Chairman
Save the Township Committee[1]

The committee whose work was most evident to the general public was the Speakers Committee, which provided men and women to address city and township groups and to debate the Jaycees. Edward Sinelli was the pivot around which the committee functioned. After speaking on the same platform with Jaycee representatives early in March, members of the Speaker's Committee realized that the questions were usually directed at their rivals. Consequently they organized a team to attend each meeting at which their representatives spoke which was armed with a prepared list of questions for their side alone. By late March the STTC representatives were receiving almost all the questions, and the Jaycees were given much less time to explore the positive consequences of consolidation. This developed into a workable technique for excluding the Jaycees, and the latter never became cognizant of its use.

STTC Financing

While we were able to observe first hand the financial efforts of city leaders, the STTC excluded us from meetings of their Finance Committee. Attendance at all public meetings, private conferences, and meetings with members and workers provided abundant information on the fiscal phase of the campaign, e.g., records of the number of posters, newspapers, cards printed, and requests of funds by the Township Businessmen's Association representative of the STTC to his organization.

How did the STTC raise and use its money? At the first meeting of the committee in township hall a solicitation was made. Some of

1. *The Woodruff Press,* March 3, 1958.

the farmers present and other large-property owners contributed as much as $10.00 each. A total of $150 was collected. No other solicitations were made at public meetings. The chairman of the Finance Committee, organized ten to fifteen men and a few women to solicit funds from township businessmen and interested citizens. The committee tried to reach every township businessman who was unaffiliated with the Township Businessmen's Association, discussed below, and to reach those private citizens able to contribute a few dollars. The committee earnestly solicited funds from those businesses that required the issuance of a license by the township board, such as the "Tabletoppers," owners of liquor by-the-glass establishments, and the construction and building contractors. Most of the contributions from these sources were less than $50.00. The two largest contributors in the township were Joseph Zeller and Ronald Paster. Both were large property owners, felt they had much to lose if taxes were increased, and had histories of financially supporting township projects and the political candidates of both parties. Both had received preferential treatment at some time from representatives of local government. Any deference pattern that existed in the township would have had to function with them in mind.

The Township Businessmen's Association was organized in part to provide financial support for the STTC. Generally speaking, assessments on many business properties in the township were considerably below the established level of 20 percent of market value. The owner could not be assured that such an oversight or preferential treatment would continue if consolidation took place. A number of businessmen were willing to contribute campaign funds to maintain the *status quo*.

Bills for supplies and literature were sent to the Township Businessmen's Association and handled by its executive secretary. At the end of the consolidation campaign the association had given approximately $1,200 and was $800 in debt. While the Jaycees budgeted and spent $6,000, STTC expenditures totaled little more than $2,000. None of the money was used for salary for a professional. All of the funds were spent for publicity—mimeographing, printing, signs, and newspaper advertising.

The financial arrangements of the STTC were not as formalized as those of the Jaycees. In the proconsolidation group a budget was prepared and a special, high-level group was organized to raise funds. In the township, a drive was organized and carried out by a committee representative of the various levels of township society. The counterpart of the top leadership money raisers in the city was the township businessmen's group. Members of the latter, however, were not top community leaders and often carried out STTC programs themselves, e.g., ordering and paying for additional posters. They then used the STTC to distribute material. Zeller, who organized the drive for large sums of money, was Davenport's township counterpart.

The Township Businessmen's Association

Organized by Joseph Zeller and paralleling in time the organization of the STTC, the Township Businessmen's Association supported the latter committee by supplying leadership and financial backing. Approximately six meetings were held before the vote on April 7, and seven meetings were held between May and October, 1958. Dissatisfactions resulted in the group's quiet demise approximately six months after the election.

The association attempted to function as Woodruff Township's Chamber of Commerce. Unlike the city Chamber, it was to have a real concern for township affairs and was to be an organization in which township businessmen would feel welcome. The consensus seemed to be that township businessmen and "leaders" were not welcomed into many city organizations. They were merely tolerated and seldom were permitted to hold positions of influence and prestige.

To solve the problem, as they saw it, township businessmen established a township organization fusing business and social functions. The group sought recognition as the Woodruff Township Chamber of Commerce. Official status was denied after the Woodruff City Chamber protested that it served the entire Woodruff area. With Zeller as president, township businessmen proceeded to chart their new organization.

The six association meetings before the election were characterized by a general concern for defeating consolidation. Five meetings focused on reports of the STTC efforts, stories, "surveys" of city ineffectiveness, and the selection of suitable charter candidates. Only a few of the association's members belonged to the STTC and these men were usually referred to as association members who were assisting the committee. Zeller met privately with the STTC. In some respects the participants of the two groups differed in amount of status and prestige. The STTC workers were, as a group, on a lower economic level than the businessmen. The latent functions of the association and the committee allowed two different status levels of participation for anticonsolidation workers.

The STTC and the Township Businessmen's Association were the offsprings of the needs of the township during a period of crisis. The fact that they were not able to survive as township organizations suggests the strength of the long-term prestige factor attached to city clubs. By admitting a few township residents over the years and by adding to the status position of those selected in both political units, city organizations maintained an allure, even after severe community crisis.

Consolidation Court Hearing

The commitment of all of the township board, with the exception of the supervisor, to the defeat of consolidation led to another campaign tactic. The township clerk and treasurer, utilizing township funds, co-operated to the full extent of their office's with anticonsolidation forces by challenging the legality of the consolidation process. This use of public funds enabled the anticonsolidation groups to gain favorable publicity for their cause through the manipulation of legal processes. Public expenditures added to STTC resources far exceeded the $6,000 spent by the Jaycees.

In February, 1958, petitions were circulated for a week by the STTC during which 2,012 signatures were obtained requesting that the township board demand a legality check. Early in March, above the protests of the township supervisor, the board employed Sinelli's Township Businessmen's Association attorney.

On March 26 and April 5, 1958, respectively, hearings were held in the Iroquois County Courthouse on two issues: first, a request for an injunction to set aside the consolidation election; and second, a suit for a show cause on why the court should not grant the township's request to halt the election or require separate tabulation of city and township ballots.

The injunction suit that would have halted the April 7 election was dismissed on March 26, after a brief hearing. The court ruled that the petitions for suit brought by attorneys for Woodruff Township were at fault on four counts:

1. The suit was brought at the wrong time.
2. In naming the county clerk and the county board of canvassers as defendants, the suit named the wrong parties as defendants.
3. The township treasurer was without authority to sign the suit.
4. The suit was brought in the wrong court (it should have been brought in a court of law not equity).

Between the March 26 dismissal and the mandamus hearing of April 5, the newspapers reported daily on the County Seat City attorney's attempts to set a new hearing and his plans to challenge after the election. At the hearing on April 5, the judge dismissed the suit brought by the township to secure separate ballot countings. The dismissal was based on three grounds: defendants in a mandamus action must have a clear legal duty to perform an act and they did not; there was no basis to sue the city of Woodruff; and in a mandamus action there must not be any other available remedy.

The township board lost the two court battles, but won the election. What did the hearings really accomplish? Did the township attorneys believe the court would rule in their favor? Although it is difficult to answer these questions, certain facts and observations are pertinent.

First, precedent is against halting an election that has been petitioned for by the citizens if the petitions are in order. If redress is required, it is requested after the election. Since consolidation did not win there would have been no reason to seek relief. In turn, the large sums of money spent for attorney and court fees during the pre-election hearings would have been saved. When the court set aside both the injunction and mandamus it indicated that relief should be sought after the election. Why, then, after the injunction hearing, did township attorneys seek a mandamus order? Second, the hearings were brief, less than an hour, and the number of lawyers present, both as participants and observers, represented half the spectators present in the courtrooms. The merits of the cases were never considered nor could they be considered given the choice of court of suit. It seems unlikely that the attorney of the Midstate Township Association, whose speciality was municipal law, and his local attorney associate could have been unaware of the possible disposition of the suits. The Woodruff Township attorneys' firm had functioned in this area of law for a number of years and was employed in the injunction suit during the 1950 township annexation attempt.

In addition to the large legal fees, which benefited a few participants, what advantages were derived from the court actions? The court action provided a fertile source of favorable publicity. During the last weeks before the election the major sources of newsprint on the movement were the court hearings. Accusations and debates between Jaycees and STTC members and government representatives were "old hat." From March 6, 1958, when the outside attorney was employed, the possibility of court action held the headlines. Reports of the hearings were even printed in the Metropolitan City newspapers. Between March 5 and April 5, twenty-four headlines or large subheadings appeared in steady succession in area papers.

The cases afforded the STTC opportunities for keeping the consolidation attempt before the public in a way that placed the township in the position of underdog in the eyes of many township and city voters. To the layman it appeared as though "even the courts are with the city" and against the township. It also enabled Sinelli to maintain the work level of the STTC at a high pitch through the creation of a conflict area that drew members together. The conflict was dual in nature, centering first on the areas of the suits and second on whether township funds could or could not be spent for legal fees on a controversial issue. It permitted the protesting groups to retain through election eve the frenzy that characterized their early efforts to defeat consolidation and save the township.

Although township forces were limited in the level of leadership involved and the private monies at their disposal, they were able to supplement their supplies from the public coffer. This added an official status to their activities which the Jaycees did not have. In addition, these resources more than balanced the township committee's campaign with the larger, privately financed public relations program of the Jaycees.

Summary

STTC leaders demonstrated, campaignwise, a more overt ingenuity, inventiveness, and determination than the Jaycees and their supporters. Their reward was the preservation of township autonomy. City leaders and many Jaycees conducted a campaign of covert inactivity. Their reward was the maintenance of city autonomy.

Although, the comparison of the efforts made by a small number of Jaycees and a smaller number of city leaders with the township action that involved several hundred men and women is of considerable significance, there were important considerations. At least 7,000 township and city residents who voted on the issue had not worked on either campaign nor had they even attended a meeting. The knowledge they exhibited or expressed was gleaned from newspapers, roadside posters, or back-fence exchanges with neighbors. For most township voters the question of *Gesellschaft*-city versus *gemeinschaft*-township government was not as important as living as well as possible for as few dollars as possible. Many city and township residents were convinced that consolidation would cost them money, that it would result in tax increases for both. While low public expenditure was part and parcel of the city's decision-making policy, township residents felt that a decaying core city would add an unnecessary financial burden to the pressing expense of service expansion which they faced.

The Election

On Monday, April 7, 1958, the voters of Woodruff City and Woodruff Township went to the polls to translate their decision concerning the six-months controversy into hard, cold fact. The issue was defeated by a combined total vote of 5,502 to 3,048. City residents cast 2,247 votes for the proposal and 687 against; township residents cast 801 votes for the proposal and 4,815 votes against.

By 9 P.M. election night the corridors of Township Hall were crowded. A public address system triumphantly roared out each new return that indicated the inevitable defeat of merger. Individuals moved about from group to group exchanging stories of the campaign and of city injustices. The few proponents of consolidation observed from the sidelines and left the hall one by one as defeat became inevitable. When defeat was a certainty, Edward Sinelli addressed the hundreds who crowded the halls. He observed, "The people of Woodruff Township have proved today that they are not ready to buy so ambitious a plan as incorporation of 36 square miles of territory, without a carefully planned and detailed study, including the costs involved." He stated further, "This does not represent a victory for the Township or a rebuke against the people of the city. Rather, it indicates that Township residents want further study and information, which will be unbiased, without prejudice, without preconceived ideas, without speculation, theory, assumption or sheer guesswork." He congratulated the people of Woodruff for turning out such an overwhelming vote on the issue and added: "This was an inspiring demonstration of what people can do in the finest American tradition, using the most potent weapon which we possess."

He paid tribute to the leadership of the STTC and the many people who had volunteered their services during the campaign and on election day. In conclusion he indicated that the techniques employed by the workers, " . . . may have been old fashioned, but certainly most effective. Particularly inspiring was watching Democrats and Republicans working together on this vital issue. Both realized that this was not a partisan issue, but one which involved all segments of the population. Future elections may elicit great interest, but, it can hardly be expected that the overwhelming enthusiasm displayed in this area today can be reenacted again for some time to come."[2]

Deafening cheers followed the Sinelli statement. By midnight the hall finally cleared, leaving behind floors and desks littered with campaign materials, dittoed and handmade tabulation sheets, empty coffee cups, and dead cigarette and cigar butts. The air of the building was filled with the unpleasant stifler of old smoke and human bodies, endurable only to those who lingered in the ecstacy of victory.

2. *The Woodruff Press,* April 8, 1958.

Sinelli was wrong on several counts. Township leaders were not interested in a "carefully planned and detailed study including the costs involved." They were interested in one thing: maintaining the township as a separate unit of government. Because of this, they proved Sinelli wrong on a second count. He had stated, "It can hardly be expected that the overwhelming enthusiasm displayed in this area today can be reenacted again for some time to come." Six years and one month later, township leaders waged a second, enthusiastic campaign against an almost total annexation of the township by the city and won.

10. Unification 1963-1964[1]

This account of a second election campaign for the political reorganization of the Woodruff area should strike the reader as a "rerun"
of the preceding contest. While the identity of many participants and
the specifics of the unification proposal differed from those of the
earlier campaign, the forces contributing to the election outcome
and many of the critical issues resembled those discussed in the
previous two chapters. The pattern of events, both before and during
the merger campaign, reflected the operation of influential groups
committed to each municipality's decision-making patterns.

The Interim, 1958–1963

As in the previous campaign, prospects for success were greatly
influenced by events occurring before the filing of election petitions.
The chances of success would be enhanced if initiation of the cam-

1. The researchers became observers in the second campaign when leaders
were attempting to decide whether to initiate the merger effort while previously involvement began immediately after the decision had been made. While
the researchers personally studied the entire first campaign, this was not possible for the subsequent effort as they left Woodruff in August, 1963, nine
months before the election. Data on the electioneering were obtained from
newspapers, correspondence, phone conversations, and a few interviews.

paign had been the final step in a long-term trend toward greater co-operation between the two municipalities or the result of a pronounced increase in support for merger among township residents. Neither of these changes had preceded the emergence of the 1963 merger effort. Despite this, a number of new elements held out some promise for more favorable results.

First, the editor of *The Woodruff Press*, which had been purchased by the Kent Group, adopted a strong position in favor of unification. The newspaper would support merger throughout the campaign.

Second, the basis of opposition to merger from an important township interest group—owners of liquor licenses—had been removed when city voters, in 1962, approved the sale of liquor by the glass.

Third, the men who initially took charge of the campaign were much closer to the fiscal organizations of the city and were in a better position than their predecessors to obtain the financial and human resources required for an election victory.

On the other side were situational changes that reinforced prevailing township opinion on the desirability of maintaining township autonomy. In the five-year interim the township government had improved its functional effectiveness. It had acquired the ability to serve virtually all urban areas and many undeveloped sections of the municipality by extending trunk-line water and sewer mains to areas west of the city. Service to these areas also was improved by construction and staffing of three fire stations. To fill needs that previously had been neglected, the township board established a recreation program and gave partial support to a library system. In no significant area of community life did city and township governments engage in new co-operative or joint programs. Although Midwest Motors pressured the two governments to jointly operate a new sanitary land fill in the township, this change represented little progress. The township for a number of years had paid for the privilege of using the city's dump.

Normal processes of population and economic growth also de-

These circumstances, combined with the desire to avoid as much repetition as possible, resulted in the initial policy-making phase receiving more and the electioneering phase less attention than the corresponding stages of the earlier campaign.

creased the likelihood of unification. The township's tax base increased at a rate more than six times greater than that of Woodruff. While the city's tax base, between 1957 and 1963, increased by a mere 5 percent, from about $33.5 to $35 million, that of the township increased by a third, from $57 to $76 million. The almost 40 percent increase in the city's tax rate, from less than 17 to over 23 mills, and a two-mill increase for the township failed to enhance prospects for merger.

No governmental crisis occurred during the interim. There were no breakdowns in the water or sewerage systems, no outbreaks of violence that embarrassed law enforcement agencies, no scandals in government, no event that dramatized the inadequacies of area governmental structure and the necessity for change. There were no major improvements in the communities that could be attributed to increased co-operation between the two municipalities. There was little to demonstrate to residents that social life could be improved if the two municipalities became one.

Under these circumstances, one would expect the majority of township citizens to oppose a merger of the two governments. A thorough and competent study of the two governments and of various alternative arrangements seemed to be one of the few remaining agencies suitable for modifying public opinion. The attacks on merger by the STTC indicated the need for information on the consequences of the present arrangement and on the gains, if any, to be achieved by adopting an alternative plan. The expressed willingness of Universal Motors to help finance a study of local government provided local leaders with an opening that could have been exploited, but no action was taken on this matter, except for an independent and unsubsidized effort by the Woodruff League of Women Voters. In the winter of 1962, the league assembled data on the expenditures of both governments. The contribution of the report to an understanding of the pattern of divided government was limited by its narrow scope.

A 1958 decision of the Midstate Supreme Court on the method of tabulating votes in a merger election also increased the need for an objective study. The votes of the two municipalities could not be counted together, as had been done in the previous campaign. This ruling gave township citizens veto power over any merger proposal.

The defeat of unification left proponents in disarray. The Jaycee organization had been decimated by the withdrawal of members who opposed merger or who believed that the officers had erred in assuming leadership of the campaign. To prevent a recurrence, the organization decided to remain neutral in subsequent community controversies. The difficulties that Davenport and his colleagues experienced in seeking support for merger demonstrated the risks of accepting such responsibilities. Since the leaders of the movement were likely to fail, it was foolhardy to jeopardize one's position as an influential. The task of assembling a competent staff to initiate and manage the campaign had been made more difficult by the outcome of the previous effort.

City leaders had not faced up to the question of whether retention of nonpartisan, at-large elections and a weak mayor would increase or decrease the prospects of merger. This issue had not been considered in the previous campaign since the charter commission never had the opportunity to serve. Township opposition to these forms of city government could put advocates of merger in the position of simultaneously seeking to annex township land and to change the structure of city government. This task seemed too complex to be dealt with in one unification election.

The five years that had elapsed since the previous unification election had not been utilized by city leaders and organizations to improve the chances for area political reorganization. Township leaders, on the other hand, had strengthened the effectiveness of township government by providing services to areas that previously lacked them or that had been unavailable throughout the municipality.

Genesis of the Unification Campaign

Despite dim prospects for success, another effort to reorganize area political structure developed in the spring of 1963. Two separate events triggered the campaign. First, City Manager John Dowling, who had held the office for only a year, became increasingly aware of the inadequacies of Woodruff's tax base. He had had considerable difficulty in preparing the municipal budget for the coming fiscal year, and the millage rate subsequently was raised from 21.86 to 23.36 mills. Dowling concluded that the acquisition of the township's industrial tax base would alleviate many municipal problems, and his annexation suggestion was accepted by Mayor Matthew Hensil.[2]

The second factor concerned the rumors that began circulating at this time in the township concerning the possibility of incorporating the municipality into a home-rule city. The two leading township politicians were competing for the office of supervisor. The intensity of this contest sparked rumors that one or the other of the candidates had township incorporation under consideration. Certain city leaders refused to regard these reports as campaign oratory.

Employing a Law Firm

Since the annexation plan was complex and might involve the city government in litigation, Dowling and Hensil sought the assistance of a law firm. The only city firm available at the time was that of R. Jason Lockwood, one of whose partners lived next door to Dowling. Before taking the matter to the city council and without mentioning it to the city attorney, the mayor approached Lockwood and two of his partners.

Although the partners favored the annexation plan, Lockwood was less than enthusiastic. Familiarity with the recent history of city-township affairs and the prevailing prejudices toward township leaders and residents disposed him to doubt the possibility of an election victory. Recent developments offered little hope that Woodruff's leaders would provide the necessary assistance.

The factors that led city officials to seek the services of the Lockwood firm did not strengthen confidence in official loyalty. First, municipal officials came to Lockwood because no other firm was available and not from recognition of the considerable legal and related talents possessed by the firm. Second, during the more than thirty years Lockwood had practiced law in Woodruff, the firm never had been asked to handle any of the legal problems of the municipality. The firm never had received honest consideration or fair treatment, in Lockwood's opinion. Just a few weeks earlier his firm and that of another had submitted estimates for handling the

2. Mayor Hensil was employed by the Edmunds Real Estate Agency. He had been a Universal Motors automobile dealer at the time of consolidation. Hensil later served as president of the Chamber of Commerce.

legal details of the city's urban renewal program. The rival attorney received the contract although the Lockwood firm was widely respected throughout the Negro community in which the renewal project was located. Third, Lockwood believed that accepting the municipality as a client would compel the firm to neglect other and better paying clients. The municipal treasury lacked the funds to adequately recompense the senior partners for their efforts.

Lockwood and his associates considered the request for many days. They recognized that the firm, in addition to legal services to the city, would also be involved in campaigning for the acceptance of the annexation proposal. Weighing in favor of acceptance was Lockwood's confidence in his abilities as a campaigner, a confidence that had been boosted by recent successful experiences as a candidate to the state's constitutional convention and as campaigner for adoption of the new constitution. The decisive consideration in the firm's affirmative decision pertained to actions allegedly occurring in the township. The titular leaders of the Democratic and Republican parties, Strite and Jones, were competing for the office of supervisor and for their political careers. Rumors abounded that the Democratic candidate, Strite, as township clerk, had prepared petitions for incorporation of the eastern section of the township into a city. A second rumor affirmed that a prominent township businessman intended to prevent this action by incorporating the Universal Motors' plants and a southeastern township area, excluding the remainder of the township.

This report caused considerable concern among leaders and officials of Woodruff. The legal steps for incorporating a portion of a township were relatively simple to execute. Since residents of the area excluded were not allowed to vote on the question, boundaries could be drawn to include a majority of residents who favored the change. Second, the person who allegedly was interested in this plan had at least one grievance against the city and was thought capable of taking such an extreme step.

The possibility that some township leaders might move to incorporate a portion of the municipality as a separate city placed the Lockwood firm in a difficult position. The prospects for a successful merger campaign were slender. Lockwood not only would be endangering his leadership position, but for the reasons stated above, the law firm might suffer also. Other considerations compelled Lockwood to accept these risks. Should an incorporation movement develop and succeed, Lockwood would be blamed for the failure to prevent this eventuality. He had been forewarned and city officials had requested the assistance of the firm. Lockwood would be the scapegoat if a city were organized in Woodruff's backyard.

While Lockwood recognized the fact that he would have to accept responsibility for preparing and filing annexation petitions ahead of petitions for separate incorporation, he also realized the importance of a clear delineation of the respective responsibilities of the city council and of his law firm. Toward this end he insisted that the city council authorize in writing the employment of the firm. The city council thereby would accept responsibility for the initiation of the campaign, and the law firm would function as its legal representative. If matters went wrong, the mayor and the city council would have to shoulder their share of responsibility for events. Lockwood also gained assurance from the mayor and city manager that he could select the persons with whom he would work on the campaign. This request indicated that Lockwood was willing to accept the risks of leading the merger attempt. He thought of his role in terms of policy making and electioneering and not solely as legal advisor to the city council.

The city manager and mayor presented Lockwood's conditions to the city council at a special session on Monday, March 18, 1963. The council, with one member absent, was informed of the course of events. The councilmen were persuaded to authorize the employment of the Lockwood firm for the purpose of annexing the Universal Motors plants and only that territory required to make the plants contiguous with the boundary of the city. No residential population, or at the most a few families, were to be included. The letter that the city manager prepared for submission to the Lockwood firm over the signatures of the councilmen "asked the firm to represent the city in the annexation 'of the Universal Motors property' in the township."[3] Six of the seven councilmen signed the letter, including the mayor. Thomas Barker, a Democrat and Negro, did not attend the special council sessions on annexation and refused to sign the letter.

3. *The County Seat News,* August 6, 1963.

Initiating the Campaign

After receiving the letter of authorization from the city council, Lockwood and his partners deliberated over the steps for accomplishing annexation. To provide assistance, Lockwood invited to a series of meetings the young man who had managed his campaign for delegate to the constitutional convention and who was the chairman of the city Republican party, Christian Endicott. Lockwood also invited the editor of the newspaper, William Bowes, the mayor, the city manager, two partners of the law firm, and the authors.

The planning meetings that followed were not limited to consideration of the method for annexing the Universal Motors plants. The area to be annexed as well as the method of annexation were subjects of considerable discussion and controversy. The participants also discussed the mechanics of preparing and circulating petitions and the selection of an appropriate date for the election.

Two factors led participants to realize that the original plan had to be modified: the impossibility of securing annexation of the plants without the approval of the township board and the newspaper editor's statement that he would oppose it editorially (see Chapter 7). The participants were forced to consider alternative annexation proposals. Two plans were suggested. The first sought to annex the automobile plants and only those neighborhoods near the plants whose inhabitants might prefer joining the city. These neighborhoods were predominantly middle class with a higher proportion of Republican voters than other township areas. The second plan called for annexing all of the township except the southern tier of rural farm and nonfarm land.[4] The area included all of the township's industrial tax base, utility plants, and over 90 percent of its population.

The participants considered the merits of each plan at several meetings. The first plan seemed to have a better chance of gaining voter acceptance, as a larger proportion of residents in the neigh-

---

4. Midstate statutes required rural land in a municipality to be taxed at the same rate as urban land. This law handicapped merger advocates in 1958. It influenced the decision in 1963 to exclude the township's southern tier of rural land from the area to be annexed.

borhoods had ties to the city of one kind or the other and were of similar political persuasion. Some felt that the second plan had the better chance for it showed the willingness of the city administration to include all urban areas, whether Democratic or Republican, good residential or Shady Lea slum. Lockwood made the decision for the group. Recognizing that city voters might reject the remainder of the township if the plants and middle-class neighborhoods were annexed, Lockwood felt that only the second plan could be justified to township voters. Lockwood made it clear that he could not take responsibility for advocating and defending the first plan.

This decision led to one other conclusion concerning the character of the campaign. As the number of city voters would not exceed the number of voters registered in the section of the township to be annexed and the votes of the two would be counted separately, a major effort would have to be made to overcome township resistance. Since the campaign would begin with most township voters opposing annexation, changing their attitudes and opinions was the prerequisite for victory. For this purpose the campaign was to have two phases: first, the completion of a study of local government and municipal finance which, hopefully, would demonstrate convincingly the need for the proposed annexation; and second, the electioneering. This plan required time for implementing the study and for publicizing results. The group expressed a preference for an eighteen-month period between the filing of petitions and election day.

One staffing problem concerned that of mayor of the new city council. Since the spring election was imminent, it was imperative that the next mayor be an enthusiastic supporter of unification. Lockwood endorsed the only woman on the council, and the others, including the incumbent mayor, who was not a candidate for reelection, and the city manager, approved. In a few days the annexation petitions had been prepared, and on the night of April 4, forty-four city and township men and women gathered signatures. When the county clerk opened her office the next morning, the petitions were filed.

At the close of this phase of the campaign, prospects for success were enhanced by several factors that had not existed during the two previous unification efforts. First, the movement had the solid support of the newspaper editor. During the two weeks following the filing of the petitions, three editorials responded to official township criticism of annexation. Bowes became a spokesman for and defender of unification. Second, the initiation of the campaign by leaders of the city administration and the employment of the Lockwood firm made unification an official act of the city council. The sponsors of the movement were visible to all. Charges of stealth and secrecy would be difficult to sustain. Third, participation of the city manager gave campaign leaders access to information on government operations which was in the files of the various municipal departments. Fourth, and perhaps most important of all, the movement had Lockwood.

R. Jason Lockwood

Lockwood's selection as president of the Woodruff National Bank in the spring of 1963 gave the merger campaign an important link with the banking interests of Woodruff. As president, he would have the respectful attention of all bank directors and officers in any effort to obtain support, financial and otherwise, for the unification effort. Also, he would command the attention of leaders of other business and professional groups in the community. While this did not guarantee the support needed, the chances were improved considerably.

Involvement of Lockwood in the campaign came at an important point in his career as a leader. By expanding leadership activity into several different areas of social life, Lockwood had become one of Woodruff's most important leaders. As a delegate to the constitutional convention, Lockwood worked with and earned the respect of some of the leading political figures in Midstate, including the man who was to become the next governor, and some important political scientists. Lockwood had access to these men during the unification campaign. As a reward for service as a convention delegate and for campaigning for adoption of the constitution, Lockwood was appointed to the governing body of the local university.[5] This position gave Lockwood important ties with the academic community. Lockwood induced the president of the university in April,

5. In 1963, Lockwood was appointed to the university's first board of trustees.

1963, to accept the chairmanship of the Citizens' Committee formed to assist unification.

Lockwood knew and was respected by a number of township leaders. During eight years of service as township attorney, 1941–49, Lockwood had worked closely with Donald Nelson in acquiring the township utility system. Nelson had helped Lockwood with the suit in 1950 to prevent the merger election. They had collaborated in detecting errors in the annexation petitions concerning the boundary lines of the area to be added to the city. Although Lockwood and Nelson were loyal to their political divisions, the respect and esteem with which each viewed the other and their almost twenty-year-old friendship might have facilitated communication between officials and leaders of the two municipalities.

Lockwood was the key man in the unification movement. He had assembled a staff of persons whom he knew personally and whom he felt were competent in activities necessary for the campaign. As president of the National Bank, Lockwood might persuade financial leaders to be generous in aiding the unification program. He also had access to key township and state leaders. From a leadership standpoint this merger campaign seemed stronger than its predecessor.

The strategy for gaining quick approval of annexation from the city council was destined to become the "Achilles' heel" for Lockwood and the merger movement. The city council was led to believe that it was possible to annex a major portion of the township's industrial tax base. In actuality, township land uninhabited by people could not be annexed by a city unless the governing body of the unincorporated municipality gave its consent. If this had not been true, the city council long ago would have annexed the township's factories. Lockwood and his colleagues knew of these provisions and related statutes. The firm had acquired this expertise first hand while representing the township board in the forties and Pacific Motors in the fifties. Why did Lockwood and his partners, along with the city manager and mayor, rely on subterfuge?

The possibility of a determined move to establish a city in a portion of the township necessitated a swift response by Woodruff officials. Annexation petitions had to be filed before those of the township to forestall an election on incorporation. The strategy worked and the city council acted quickly and covertly, enabling petitions to be prepared, circulated, and filed before those of township leaders.

Once the truth became known, some councilmen felt that they had been tricked, that under the guise of approving one annexation plan they had approved another. Whatever the justification for this situation, some councilmen might object strenuously. Barker, as representative of the black minority, had for some time felt that city government should be concerned more with improving conditions for its Negro citizens than with territorial expansion. Barker also may have feared that merger with the essentially white township would dilute the political power of black voters. The strategy used to obtain city council approval gave Barker and several colleagues a weapon to use against merger.

Campaign Development

Success in preparing and filing petitions brought into prominence the next phase of the annexation plan, a thorough analysis of city and township government.

A Citizens' Committee, composed of city and township residents, was selected to examine the ways by which an adequate and objective study could be made of governmental structure. It was assembled to provide the planning necessary for finding and employing the proper agency to conduct the inquiry. The committee was not conceived as an action or campaign group. A number of persons agreed to serve on the committee with the understanding that membership did not imply or suggest endorsement of annexation, although many members had made such a commitment.

The persons or agency engaged to conduct the investigation and the means of meeting the cost had to be determined. While these problems were under consideration by the executive committee of the Citizens' Committee, two important changes in campaign personnel occurred. These changes and the inability to obtain support for the government study were manifestations of the continued vitality of the city's decision-making pattern.

The Campaign Stalls

After the decision had been made to annex all but the undeveloped section of the township, the city manager and mayor informed the councilmen of this change in the original plan. While formal approval was not required, it was essential to retain council support for unification. It became evident that Lockwood's doubts concerning the constancy of council backing were well founded. Two councilmen objected, the Democrat Barker and a councilman who opposed the addition to the city of township Democrats and "hillbillies."

The spring elections produced further uncertainties. The preferred candidate for mayor lost by one vote to a minor official of Midwest Motors. The mayor *pro tem* also was employed by this company. Since these two officials could be influenced by the preferences of superiors at the auto plant, their support for unification could not be taken for granted. Only three of the seven councilmen were firm advocates of unification.

Dissatisfaction of several councilmen with the annexation procedure persisted after the petitions had been filed. At first Lockwood dismissed the objections as unrepresentative of the feeling of the councilmen; the verbal opposition of two councilmen would not be permitted to destroy unification.

Lockwood exhibited concern over the position of the city council early in May. Repeatedly, friends and associates informed him of council dissatisfaction with unification. One councilman told the minister of a prestigious Woodruff church that annexation was dead. To have it widely known that the city council was about to desert the field of battle intensified Lockwood's initial fear of leader opposition to merger. In an effort to rally support and bring pressure on the recalcitrant councilmen, in effect to unite officials and leaders in behalf of merger, Lockwood and Dowling took what some might regard as extreme measures. Lockwood acted privately and informally, Dowling publicly and dramatically.

Lockwood let it be known that if conditions did not improve, the firm would withdraw completely from the campaign. Should Lockwood carry out his threat, the movement would be greatly weakened. The threat was intended to rally support for merger and to silence the objecting councilmen. The maneuver did not work. The councilmen were not disciplined by city leaders. Sampson, for example, was noncommittal when asked by a council member to use his influence in behalf of unification.

Since all council members but one were Republican, Christian Endicott, chairman of the Woodruff City Republican party, might have been able, directly or through others, to obtain a more cooperative attitude. His personal loyalty to Lockwood, as a close friend and as his former campaign manager, also might have led him, if not for the sake of merger at least for the protection of Lockwood's leadership position, to find ways to quiet the dissidents.

Other factors weighed heavily with Endicott. Merger, to succeed, would require a long and difficult campaign. Since the rivalry between the two political parties in a unified city would be intense and the dominance of the Republican party would be severely tested, Endicott may have had some serious misgivings about the desirability of the change. For whatever reason, Endicott, like Sampson, failed to respond positively to the crisis.

Despite the many reports Lockwood had received on the intransigence of certain councilmen, Endicott suggested that the situation was not as serious as Lockwood believed. He ignored a suggestion that an effort be made to have citizens write and phone the dissident councilmen although several experienced women would have willingly undertaken such a campaign. For appearances, Endicott refused to recognize the gravity of the situation and did nothing.

Events reached a climax at the meeting of the city council early in June. The council refused to act on a partial bill submitted by the Lockwood firm at the request of the new mayor. One councilman suggested paying a fraction of the bill and negotiating the balance. Lockwood would not haggle. A second councilman repeated his frequently stated position that he was only interested in annexing the plants. When the motion was made to pay the $1,500 bill, no second was offered.

The following day, June 6, Lockwood kept his promise. He disassociated himself from the unification campaign although officially the firm did not withdraw until early in July when the Board of Supervisors scheduled the election for May 5, 1964. Lockwood reluctantly recognized that he could not obtain the support from key people needed for an election victory. Lockwood was faced with the dilemma Davenport had been confronted with when it became evident that financial and leadership support was not readily available.

The harping and haggling of the councilmen was only one consideration. Another was the more important index of upper-level leadership reaction to unification—the chances of obtaining financial support for the study and for the campaign. More than $10,000 would be required to conduct a proper study and the electioneering drive. Lockwood had little hope of convincing the directors of the National Bank to give generous financial contributions. Since the bank had both Universal and Midwest Motors companies as customers, as well as clients in both the township and the city, bank officers and directors preferred neutrality. The men at the Savings Bank were in accord.

These circumstances placed Lockwood in an awkward position. He had planned to meet with the manager of one of the divisions of Universal Motors. Lockwood intended to ascertain whether or not Universal Motors would keep the promise to assist a study of governmental problems to be made during the consolidation campaign. A sizable donation from Universal Motors would improve chances for obtaining similar responses from Midwest Motors and other absentee-owned enterprises. A refusal would place the entire financial burden on local leaders and reduce the likelihood of implementing the investigation.

Lockwood anticipated that, as president of the National Bank, he would be asked how much money his institution would give. Since the matter had not been discussed by the bank's directors and he feared the worst, Lockwood preferred to avoid embarrassment. This fact and the absence of leaders allied with him who could unite the councilmen in behalf of unification led to Lockwood's withdrawal. Lockwood refused to invest additional time and energy in a cause that some councilmen openly opposed and that other leaders refused to support.

Lockwood did not accompany Mayor Hensil to the meeting with officials of Universal Motors. His absence was noted and interpreted correctly: the proposed study of city and township government did not have the financial backing of affluent Woodruff leaders. The executives of the automobile firm refused to underwrite any part of the cost of the study.

Other consequences of Lockwood's withdrawal were equally serious. Lockwood took no part in merger; he did not attend meetings of the executive committee. One law partner attended meetings until early in July. He then moved to the fringes of campaign activity. Expectedly, Endicott lost all interest in merger. While the president of the local university held occasional meetings of the executive committee during the summer, inability to raise money for a study compelled him to admit that odds were heavily against merger success. When the campaign reached the action stage, the president dropped out of the movement. The staff that Lockwood had assembled went out of existence by mid-summer.

During this period, relations between the city manager and the city council also deteriorated. The resentment of certain councilmen against merger was not directed solely against Lockwood. Dowling, as their employee, was especially vulnerable. At least one councilman adopted the practice of bypassing the city manager in transacting business with the head of a municipal agency.

Whether Dowling and Lockwood co-ordinated their strategies in a combined, last ditch effort to save unification is unlikely. Dowling's response was not entirely motivated as an effort to save unification, for his family situation also had intensified the pressures operating on him. In any event, his move was public, made without any prior warning, and a surprise. At the city council meeting for May 13, 1963, Dowling read a statement before representatives of the press in which he criticized the city council for its lack of unity in several policy areas and for undermining his authority with department heads. He called for a vote of confidence and a sizable increase in salary along with salary increases for other municipal employees. Dowling left the meeting after reading the statement.

While Dowling's actions cannot be attributed solely to the merger controversy, this issue was deeply involved in his relations with the city council. The strongest supporters of Dowling on the city council and his severest critics also disagreed on the merger question. Barker and the councilman whom Dowling believed to have undermined his authority favored the dismissal of the city manager.

The city council later issued a mild statement of support for Dowling that failed to mention a salary increase. On May 23, 1963, Dowling resigned.

The Study

Although the initiators of unification did not know the exact cost of a study of local governments and of the campaign, it was obvious that a considerable sum would be needed. At every meeting in May of the executive committee of the Citizens' Committee, selection of a chairman and members of a finance committee was discussed. Recognizing the difficulties of raising the required sum, the members could not agree on a chairman and made no effort to approach any of the persons mentioned. After the director of the Public Administration Service informed the committee early in June that an adequate study would cost $10,000, the committee was forced to decide whether an attempt would be made to raise this sum.

The Citizens' Committee met to settle the issue on July 8, 1963. The position of Chamber officials would be decisive, for the organization represented both the more affluent residents of the area and the men who would be called upon to solicit funds. The Chamber's executive secretary and the chairman of the consolidation committee took a firm stand against the proposed study of local government. They insisted that such a study was unnecessary since the information required for an effective campaign already was available. In addition, they pointed out that there was no assurance that the Public Administration Service study would favor the annexation proposal. The study might recommend continuation of the pattern of divided government or a different method of unification. Expenditure of a large sum of money for a study that might criticize the annexation plan was unjustifiable.

Although the committee voted to employ the Public Administration Service, the resolution could not be implemented. Leaders of the Chamber would not and did not raise money for the study. The mayor had expressed the belief that the city council would contribute some funds for the study, but the council later rejected his suggestion that it pay a fifth of the cost, $2,000.[6] The township clerk took the position that the township board could not contribute funds for a study that was part of the annexation effort. If annexation petitions were withdrawn, the board would support the study.

The refusal of Woodruff leaders to finance the study of area political structure changed the character of the campaign. Without the study the campaign could not perform its planned educational function; it could not modify opinions and viewpoints. Existing

6. Some months later the former mayor became chairman of a committee that raised $200,000 for Woodruff's repertory theater.

prejudices and antipathies would be strengthened. The campaign reverted to the type of propagandizing that prevailed in the consolidation controversy. The year that unification supporters had designated for a thorough examination of local governments was squandered.

Preparation for the Sharing of Power

A subcommittee of the Citizens' Committee considered the implications of merger in the light of the differences between city and township forms of government. One problem resulted from a provision of the city charter which specified a three-year residence requirement for persons seeking elected office. Should merger succeed, township citizens might not be able to run for public office for a three-year period. Despite occasional merger and annexation elections, city officials had not modified or clarified this residency requirement. The provision had been used as recently as 1958 to discourage a person who resided in the area annexed from running for a seat on the city council.

At the suggestion of the committee, the city council took steps to rectify the situation. Superficially it appeared that the city council's recommendation signified a sincere and earnest desire to share political power and responsibility with those persons from former township areas to be elected to the city council. An amendment to the charter was placed on the election ballot in the spring of 1964. It provided for the election of at least seven and possibly eight persons to the city council from the annexed area. These officials would have the same powers and rights as the councilmen elected by city voters. At the very least, representation on the enlarged city council would be equally divided between residents of the city and of the annexed territory. The amendment was approved by a nine-to-one ratio in a very light voter turnout.

This change in the city charter was not sufficient. Elections in the city remained nonpartisan, and if the outcome for the new city would resemble that for the former city, the majority of successful candidates would come from the western sections and would be Republican. Furthermore, merger still would destroy important institutional supports for township leadership, partisan elections, strong political parties, and full-time, elected offices in township government.

City leaders had ample time to place on the spring of 1964 ballot an amendment establishing partisan elections. The Midstate attorney general had ruled in October, 1963, that adoption of partisan elections and direct election of the mayor for a two-year period could be accomplished by election. A return to the ward system of elections, however, would require a revision of the city charter.

Adoption of partisan elections was supported by Bowes editorially on March 3, 1964. It had been an objective of a dissident group in the Negro community, and various city leaders had talked of this change off and on for many years. One month before the 1958 merger election, the mayor and city council had agreed to investigate the desirability of adopting the ward system, but no action was taken after merger had been defeated. City officials responded to arguments for partisan elections and direct election of the mayor by repeating the suggestion that these matters should be considered after the election.

At this time, shortly before the merger election, the city council took a step that clearly indicated its concern for maintaining the dominance of the Republican party. At the first or second session of the council following the spring election, council members usually reappointed the five representatives to the County Board of Supervisors. Supervisors generally held these positions until death or retirement. On April 13, 1964, without warning, the city council replaced the two Democratic appointees with two Republicans. All of the city's supervisors were Republican. Barker, the lone Democratic councilman, supported the action.[7]

Whatever the reasons for this action, several consequences were obvious. First, in the event of a merger success, the councilmen could select Democrats for the two or three additional supervisors whom the enlarged city would gain and retain the Republican majority. Second, Republican leaders served notice on all Democrats that no concessions could be expected in the enlarged city. This message was made unmistakable in refusing to reappoint as super-

---

7. In 1965, Democrat Barker was named to the County Board of Supervisors, replacing a Republican appointee. The newly elected mayor, also a Republican, was named to the Board. In 1967, Barker became Woodruff's first Negro mayor. He retired from public life two years later.

visor the woman who, for many years, had been chairman of the Iroquois County Democratic party and who had held a seat on the party's state central committee.

Residents of the area to be annexed were asked to exchange the customary forms of township government for those of the city. They were asked to accept forms of government that would weaken the Democratic party and the traditional basis of leadership for influentials of both parties. They also were asked to accept higher tax rates and to yield the township's rich industrial tax base to city officials. To many residents, this hardly seemed like a fair exchange.

Electioneering

Electioneering by Annexation Supporters

After it became obvious that no study would be conducted as part of the unification campaign, the Citizens' Committee disbanded. During the fall of 1963 little was done to promote unification. Late in February, 1964, an action committee was organized which concerned itself primarily with preparation and dissemination of information on the unification election. An attempt was made to co-ordinate the activities of this group with the appropriate committees of the Chamber of Commerce and the League of Women Voters, both of which had endorsed unification. The Chamber conducted a fund drive to support unification. The volume of propaganda indicated that several thousands of dollars were raised and spent. Seven separate fact sheets were prepared and distributed in the community. These explained the characteristics of the current annexation, its impact on the taxpayer's pocketbook and on the schools, the increased revenue that annexation would bring to the new city, characteristics of the current city charter, and alternatives to annexation. About eight flyers were mailed to township homes extolling the virtues of unification and emphasizing the theme that Woodruff should be "one united community." Many of these were sent out under the joint auspices of the League of Women Voters, the Chamber, and the United Community Committee.

Newspaper advertising was used extensively. Seven ads appeared in the paper in the ten days preceding the election. One was a full-page ad; the others filled approximately one-third of each page. Several thousands of dollars must have been spent for the mailings and newspaper advertisements. A poorly implemented effort was made to personally contact township voters by means of neighborhood coffee hours and doorbell ringing.

Undoubtedly the most important advocate of unification was *The Woodruff Press*. If the editor committed any error it was overzealousness in pleading the cause of merger. From the time the petitions were filed on April 5, 1963, to the day of the election, thirteen months later, over forty editorials favoring unification were published. The editor explained the nature of the annexation proposal and the reasons for excluding certain areas of the township. He selected arguments used by opponents either in speeches or in letters to the editor and responded to them. To increase the effectiveness of the editorials he did not publish them at random intervals but clustered them together, at the very beginning of the campaign, early in February, 1964, and again in the days just before the election. During the last days of the campaign Bowes ran a number of stories on the front page which emphasized the many advantages of a unified city. One article pertained to the progress that a "unified" city nearby had made in recent years. Several editorials described a number of services provided by the city, such as caring for the elm trees, which were not available to township residents. Another article dealt with the inadequacies of police protection in the township as contrasted with that in the city, and one report concerned the need for improved roads in the township. Bowes sought to convey the impression that Universal Motors favored merger and quoted a statement by the president of the company in 1961 which endorsed unification in another Midstate community.

In the last weeks of the campaign virtually all of the news stories and editorials emphasized the advantages of unification. Except for some letters to the editor, antiannexation material did not find its way into news columns. Many township residents may have reacted by ignoring the stories and editorials on the issue, knowing in advance the bias of the editor.

For days before the election, a table was published on the editorial page listing the probable changes in tax rates that residents of the various school districts could expect to pay in a unified city. The figures were based on a report issued on January 15, 1964, by the new city manager. He estimated a general increase in the township tax rate of slightly less than ten mills and a decrease in city tax rate of slightly more than ten mills. Since the increases for township property owners were small, the editor hoped that resistance on the basis of taxes would be more than offset by the benefits to be received. To many township readers the table confirmed the allegation that city officials were interested only in the automobile plants; the city would gain at the expense of the township.

Saving the Township
The effort to save the township from the perils of unification both resembled in important respects and differed from the anticonsolidation attempt of 1958. The usual bipartisan committee was established to organize and direct the counterattack, and a thousand dollars was spent to defeat merger. As in the previous campaign, doorbell ringing played an important part in the propaganda effort, and tax increases were a central theme. The campaign differed in several ways. The assistance of Sinelli, the paid executive of the Midstate Township Association, was not requested, and little effort was made to get the antimerger case into the local paper. The committee preferred to distribute its information in other forms. Legal maneuvering to gain favorable newspaper publicity was not employed.

Most of the activities of the new STTC were concentrated in the final month of the campaign, with important propaganda material distributed the weekend before the election. Early in April, homes in every precinct of the township were contacted ostensibly to survey sentiment on unification. Approximately two thousand homes were "surveyed"; of those who had made a decision, over 80 percent opposed annexation. Those who gave noncommittal answers or who expressed partiality for the proposal were given reasons for voting "no." The willingness of many STTC members to speak directly to as many township citizens as possible contributed to the large turnout on election day; 62.4 percent of registered voters went to the polls, as compared with 35 percent in the city.

The propaganda campaign emphasized the slogan of the STTC:

KEEP TAXES LOW
LET'S GROW
VOTE NO
MAY 5

The committee selected the Trojan Horse to symbolize its view of the unification proposal, and a model was built on the lawn in front of Township Hall. While the customary forms of propaganda were used—bumper stickers, signs, and posters—effective use was made of one short pamphlet distributed ten days before and one newspaper distributed the Saturday before the election. Although the newspaper editor, late in April, offered the STTC space for three articles, the committee declined. Had they accepted the offer the editor would have had the opportunity to rebut their arguments in the final days of the campaign.

The themes emphasized by the STTC had been used in the previous campaign. The lead article in the lone newspaper issue began in this fashion: "The Power Structure of the City of Woodruff is making what they consider to be 'one last effort' for the tax base and utilities of the most progressive Township in Midstate . . . they [the persons in the power structure] are going to save us! Save us with our own money! Save us with our own utilities! Which are ample, modern and growing! We are reminded of the drowning man offering swimming lessons."

Unification was described as a "grab," and the township was put in the "underdog" position by frequent reference to the unfair tactics of the opposition. This characterization gained credibility by mention of the difficulties of placing antiunification viewpoints and news in the local press. Attacks were made on the city manager system and nonpartisan elections. City leadership was characterized as ineffective and unable to solve municipal problems. Woodruff was a dying city with old buildings and unsightly streets. Above all else there were taxes, taxes, taxes!

These appeals to the fears of township citizens of economic penalties in a unified city and to the animosities toward Woodruff which had existed for decades were as effective as they had been five years previously. Over 85 percent of the voters in the area to be annexed voted against the proposal, 5,885 to 982. While 87 percent of the city voters voted for the proposal, 2,340 to 358, the battle was lost in the township. City annexation leaders could find a little consolation in the fact that consensus among city voters for unification was higher than in the previous election, when about 77 percent of the voters affirmed consolidation. This increase might well be attributed to the vigorous support given by the newspaper to unification and to the explicit statements that taxes for city residents would decrease.

The campaign illustrated again that the formula used by city annexation leaders to gain unification provided for an exercise in futility. In Woodruff it seemed impossible to persuade a majority of township voters in the heat of a campaign that unification would benefit the area.

Conclusion

The 1963–64 annexation campaign possessed several important elements that were similar to those of the two previous efforts. It was sparked by fears that an attempt might be made to incorporate the township in whole or in part. Whether the reports of such a development were real or fictional, self-interest on the part of the city and the Lockwood firm seemed to require swift, preventive action. The interest of the councilmen in unification was stimulated by a plan that promised no change in the balance of power while the tax base would more than triple. The councilmen were interested in a risk-free strategy that would "solve" financial problems, retain the Republican business and professional groups in power, and give city voters the option of selecting which township areas were "suitable" for annexation. The original annexation plan suggested by the mayor and city manager was thought capable of providing these benefits without modifying one component of the restrictionist decision-making pattern.

Once it became clear that unification might result in a shift of political power and that the effort would require a sum in excess of ten thousand dollars with no certainty of success, the city's leaders responded as they had in 1958 to Davenport's appeals. Unification deteriorated rapidly into a propaganda ritual that culminated in another resounding defeat.

11. Unification Efforts and the Decision-Making Pattern

The state statutes specifying procedures for merging an incorporated and an unincorporated municipality and those permitting annexation provided mechanisms whereby communities could adapt political organization to urbanization and industrialization. Within a period of thirteen years three attempts at merging Woodruff City and Woodruff Township took place, either directly or indirectly through large-scale annexation. The annexation of 610 acres in 1958 and a number of other efforts suggest that the forces for political change within Woodruff were strong and active. Our analysis prompts the opposite conclusion: that the groups committed to these changes were weak and that merger campaigns served mainly to preserve the existing political structure.

The uniformity of the circumstances attending the initiation of and the main events within each campaign suggests the operation of powerful social forces. Comparison of these elements with the basic decisions on sanitary services indicates merger did not represent a sharp discontinuity from past policy: it was a remarkable extension of the decision-making pattern.

Analysis of the Campaigns

The factors influencing the outcome and consequences of the three campaigns will be analyzed by relating the Woodruff experience to hypotheses based on similar events in other communities. Certain features of the Woodruff community which preceded the initiation of the controversy came close to predetermining an election defeat. One set of factors concerns the availability of essential services. The likelihood of outlying municipalities voting to merge with a central city varies inversely with the degree to which the former have invested in the provision of these services.[1] Where investment is low, merger or annexation enables these communities to obtain the services that their citizens require.

The Woodruff experience strongly supports this hypothesis. Township officials had developed water and sewerage disposal facilities equal to or better than those in the city (see Chapter 4). The decisions and nondecisions of city officials which assisted the township to gain self-sufficiency in this area and which hindered the development of Woodruff's water and sewerage disposal systems greatly dimmed the chances of merger.

Complex changes in political structure seldom are accomplished quickly but usually require a lengthy period of time. Generally the advocates of change, in this instance of merger or some plan for intermunicipal co-operation, learn from past defeats. They come to recognize the weaknesses in the original plan and the reasons for resistance. Proposals are changed to satisfy criticism and increase the base of support for the change.[2]

The Woodruff experience supports the hypothesis that success in reorganizing patterns of local government requires a particular type of implementation process, lengthy in time and characterized by feedback and learning from past defeats. This type of process did not occur in Woodruff. Each merger campaign developed as a defensive reaction to a group of township leaders who threatened

---

1. The municipalities supporting metropolitan integration in Cuyahoga County lacked sewer and water facilities. Norton E. Long, *The Polity* (Chicago: Rand McNally, and Company 1962), p. 208. The difficulties that suburban areas in Davidson County had with septic tanks, inadequate water, and firefighting facilities played an important part in the success of the campaign to consolidate county government with that of the city of Nashville. See Roscoe C. Martin, *Metropolis in Transition: Local Government Adaptation to Changing Urban Needs* (Washington, D.C.: U.S. Government Printing Office, 1963), pp. 103–4. For other studies subscribing to this point of view see Roy H. Owsley, "An End to Freeloading," *National Municipal Review,* 66 (April, 1957), 181–88; John C. Bollens, "Elements of Successful Annexation," *Public Management,* 30 (April, 1948), 98–101.
2. Martin, *Metropolis in Transition,* pp. 13–31, 132.

to incorporate the municipality in whole or in part as a separate city. They were "spur-of-the-moment" responses, initiated with little or no advance preparation amid haste and secrecy designed to prevent interference from city leaders and from township officials. Given the absence of intermunicipal co-operation in the solution of area problems and the lack of any reputable and systematic body of information to justify governmental reorganization, unification efforts might be expected to fail.

After a merger proposal had been defeated, Woodruff officials and leaders ignored area problems. Various changes in municipal policies which might have lessened the opposition of township residents were not made. City and township government continued to operate in the interlude between merger elections in a manner that would maintain autonomy and self-sufficiency.

A third hypothesis pertains to a type of change necessitating a lengthy period of time before merger success. The probability of large-scale changes in intermunicipal relations improves if similar changes on a lesser scale have occurred. Merger is more likely to occur where the municipalities have established formalized patterns of co-operation in areas of importance to the citizenry and local institutions.[3] Presumably the willingness of citizens to endorse major realignments in area government increases if co-operative programs have yielded substantial benefits.

City and township officials, in the periods between elections, were concerned mainly with internal matters. Despite periodic suggestions from editor Bowes and his successors for joint performance of certain municipal functions, little was done to move in this direction. The failure of city and township officials to establish co-operative arrangements for services such as sewer, water, garbage collection, fire protection, library, recreation, and maintenance of roads tended to confirm prevailing beliefs that each municipality could operate as or more effectively as an independent unit rather than jointly.

Political Factors

Several researchers have suggested that prospects for integration of local governments vary with the degree of heterogenity of the popu-

3. *Ibid.*, pp. 112, 125.

lation of the central city and the outlying communities.[4] Banfield and Grodzins translate socioeconomic differences into political divisions and conflicts, based on class, race, and party affiliation.[5] The middle-class citizens of a suburb will reject merger with a working-class city to maintain the distance and separation in identity achieved by outward migration. Racial differences operate in a similar manner. Woodruff's experiences with merger partially supports this hypothesis. Many in the Negro community feared the dilution of its political power if merger with the township took place. They also preferred to have Woodruff officials concentrate on improving conditions in Negro neighborhoods. Some Negro leaders, especially Barker, attacked the principal advocates of merger and helped defeat it.[6] Despite these considerations, the differences in racial composition of city and township do not appear to have been as influential as another type of conflict.

Despite similarities in the population of the two municipalities (see Chapter 2), the Democratic party was much stronger in the township than in the city. Partisan elections in the former and nonpartisan elections in the latter contributed greatly to this variation. These and related differences in forms of government also influenced the power of political leaders in relation to economic leaders. Nonpartisan elections and the weak mayor impeded the efforts of Woodruff's elected officials to consolidate control over the political

4. Thomas R. Dye, "Urban Political Integration: Conditions Associated with Annexation in American Cities," *Midwest Journal of Political Science,* 8 (November, 1964), 430–46.

5. Edward C. Banfield and Morton Grodzins, "The Desirable and the Possible," in Edward C. Banfield, ed., *Urban Government: A Reader in Politics and Administration* (New York: The Free Press of Glencoe, 1961), pp. 82–88; Edward C. Banfield, "The Politics of Metropolitan Area Organization," *Midwest Journal of Political Science,* 1 (May, 1957), 77–91. For a comparative study presenting contrary results, see Brett W. Hawkins, "Fringe-city Life-Style Distance and Fringe Support of Political Integration," *American Journal of Sociology,* 74 (November, 1968), 248–55.

6. Negroes in other communities reacted in a similar manner to proposals for political merger. Nashville Negroes opposed the first plan for consolidation of city and county governments. John C. Bollens and Henry J. Schmandt, *The Metropolis: Its People, Politics and Economic Life* (New York: Harper and Row, 1965), pp. 491–524.

The Negro community also opposed metro government in St. Louis and Cleveland. Long, *The Polity,* pp. 207, 209–10.

apparatus. Political leaders did not have a strong following among the voters. Economic leaders and the Chamber exercise a large role in shaping public policies. Partisan elections and three full-time board positions help to make political position a major basis for influence in township affairs. Resistance to merger derives partly from the fear of leaders in each municipality that changes in government will affect adversely the institutional sources of power. Although merger had scant chance of success, each campaign was important for city and township relations, for various participants, and for merger as a mechanism of political change.

An Overview of the Campaigns

Many city leaders anticipated serious negative consequences from merger success and hence failed to contribute substantially to the several campaigns. In this way these persons tacitly or unknowingly co-operated with township leaders to defeat the proposal for combining the two municipalities. The court handling of the 1950 annexation represented an ideal procedure for disposing of the issue. After the court issued an injunction prohibiting the election until a hearing could be held, both sides found ways to prevent the matter from reaching a judicial decision. This procedure avoided the expenditure of several thousands of dollars for electioneering and the bruising of egos in the midst of campaign exchanges. The financial burden for legal actions was borne by the public treasury and not by community leaders. Since the latter assumed no responsibility for actions of the court, none of the leaders promoting merger felt betrayed.

As township opponents of merger had no legal basis for obtaining an injuction or for preventing the elections in 1958 and 1964, the campaigns could not be avoided. Leaders of the Chamber, the banks, and other Woodruff organizations weakened the movement by withholding resources that were badly needed, money for a study, money for campaign expenses, and other assets they possessed—prestige, ideas, organizational skills, and contacts with industrial executives and higher levels of government. The established leaders who had committed themselves to merger responded in one of three ways. Harding and Erickson worked outside the spotlight of publicity, where they were less vulnerable to criticism. Davenport performed his duties in a half-hearted, routine fashion to avoid offending upper-level leaders opposed to the change. Lockwood, his law partners, and Endicott withdrew entirely once they recognized that opponents in the city could not be won over. The campaigns for merger were waged by persons not generally acknowledged as leaders, persons who erroneously considered the campaign as the appropriate stage for demonstrating leadership abilities or citizens so interested in community betterment that they were blind to the signs of leader resistance.

At first glance the merger campaigns had all the signs of an earnest, wholehearted confrontation, of a major struggle on an issue basic to the future of the Woodruff area. Sincere men made strong speeches, propaganda filled the newspapers, posters and bumper stickers were everywhere, and the campaign was a favorite topic of conversation at informal meetings of business and professional men at the customary gathering places. The "insider" recognized these activities and symbols as window dressing, a "cover" concealing the fact that the leaders were co-operating indirectly with merger opponents. The ritual of citizen participation in political decision making hid the actual purpose of the campaign—preservation of the political structure.

The behavior of Woodruff's more influential organizations and leaders during a merger campaign can be described as a "slack" system.[7] Most of the sources of influence, the basic weapons, were in cold storage; they were not available to the men waging the election fight. Township organizations and leaders, although possessing fewer resources, used a higher proportion of what was available and used them more effectively. Most if not all economic notables, Zeller, Paster, and several others, contributed financially to the 1958 campaign. Those who had liquor licences depended on annual renewals by the township board. Virtually all enterprises benefited from lower than customary tax assessments at the time of the 1958 campaign. Zeller also organized the business and professional men of the township in opposition to merger. The Jaycees received far less proportionate support from Woodruff's economic notables.

7. Robert A. Dahl, *Who Governs? Democracy and Power in an American City* (New Haven: Yale University Press, 1961), pp. 271–275, 305–10.

Township leaders involved and sustained the interest of large numbers of people. They relied on personal contacts with voters to a degree that merger proponents could not duplicate, in the form of a voter registration drive in 1958 and an opinion survey in 1964. In both campaigns, many workers walked through neighborhood after neighborhood ringing doorbells. While merger supporters relied extensively on published propaganda, opposition leaders used face-to-face contacts, the personal touch that characterized so much of political activity in the township and that occurred so rarely in a municipality lacking partisan elections. From a financial standpoint, in consolidation, if not in the 1964 campaign, expenses were greater in the township than in the city because of the hiring of additional legal assistance to fight merger in court. Including this item as a campaign cost increased the township bill for defeating consolidation to a level above that of the city. Since the leaders of the township openly and ardently fought merger in both campaigns while their city counterparts sat on the sidelines, the "taut" system of the township was more effective than the "slack" system of the city. Indeed, the slackness of the merger organization was intended to limit operational effectiveness. It was intended to be dysfunctional to merger advocates and functional for the city's top leaders.

The intangible differences between city and township election activities were no less significant. The township leaders were more skillful in appealing to the basic emotions of township voters. To accomplish this end, merger was described to township voters in largely fictional terms that were believable although far from true. Merger was a huge steamroller set in motion by self-seeking, powerful "city fathers" who were anxious to take advantage of weaker, more vulnerable township neighbors. The township was the underdog, subject to severe exploitation if the "city fathers" were successful. Fears of subjugation to the city, once aroused, were sustained until the last vote had been cast. Defeating merger was akin to a "holy war."

The advocates of merger, during two campaigns, never countered opposition tactics. In a rational manner they sketched the ways by which life would be better in a unified city. Reports of additional funds forthcoming from the state and of the improved services available to all, especially to those in the township, seemed to many to be "pie-in-the-sky." If these justifications had any beneficial impact they were offset by intimation in 1958 and by admission in 1964 that property taxes would increase for township residents. Advocates of merger had the impossible task of persuading persons who saw little wrong with the existing system of divided government that it operated badly and that merger would remedy most ills. The day-to-day experiences of township residents—the water in the tap and the excellent plumbing in the bathroom, the fire station a few blocks away, the state highway and county patrol cars cruising through the area every few hours—did not lend credence to the claim that life would be beautiful if only city and township marched to the altar. Life was sufficiently beautiful, at least at the existing tax rates. Furthermore, many merger advocates found it difficult to be convincing day in and day out when so few city leaders had demonstrated agreement in any positive and meaningful way. For those who knew of the opposition of the city leaders, the taste of bitter defeat made it difficult to extol the glowing city of the future, a unified Woodruff.

The Role of Specific Structures

Government
The participation of city government leaders in each of the three campaigns was similar except for superficial differences. The city manager played an important part in initiating the 1950 and 1964 annexation drives. In 1958, government officials remained in the background or took little overt interest in the campaign. The similarity between the 1958 and 1964 campaigns increased after the initial stages. Government leaders were not in the forefront of the campaign after Dowling's resignation and Lockwood's withdrawal. A voluntary group comparable to the Jaycee leaders took charge of the electioneering.

Township government leaders were among the most active opponents of political reorganization. They helped to organize and develop strategy for resistance. Their views on the campaign were considered newsworthy items. This contrast in the participation of political leaders was a product of several differences in the political action in the township whereas a variety of private organizations—

service clubs, civic association, and the Chamber of Commerce—operated in Woodruff. Second, the development and maintenance of strong voter appeal was not a prerequisite for the office of mayor since he was elected by the council. In contrast, the three salaried, full-time township officers had to be top vote getters. Third, township government leaders were key members of the power structure whereas the city political office holder often was not. The latter was more beholden to those who were and less inclined to fight for changes that ran counter to the decision-making pattern. Important campaign roles were filled by heads of township government while city politicians and city government were subordinated to voluntary groups of private citizens.

The merger conflicts revealed some of the strengths of township government and some of the weaknesses of city government. These differences can be attributed largely to partisan elections and direct election of several, full-time office holders in the case of the former and nonpartisan election of part-time officials combined with indirect election of the mayor in the case of the latter. Partisan elections waged by two evenly matched parties developed and broadly distributed the skills and motivation necessary for performing the routine tasks that turned voters out in large numbers. Nonpartisan elections could not match this achievement, for gaining a public office depended not on organization but on the "popularity" or "suitability" of the candidates. Engaging regularly in bitter struggles for township offices had an additional advantage. It developed in many officials and party leaders the abilities and techniques for reaching voters which proved invaluable in fighting merger. Their propaganda techniques, slogans, and symbols had more appeal and impact that those of merger supporters. These skills for political campaigning offset to a considerable degree the greater affluence of city influentials.

The Chamber of Commerce

The activities of the Chamber deviated little in the two recent merger endeavors. The Chamber played a dual role, limiting the financial burden on the city leaders and supporting the campaign efforts of the action group. In neither campaign did the Chamber, as an organization, spearhead the election activities.

The Chamber was judicious in the support given merger. In the

1964 campaign, by rejecting the plan for a study of local government and by refusing to assist the fund raising, Chamber leaders helped eliminate the study phase of the movement. Once this goal was accomplished Chamber leadership raised money for meeting the costs of electioneering. In 1958, the Chamber assisted Davenport to raise funds by providing some of the more effective solicitors and its membership list as a source of potential donors. The organization publicly endorsed both merger proposals, an action that had little or no positive effect on township voters. Whether from opposition by campaign leaders or from awareness of the liabilities to the members, the Chamber organization was not prominently involved in the initiation, organization, and conduct of the two election contests.

The Bankers
In the 1958 and 1964 campaigns, bankers and bank directors provided little or no help to merger leaders. Bank directors participated in the 1958 campaign in the same manner as most other economic notables, by making minimal financial donations. Nor did the banking leaders contribute to the management or planning of either campaign.

Since Lockwood accepted responsibility for initiating merger in 1963 at about the same time that he was elevated to the presidency of the National Bank, it might appear that the directors approved of his role and of the plan for political reorganization. Several facts contradict this view. First, Lockwood accepted this task as a lawyer and not as a bank president. Second, he had little choice in accepting the assignment offered by city officials. The possibility of township incorporation, even if slim, entailed too many risks for the city and for the law firm. Third, the unwillingness of banking leaders to contribute generously to the merger effort placed Lockwood in a difficult position. Having failed to gain support from his associates, he could hardly expect better results from requests to industry executives. For this and other reasons, Lockwood withdrew once the prime objective of preventing township incorporation had been achieved.

The Newspaper
The role of the newspaper in the merger campaigns conforms in certain respects with experiences in other communities. Campaigns

for metropolitan government failed in St. Louis and Cleveland despite the total editorial support of the dailies.[8] One explanation, opposition to the plan from suburban newspapers, does not apply to Woodruff. The absence of mass media committed to defeat of merger strengthens the view that the local newspaper was ineffectual in changing the opinions of township residents. This view gains additional credence from the change in editorial policy which accompanied the change in ownership from an "old" Woodruff family to an absentee-owned newspaper group. Despite the change from neutrality to advocacy, the election results were the same in both campaigns.

The Woodruff experience demonstrates the inability of the newspaper editor to carry most of the burden for changing public opinion on an issue as complex and basic as reorganization of area government. The daily experiences of residents with the operations of their governments also shapes opinion on proposals for change. In the absence of benefits produced by and attributed to intermunicipal programs and organizations, few citizens can be convinced of the desirability of exchanging community identity for merger. The Woodruff experience also suggests that a consistently outspoken position in favor of a controversial proposal will discredit the newspaper's authority in the eyes of many readers.[9] These persons reject the editor's arguments as biased and unreliable. They turn to other sources of information, antimerger groups, opinion leaders, and friends. Possibly the newspaper and other mass media can be more effective instruments for developing public opinion on complex issues by occasionally recognizing the merits of the opposition position and, in general, according it sympathetic treatment.

The long-run influence of the newspaper editor should not be dismissed too lightly. Unlike Amdur, Bowes and his successors were responsible to executives of the newspaper group in addition to the local readers. The pressure to produce an interesting, readable paper probably was greater than the pressures that led Amdur to silently acquiesce to Woodruff's decision-making pattern. Bowes's successors have continued to comment editorially on local issues, to take

8. Long, *The Polity,* pp. 208–11.
9. Many leaders of New Haven rejected the views of the owner of the city's two newspapers as "politically biased and even eccentric." They had little or no "confidence in the source." Dahl, *Who Governs?* pp. 258–59.

public positions, and to advocate intergovernmental co-operation for the performance of important functions. For these reasons the newspaper editor and his publication represent important agents of change, which contradict the decision-making patterns of both municipalities.

Absentee-owned Industry
While Pacific Motors financed the legal maneuvers to defeat annexation in 1950, Universal Motors and Midwest Motors were more restrained in the two subsequent campaigns. Except for encouraging several employees to work against merger, auto executives participated to the same extent as most of Woodruff's leaders. How the automobile companies would have responded had all the major leaders of Woodruff actively worked for merger is problematical. The companies adapted policy to the occasion. The absence of city leadership support for unification made it difficult for the automobile executives to do otherwise. The outcome of the three merger endeavors was determined more by the responses of city and township leaders than by the actions or inactions of company officials.

Potential Agents of Change

The men who took the initiative in launching and carrying out the merger efforts acted in opposition to Woodruff's restrictionist pattern. Had they succeeded or had the result of even one campaign held out strong promise for success on a subsequent effort, these men could have become major agents of social change. To understand the conditions that encouraged these men to work in behalf of an ambitious plan for political change is to explore the question of the sources of change within the Woodruff area.

The men responsible for the 1950 effort were marginal while those who initiated the other two campaigns were closer to the center of community life. Despite this difference, these two sets of potential change agents had come under the influence of a doctrine of local government expounded by specialists in the larger society, namely the virtues of metropolitan government and urban planning. In this sense both sets of actors were more oriented than most other local leaders to a feature of the external social system.

A handful of former GI's and their wives, residents of Shady Lea

Village who were students either at Midstate University or the university in Woodruff, became convinced of the need for redeveloping the village and that the method for accomplishing this end was through merger with the city. Their interest in and willingness to work for this program, despite their intention to leave the community after graduation, is indicative of their idealism. They were convinced that a democratic polity and the tools of planning could improve the community. They were determined to make their point.

Ignorance also played an important role, as it did in the case of the Jaycee leaders seven years later.[10] As young persons who were not well acquainted with the community, the former GI's were unfamiliar with Woodruff's restrictionist decision-making pattern, and they were possibly unaware of the hostilities born of wartime experiences toward Shady Lea Village, even when many inhabitants were college students and not "hillbillies." These men and women either underestimated the difficulty of accomplishing major structural change or exaggerated their powers, perhaps because of recent election success in gaining seats on the Shady Lea School Board.

The Jaycee leaders who took the lead in the 1957 campaign and Dowling, who played a similar role in the subsequent effort, also had certain characteristics in common with the former GI's: namely, youth, an underestimation of the difficulty of accomplishing change, and a belief in the validity of the doctrine of area political unity. The influence of this doctrine on the Jaycees was indirect, through Harding and Erickson. The familiarity of these men with contemporary ideas on government and planning is suggested by the fact that Harding had played an important part in the mid-fifties in the unsuccessful effort to establish an area planning commission. Erickson had served for some years on Woodruff's Planning Commission. Dowling's training as city manager exposed him to the tenets of this doctrine and the city's budgetary difficulties persuaded him to apply it.

The factors operating on Davenport and Lockwood reveal some of the circumstances inducing established leaders to play the role of change agents. Neither was especially concerned with theories of

10. For a discussion of the importance of ignorance see Wilbert E. Moore and Melvin M. Tumin, "Some Social Functions of Ignorance," *American Sociological Review*, 14 (December, 1949), 787–95.

local government; nor could it be said that they were unfamiliar with municipal policies. Since Davenport had served a long time as mayor and Lockwood as township attorney, both had helped to make and carry out these policies. Both recognized the many difficulties of merging city and township. Davenport's acceptance of fund-raising responsibilities, which gave the green light to the Jaycees, and Lockwood's decision to accept the city government as a client were for different reasons. Davenport's leadership of merger was an extension of the role played in the adoption of the manager form of city government in 1946, which led to service as the first mayor under the new form of government. History would repeat itself if Davenport became the first mayor of the enlarged city. This would culminate a distinguished record of service to the Woodruff area and brighten the Davenport name.

Lockwood's major reasons for initiating merger had little or nothing to do with aspirations for public office. The role of change agent was forced upon Lockwood by a combination of factors, especially the possibility that a new city might be established in the township. Lockwood was more interested in preventing what appeared to be an impending disaster for both municipalities and in protecting the standing of the law firm.

None of these factors indicate that the forces for political reorganization were strong and powerful. Ignorance, ambition, exaggerated self-confidence, recognition of internal difficulties, and awareness of an alternative suggested by practitioners of a social science were important elements. Missing was the conviction that local conditions were deteriorating or that public opinion in the township was moving toward a more favorable view of merger, that the "tide of change" now was on the side of consolidation. It is no surprise, therefore, that each merger campaign was launched after threats of separate incorporation had been made by township leaders.

The three township personages who vigorously supported merger also suffered major setbacks. One township resident, a graduate student in public administration at Midstate University, spent a considerable sum of money to assist the 1950 campaign. Disillusionment led him to contribute substantially, as a township businessman, to its defeat in 1958. The Democratic supervisor for 1957–59, the lone township officer to endorse merger, allowed himself to be persuaded that this course of action would further his political ambitions. Instead, this action led to recall procedures in 1958, defeat in the Democratic primary in 1959, and the end of what appeared to have been a promising career in politics. Another township resident, a businessman who was largely self-educated and had some familiarity with political science literature, spoke openly for merger at township meetings. Retribution also came in the 1959 election contest when the businessman was the sole Republican candidate defeated for township office. He subsequently reversed his stand on unification and served for several years as assessor in the office of Supervisor Jones.

Leading and openly working for merger was a punishing experience. Those who had played an active role once did not care to repeat the performance. By thinning out the ranks of influentials committed to merger and by strengthening township leaders opposed to merger, the campaigns endowed the pattern of divided government with increased longevity.

12. System Conflict and Integration

To understand the factors preventing the adoption of various forms of organized co-operation between city and township government, the factors responsible for the continuity of the spatial domain of each municipality much as it had been for half a century or more, requires consideration of a number of factors. The answer is complex and must consider the impact of conditions antecedent to rapid economic growth, aspects of the depression experience. These conditions were reinforced by reactions to wartime industrialization and established continuity of certain features of political structure as top-leader goals. A second set of factors concerns the processes by which economic, social, and demographic change were confined to the framework of two officially independent governments. The decision-making pattern and inaction were critical factors. Third, we take a backward look from the vantage point of the present and consider the ways by which traditional features of area political structure have been functional.[1] What groups have benefited from

1. Structural functional theory has been criticized for its teleological character. Defenders of the theory have emphasized the importance of the distinction between efficient and final causes. In emphasizing antecedent conditions, procedures for implementing top-rated objectives and the consequences of the forms of certain social structures we have sought to keep these criticisms in mind. For essays which debate these and related issues see N. J. Demerath

the pattern of divided government? The fourth section considers the future of the Woodruff area, and the fifth discusses in a general way the factors influencing the degree of rigidity in the reactions of a social system to conflict.

Adoption of the Decision-Making Patterns

Two sets of factors, one internal and the other external, led to Woodruff's adoption of a restrictionist pattern. Both sets of factors had similar consequences, provoking strong fears among city leaders of a political "takeover" by persons of lower socioeconomic standing and "alien" political persuasions. Woodruff's influentials became convinced that maintaining essential features of leadership and government should be top-rated objectives. The depression and wartime industrialization combined to create a sense of weakness and a loss of confidence on the part of Woodruff's officials and leaders concerning their ability to administer local organizations effectively. Powerful forces had been unloosed in the larger society that seemed likely to undo all the efforts of local influentials. City government had great difficulty meeting local payrolls and bond payments, and on at least one occasion issued scrip. The school board almost defaulted on the high school bond issue. The Country Club could not make its bond payments and had to be reorganized. The local economy underwent crisis and panic as first one and then the other bank closed and had to be reorganized, causing a loss of income for depositors and a delay in gaining access to their accounts (see Chapter 5).

The confidence and resources of local leaders were weakened further by the circumstances surrounding the failure in 1933 of the First National Bank. The one family in the community whose record of leadership most strongly manifested charisma, the family that, by local standards, for almost seventy years had an outstanding record of accomplishment in community developmental activities failed the bank's directors, shareholders, depositors, and the community. By choosing not to stand behind the bank, as his father was believed to

III and Richard A. Peterson, eds., *System, Change, and Conflict: A Reader on Contemporary Sociological Theory and the Debate over Functionalism* (New York: The Free Press, 1967).

have done in 1907, Davenport lost much prestige and respect. The inevitable diminution of the "mystique" of the Davenport family deprived Woodruff's government and associations of this resource for getting things done.

This loss of charisma would not have been so serious for the community if other families could have succeeded the Davenports. Since the local economy was becoming increasingly involved in the manufacturing function of Metropolitan City, local entrepeneurs had fewer chances to contribute significantly to the community's development than had been the case in previous decades. And few, if any, of the remaining families with strong links to Woodruff's pioneering period had compiled the record of community accomplishment that the Davenports possessed. The downfall of the Davenport family diminished the prestige of local leadership and further sapped the confidence of leaders in their abilities to meet the challenges that another world war soon would bring the locality.

Two aspects of wartime industrialization strengthened these fears and contributed to a definition of economic development as a threat rather than an opportunity to solve or remedy the shortage of territory and industrial tax base which leaders had recognized by the thirties. The first concerned the role of complex extralocal agencies —the federal government and Midwest Motors—in initiating the developments. The sheer size of these organizations and the distance of their headquarters from Woodruff, especially that of the federal government, occasioned some concern over the ability of local organizations to influence their decisions. Second, magnitude and rapidity of the changes intensified profound fears that the traditional social order would be overturned. The changes seemed destined to take responsibility for local affairs away from the families whose members, over the years, had made the greatest investment in terms of wealth, risk, ideas, and work. If the plan for the bomber plant were realized and the expectation of a hundred thousand workers came close to fulfillment, Woodruff could become an industrial, working-class city run by the United Automobile Workers.

The initial reactions of city officials established the strategy of conserving community structure against the tides of change. They refused to adopt policies that would encourage industrialization or assist the township to adjust to economic growth. City officials offered minimal water service to the bomber factory, opposed construction of Shady Lea Village, and refused to provide sanitary services to residents of the area. These decisions confirmed the predilection of city officials and leaders to look inward and to minimize as far as possible the changes that industrialization might bring. The restrictionist pattern emphasized the performance of basic housekeeping duties for the city, at what seemed minimal financial costs and risks. Officials were entirely willing to allow township officials and organizations to deal with the problems created by industrialization in the rural, undeveloped municipality. The weakening of city leadership during the depression and the enormity and suddenness of wartime industrialization led Woodruff's policy makers to reject the alternative that could have eased or eliminated the structural limitations of area political structure—organized co-operation between city and township and merger.

Township officials could do little one way or the other during the war. Once the decision to construct the bomber plant had been made and the land assembled, matters rested largely with extralocal organizations. The critical time came at the end of the war. The basic issue concerned ownership of the sanitary systems whose construction had been financed by the federal government. A number of factors entered into the decisions to acquire these facilities and to operate them in a manner that facilitated the economic and social development of the municipality. One set of factors concerned the mechanics of the acquisition. These included: first, the pressures exerted on township officials by Pacific Motors to purchase the facilities; second, the rules of the federal government permitting a virtual discount in price of 100 percent; third, the persuasive arguments of Nelson and Lockwood, assisted by Vanderpoole (see Chapter 4); fourth, the refusal of city officials to compete for the facilities. A second consideration on the part of some township officials, especially the supervisor, was the recognition that this acquisition would achieve several important goals: first, establish township government as an effective organization; second, provide the township with the facilities needed to protect itself from annexation and to punish Woodruff in this manner for what many in the township considered to be years of mistreatment.

The circumstances surrounding the acquisition, the commitment to the federal government on use of the facilities to solve health problems, and the need to encourage industrial development to maintain the solvency of the utilities department led to the adoption of the expansionist pattern. Whatever changes in economic and political structure resulted from this commitment were accepted. Officials believed that in so doing the future of the township as a separate municipality would thereby be assured.

Persistence of the Decision-Making Patterns

To understand the persistence of city and township government and the respective decision-making patterns, attention must focus on the groups that benefited from these circumstances. Attention must also be given to the groups favoring change, the reasons for their activities, and an examination of how each municipality has dealt with the conflict between proponents and opponents of political change.

Two consequences of the persistence of divided government outweigh many others. First, whether the factories were inside or outside the limits of the city mattered little to Woodruff's economy. Location of industrial plants in the township brought as much wealth to the city's economy as location within Woodruff's borders. A substantial proportion of plant payrolls were deposited in local banks and spent in local stores, and a large portion of plant expenditures were made in local enterprises. As indicated by the growth in bank deposits over the years, many different sectors of Woodruff's economy benefited from the increase in township population and in area wealth (see Chapter 5). Some of Woodruff's ranking leaders, e.g., the McDowells and Scheibles, retained positions of influence over the years while enjoying satisfactory returns from investments in downtown property and businesses and from stock in the three locally owned fiscal organizations. These leaders and many of the downtown businessmen tended to be unconcerned over the problems created by area political structure.

In one respect the limited territory and tax base affected Woodruff's economy adversely. The comparatively small industrial component of the local tax base and its low rate of growth since the mid-fifties necessitated annual increases in the tax rate since 1955.

The fiscal crisis of 1967 suggests that this trend will continue for many years[2] (see Chapter 2). The more burdensome and disagreeable the property tax becomes in Woodruff, the more local business leaders will be disposed to regard the preservation of the power structure as an expensive consequence of the continuity of area political structure. The time may yet come when Woodruff's leaders will view some redistribution of political power downward in the stratification system as more than balanced by a cut in local taxes and gains in the effectiveness of government. When this situation comes to pass, Woodruff's leaders may give wholehearted support to a merger campaign. These influentials might have reached this opinion much earlier had not the tax rate declined substantially between 1947 and 1954 while improvement of the utility systems was postponed.

A second consequence of area political structure pertains to class and leadership. Continued application of the restrictionist pattern effectively diverted substantial economic and population growth to the township. As a result, competition and conflict in Woodruff for public offices with leaders of blue-collar groups was not significantly increased. Blue-collar leaders and the groups they represented moved relatively quickly into the higher levels of the township's political structure. This movement, accompanied by the displacement of groups that traditionally had been allied to the Republican party, was symbolized by the Democratic sweep of the township board in the spring of 1957 and by the predominance of Democrats on the board for every term thereafter with few exceptions. Given the economic and organizational background of Woodruff's leaders (see Chapter 3), the blue-collar and the southern white minority groups could not have made comparable political gains in Woodruff.

The political ascendance in the township of groups in the lower-middle and upper working class constituted a situation of status incongruance that strengthened the loyalty of these groups to the

2. The mayor once again appointed a citizens committee in 1969 to consider the advantages and disadvantages of a city income tax. A similar committee several years earlier had recommended that such a tax not be adopted. Re-examination of this issue soon after the level of property assessment had been increased from 29 to 50 percent of market value indicated the growing seriousness of Woodruff's limited tax base.

township and to area political structure.[3] Having gained a measure
of political influence greater than their position in the class system
ordinarily allows, the blue-collar and southern white groups in the
township population ardently opposed proposals for political reorganization that would force them to compete for political ascendancy with Woodruff's upper classes. Maintaining township autonomy
was synonymous with preserving their political and leadership resources. By diverting industrial development to the township, Woodruff's leaders gained powerful allies for efforts to prevent merger.

Leaders of both city and township, over the years, have largely
had their way. These influentials have been among the principal
beneficiaries of the persistence of area political structure, a circumstance that accords with leader intentions.

Decision-Making Patterns and Leadership Inaction

Woodruff's officials used procedures for accomplishing their objectives which avoided arousing citizenry that reportedly had expressed
support for quite different goals. Since the voters had approved of
annexation and merger in every election held since the twenties,
city officials could have obtained support for an aggressive utilities
policy. How had the governing elite been able to maintain the boundaries of Woodruff without provoking public opinion to endorse a
contrary course of action? Three principal techniques were employed: nondecision making, negative decision making, and minimal
support for programs of change. The effectiveness of these techniques played an important role in preserving area political structure
in the postwar era. They suppressed the self-regulating tendency of
the city as a social system.[4]

3. For a discussion of status congruence and incongruence see the following: Gerhard Lenski, "Social Participation and Status Crystallization,"
American Sociological Review, 21 (August, 1956), 458–64, and "Status
Crystallization: A Non-Vertical Dimension of Social Status," *American
Sociological Review,* 19 (June, 1954), 405–13.
4. The concept of equilibrium is based on the idea of a system's ability to
protect forms of social life against disturbing forces. Vilfredo Pareto, *Vilfredo Pareto: Sociological Writings,* ed., Samuel E. Finer; trans., Derick Mirfin,
(New York: Praeger, 1966), pp. 104–7. For a contemporary interpretation of the equilibrium concept see Talcott Parsons, *The Social System* (Glen-

Both nondecision making and negative decision making occurred when opportunities materialized for establishing a new policy toward the township, one of assistance and co-operation, or for acquiring facilities that could have led to increasing dependence of the township on the city. Nondecision making refers to the reactions of city officials to happenings for which the obligation to act did not exist but the opportunity, the right, and the authority to do so could not be doubted. These were situations in which initiative in trying out a novel strategy or course of action was required, situations involving some risk of failure or disappointment. The principal example concerns the events culminating in the purchase by the township of the water and sewer systems that had been financed by the federal government. In this instance officials refused to intervene in a sequence of events initiated by executives of Pacific Motors and members of township government. To many if not all interested citizens of Woodruff, the transactions probably seemed "natural"—township officials should acquire facilities in their municipality. This reaction took city officials "off the hook." The nondecision making of city officials prevented the creation of an alternative to which federal officials, interested in obtaining a decent price for the facilities, might have given serious consideration (see Chapter 4). Nondecision making also describes the failure of city leaders to follow up the interest executives of Universal Motors expressed in 1958 in a study of city and township governments (see Chapter 8).

Negative decision making took place when city officials received a formal request that could not be ignored: a response had to be given. Rejecting the request to provide water to Shady Lea Village deprived Woodruff of the opportunity of making a large area of the township dependent upon the city for its water supply. The concern for township people expressed by this action could have been a

coe, Ill.: The Free Press, 1951), pp. 480–84, 490–92. Concerning resistance to change, Nett has written: ". . . interpreting the history of mankind even conservatively, there is too much evidence that persons in the role of conformer fail to revitalize society and sustain a healthy social organization. Under conformer dominance, institutions lose their vitality, neglecting the needs of individuals, or satisfying them only in token fashion. . . . " Roger Nett, "Conformity-Deviation and the Social Control Concept," in Walter Buckley, ed., *Modern Systems Research for the Behavioral Scientist* (Chicago: Aldine Publishing Company, 1968), p. 412.

major step toward establishing broad areas of co-operation between the two municipalities.

The third technique for eliminating opportunities for accomplishing social change pertains to the granting of limited assistance to an enterprise contrary to the policies and goals of city officials. Negative decision making could not be used for the petitioners were in a position to harm the policy makers. Such an action could have galvanized some type of opposition movement. Minimal assistance characterized adoption of Sampson's and rejection of Davenport's recommendation on fund raising for the 1958 merger campaign (see Chapter 8). Small sums were raised from a large number of persons over an extended time period in preference to large contributions from a few men. This and other forms of token support shielded leaders opposed to merger from criticism by its supporters. Responsibility for the proposal's defeat could be placed elsewhere.

The refusal of officials in 1941 to sell more than a small amount of water to the bomber plant also exemplifies minimal assistance. While it was difficult, even impossible, to refuse agents of the federal government at that critical period, it was permissible to reject other alternatives such as a pipe line to a source of water near the county seat, a plan implemented in the sixties.

These techniques either allowed changes to occur which strengthened the autonomy of the two municipalities or squandered opportunities for developing programs of intermunicipal co-operation. The secrecy attending most of the events mentioned above and the need for haste gave officials considerable leeway in choosing a course of action. The absence of an obligation to act also shielded officials and leaders from criticism. In effect, city officials and leaders were not accountable for nondecision making or tokenism.

Supporting Organizations

These procedures for stifling innovation would have been far less effective had not various organizations directly or indirectly provided assistance. *The Woodruff Press* aided city officials, especially in the forties and early fifties, by not educating the public on the significance of the township's industrial park, transportation network, and sanitary facilities. Amdur, Sr., made little or no effort to contradict in the newspaper the opinion prevalent among many city officials and leaders that the township would revert to its prewar functions and population when the war ended. Amdur, Sr., did not explore in the paper the local factors that assured the continued growth of manufacturing in the Woodruff area. He failed to inform citizens of the township's efforts to acquire the sanitary facilities and the significance of this action. Nor did Amdur, Sr., warn readers of the possibility of township incorporation and of a static tax base. The silence of the newspaper encouraged Woodruff's leaders to subordinate the adaptive needs of Woodruff to the goal of maintaining city boundaries and the ascendancy of the stratum that traditionally had influenced public policy. The case for enduring a period of intense political conflict and for yielding some political power to the Democratic party and the working class in exchange for economic and territorial growth was never made during or after World War II.

The failure of the local newspaper to serve as a critic of administrative policy and as an agency for educating the citizenry on the significance of wartime industrialization reversed the role played by the paper in the twenties. During that period Amdur, Sr., was a vigorous critic of governmental policy, including actions on annexation and sanitary facilities. The factors responsible for the change in editorial and reportorial policies indirectly served to strengthen Woodruff's decision-making pattern. The facts suggest a number of reasons. First, Amdur's newspaper criticism seldom was rewarded. Amdur, Sr., was not named to the Board of the National Bank in 1933, despite ardent efforts to assist its establishment. The other directors felt that the editor's views would embroil the bank in controversy and antagonize customers. Second, investments in local real estate seemingly proved more rewarding financially than the newspaper. In this respect Amdur, Sr., along with other local businessmen profited from the industrial and population growth of the Woodruff area. In the fifties, and until the paper was sold, Amdur, Jr., did not pay the salaries needed to hire a competent staff of reporters. Reliance on semiprofessionals also made it difficult to ferret out the stories on municipal policies and decisions.

The purchase of the newspaper by the Kent Group, and subsequently by the Clark Corporation, resulted in the restoration of a critical editorial policy and an improvement in news reporting. Although these changes were not reflected in the results of the 1964 merger election, the educational impact of the newspaper should not be discounted. It served to make citizens aware of alternatives to divided government during a period in which the mounting local taxes in both city and township induced considerable concern over the future of the area. The newspaper under new management provided advocates of intermunicipal co-operation and of merger with an instrument for persuading the public of the soundness of these innovations.

The Chamber of Commerce over the years also assisted public officials in maintaining the limited territory of the city and in diverting much of the industrial and population growth to the township. Like the newspaper, the Chamber exerted its influence in the selection of issues to be brought before the community. The Chamber helped launch and carry out the campaign for adoption of forms of government that strengthened the political grip of the Republican party and higher classes. It did not, on the other hand, make an issue of the failure of city officials to provide sanitary facilities with surplus capacity sufficient for serving outlying areas. The Chamber did not oppose the failure to expand the capacities of the utility systems at the end of the war and related actions that contradicted the recommendations of the sanitary engineers. Finally, the Chamber assisted the township rather than the city in the purchase of the utility plants owned by the federal government.

The executives of the two banks provided little or no support for efforts or proposals to modify area political structure. These men defined their interests narrowly, always in terms of the economic standing of the banks which improved as alert management enabled the organizations to benefit from the economic growth of the area. The profound emphasis that officers and directors of the banks placed on caution, on avoiding as many risks as possible, and on the primacy of immediate over long-term benefits expressed in many ways the principle underlying Woodruff's restrictionist pattern.

The principal force for shaping public opinion (the newspaper), the major agency for mobilizing community resources (the Chamber), and an important agency for legitimizing community proposals (the banks) were on the side of constancy and persistance in political structure. Each, along with the three techniques mentioned above, operated to prevent various inadequacies of city and township government from becoming issues. Each tended to stifle opposition to municipal policies and to hamper the critics of divided government.

Secrecy and effective township leadership contributed to the efficacy of these factors. Since so few persons in Woodruff knew of the action and inaction that had contributed to the above-mentioned developments, events appeared to occur in a "natural" or inevitable fashion. It was widely believed that nothing more could have been done to prevent township self-sufficiency or to accomplish Woodruff's territorial expansion. This conclusion is of some importance in a municipality whose citizens consistently favored annexation. By giving lip service to the goals of expansion, Woodruff's leaders seemed to be in accord with prevailing sentiment, while blaming failure on township opposition to merger proposals. Since this explanation was consistent with the behavior of township voters, it had credibility and plausibility.

Merger Campaigns

The outcome of the merger campaigns provides additional evidence for the view that Woodruff could not effectively utilize certain adaptive mechanisms. The campaigns were twisted to serve purposes other than unification of the two municipalities. In every instance in which a merger campaign was initiated, in 1950, 1957, and 1963, the movement accomplished a defensive goal, prevention of township incorporation. While the movements kept alive the possibility of Woodruff's territorial expansion, the two recent campaigns discouraged subsequent efforts to accomplish large-scale political change. The failure of three merger attempts convinced many people that the proposal was not feasible for the Woodruff area.

The circumstances in which each effort was initiated did little to enhance prospects for success. As the leaders of one movement generally had little or no connection with previous sponsors, they had little knowledge of the details of the earlier campaign and had difficulty correcting past errors. Plans were made hurriedly, under the impetus of a belief in the immanency of a township drive for separate incorporation. Information was scarce on the inadequacies of local governments, and data on the benefits of merger were even scarcer. These factual deficiencies combined with inadequate support from city leaders and the unyielding resistence of township leaders made involvement a punishing and, for most city influentials, a risky course of action.

Each campaign drained Woodruff of resources essential for the accomplishment of social change while strengthening opponents of merger. Those leaders and citizens who became active in the campaign found the experience painful and discouraging. Understandably, influentials who took an active part in one campaign remained aloof from the subsequent effort.

Campaign workers responded in a similar manner. The punishment handed out by the opposition and the lack of support from Woodruff's leaders quickly induced battle fatigue. Each campaign required a new crop of workers and leaders. This in itself reduced the prospect for success as the changeover in personnel decreased the amount of feedback between the previous and the current campaign.

The leaders and workers in the township thrived on merger campaigns. Township leaders demonstrated their prowess as defenders of the municipality, and the increased public exposure assisted persons interested in a career in local politics. Campaign workers also enjoyed the involvement in local affairs and gained satisfaction from the defense of their municipality.

The Functions of Area Political Structure

Considering the manner in which wartime industrialization was initiated and the extensiveness of change within a short time period, continuity of government and of local leadership manifests the resiliency and staying power of local institutions. Neither city nor township as social systems were disorganized or crushed by wartime developments. The insistence on local control of local government, the local efforts for responding to municipal difficulties, and the continued vitality of the Chamber, the banks, and other associations further supports the conclusion that the two social systems were not overwhelmed by external forces. The large voter turnouts in the township for merger elections and the energies both sides expended in the struggle also indicate the commitments to and interest in local affairs of residents of the area. Conflict, although divisive, reveals the concern of residents for their groups, organizations, and community. It is a manifestation of the large investment, emotional and economic, that residents have made in the Woodruff area. The two municipalities evolved specializations in economic and social structure which constituted a functional pattern of interdependence. The city remained the area center of stability, providing the main links with the past, while the township facilitated and encouraged growth, welcoming new industry and new residents. Each municipal role was the complement of, and indispensable for, the other. By confining its interests to stability and to retaining the configuration of its century-old social structure, the city encouraged the development of the township. Conversely, by providing an environment hospitable to factories and the families of employees, the township reduced the pressures on Woodruff for political and economic change. Township specialization in manufacturing enabled the city to remain specialized for education and services.

The combination of the city's restrictionist and the township's expansionist pattern made it possible for the Woodruff area to benefit from the accessibility to Metropolitan City and, through its airport, to every other metropolis in the nation, thereby providing the facilities needed for industrial expansion. Dominance of restrictionist patterns in both municipalities would have discouraged economic development, and expansionist patterns in both city and township might have supported rapid economic growth with far more conflict and bitterness among residents and officials of the two municipalities. An expansionist pattern in the city and a restrictionist pattern in the township probably would have led to merger of the two municipalities. Whether economic development would have been more or less rapid is problematic. This study can be thought of as an effort to understand the factors responsible for adoption of the first instead of the fourth combination.

The restrictionist pattern in Woodruff also facilitated continuity in the preferred image of the municipality as a center of commerce and education, not industry, despite the size and importance of its factories. In this respect residents of Woodruff preferred to think of their community as in the same league as County Seat City, whose prestige derived from its nationally renowned university, major research enterprises, and residential areas suitable for top executives of firms throughout the Metropolitan City area. This image of Woodruff, whatever its flaws and dysfunctions in terms of city and township relationships, supported local morale, interest, and commitment. The rapid growth of the local university in the sixties provided factual support for the image of Woodruff as an educational center and middle-class community.

The former bomber factory and the Shady Lea area remained the outward symbols of Woodruff Township. Although its occupational and class composition differed little from that of Woodruff, it was perceived by local and neighboring citizens as an industrial municipality. The heritage of Shady Lea Village also was manifest in the persistence of the notion that the township was more of a "lower-class" community than most others in the county. Regardless of the validity of these perceptions, township government with its partisan elections, strong political parties, and accessibility to blue-collar workers and their families served major integrative functions. Newcomers who showed an interest in and a talent for local politics, whether for bell ringing and transporting people to the polls or for speech and strategy making, had little difficulty finding useful work in the party of their choice. Persistence and hard work often led to a position in the party and to candidacy for local office. Meetings of the township board provided the best entertainment one could find in the Woodruff area. Only meetings on merger could prove more exciting and interesting.

The specialization of function and of decision-making pattern enabled the Woodruff area to grow economically and demographically with a minimum of institutional dislocation and conflict between "oldtimers" and "newcomers," "majority" and "minority" groups, the middle class and the working class, and the local leaders and executives of absentee-owned industry.

The Future

While the present social and political organization of the Woodruff area may continue for many years, major changes seem inevitable. The structural features of each municipality which limit the ability of each to obtain the fiscal inputs needed for effective operations will produce ever more intense conflicts as growth continues. As this occurs, the importance of the choice between merger or township incorporation, between reorganization of area political structure or permanency of the divided pattern, also will grow.

The suitability of the Woodruff area for manufacturing and the trends in the metropolitan region which increase enrollment at the local university undermine the specialization of function between city and township. Every effort to accommodate to the increasing needs for essential services has been frustrated by continued population and economic growth. Every increase in tax rates and assessment level has provided temporary relief. Each administration, city and township, moves from one fiscal crisis to the next, seeking funds to provide the services needed by the population and local organizations. Continued area development soon will compel leaders of each municipality to choose between area political reorganization and deterioration of the effectiveness and legitimacy of each unit of government.

The merger campaigns provided time for coping with these problems. No final, irreversible changes have been implemented. In this sense the political future of the area is "open-ended." A number of factors suggest that township incorporation is not inevitable. The fact that no determined and organized movement for incorporation of the township as a separate municipality had developed may indicate the existence and strength of integrative forces. Certainly, if township leaders believed that such a move had the solid support of township residents, they would have been able to circulate and file petitions before city leaders could frustrate the endeavor.

Perhaps the identity of name, the common post office, and the porousness of social boundaries in terms of churches, school districts, the Community Fund, and other civic associations has maintained feelings of unity that have not been especially noticeable in the past. Second, newspaper advocacy of intermunicipal cooperation and the joint performance of certain government functions keeps several alternatives before the public. These may be taken seriously when some crisis in the operations of one or both governments occur. Third, the establishment in 1969 of a joint city-township authority, at the instigation of Midwest Motors, to manage and develop for recreational purposes the lake surrounded by both municipalities may mark the beginning of a trend toward establishment of formal patterns of co-operation. Should this authority succeed in providing substantial recreational benefits for the Woodruff area, additional efforts may be made to use similar strategy for the provision of other municipal services. Should this trend materialize, it might forestall township incorporation and lead ultimately to merger of the two municipalities. Although the initiation of this trend in 1970 is at least twenty years late, it does not appear to be "too late." In the final analysis, this may be the decisive consideration.

Coda

This study has described and analyzed the reactions of two, interdependent municipalities to conditions of endemic conflict for a period of about thirty years. The political structure of the township and the ecological structure of the Woodruff area made extremely difficult the task of each government of acquiring the amount of revenues required for meeting effectively the service needs of a growing community. These structural factors hampered the effectiveness and threatened the legitimacy of both governments. Ultimately the conflict would be resolved if either the rate of growth became infinitesimal or fundamental changes were made in area governmental structure.

Reactions to this conflict were made within the framework of divided government. Officials sought to cope with the problems within their territory independent of the neighboring municipality. Innovations, such as the acquisition of sanitary facilities by township government and the establishment of a utilities department, were confined to the pattern of dual government. Other options, such as contractual agreements between the two municipalities for joint performance of area functions, the establishment of special districts, and merger, either have not been attempted or have been defeated. For these and related reasons, it has been concluded that municipal reactions to the conditions of conflict have minimized innovation in structure. The behavior of each municipality has been characterized by rigidity. Maintaining the two governments has taken and held precedence over establishing an adequate level of operational effectiveness by these organizations.

Analysis has concentrated on the interaction between certain normative features of decision making, the activities of several organized power centers—the banks, the Chamber of Commerce, the newspaper—as a force for mobilizing public opinion and developing issues, and the consequences for area political structure. Skillful use of such techniques as nondecision making and negative decision making by powerful agencies has permitted the supporters of the decision-making patterns to produce and maintain features of social organization considered desirable. The decision-making patterns, by defining situations and arranging priorities among objectives, helped to co-ordinate the activities of several organizations over an extended time period. Features of social organization thus have been conserved despite rapid growth of industry, university enrollment, the number of inhabitants, and the number of community organizations. Despite abundant evidence scattered throughout the volume of the pluralist character of leadership in both municipalities and the fluidity of leadership in the township, influentials largely have had their way. The continuity and exercise of decision-making patterns, not the concentration of power, has made the difference.

By providing "ready-made" policies, the decision-making pattern discouraged officials from "thinking through" the implications of their choices. The problems appeared to officials in the context of the immediate situation and its fiscal dimension.[5] By facilitating the process of reaching a decision and by discouraging a search for new procedures for disposing of a problem, the decision-making pattern enabled the day-to-day actions of local government to be conducted in a manner consistent with leader preferences on handling the conflict between adaptive and political prerequisites.

Although this study has concentrated on decision-making patterns in a few areas of government, especially those related to sanitary services, they operate also in other areas of municipal activities.

5. Richard Neustadt discusses the factors that influenced perception of several complex problems and the decisions reached by several presidents. Richard E. Neustadt, *Presidential Power: The Politics of Leadership* (New York: The New American Library, 1964).

The premises underlying the patterns of one area, especially those concerned with such matters as risk, size of fiscal investment, and the balancing of immediate and long-range benefits, may be operative in many other areas. We would expect to find policies similar to those in sanitary services in such spheres as education, welfare, and recreation.

The role of the pattern in decision making does not explain the factors influencing adoption of a particular pattern. It does not adequately explain the rigidity of response of a social system to internal conditions of stress and conflict because of refusal of leaders to consider other available lines of action. This rigidity is of prime importance, as an alternative situation might readily have occurred, one in which officials in 1941 might have viewed industrial development in the township as the opportunity to solve or greatly ease the city's shortage of land and the industrial tax base both for the present and the future. The confidence of Woodruff's leadership had been weakened by the struggle in the depression to save strategic organizations and the recent decline of a prominent family. It considered itself gravely threatened by the rapid growth of potentially hostile centers of power and by involvement in local affairs of complex organizations that were difficult to influence from the local level. Rigidity of reaction and policy seemed to be a product of both external threat and inner fear of total displacement by alien groups, fear of a complete loss of control. There appeared but one choice: struggle to prevent this eventuality, a struggle that considered the preservation of the local organization of power as a top priority objective.

To achieve flexibility in responding to a variety of complex and changing situations, both internal and external, the following factors would appear to be necessary or useful: leaders who have confidence in their abilities to cope with the problem and who do not exaggerate the magnitude of the difficulty or the inevitability of disaster; encouragement of organizations to criticize existing policies and to entertain alternative proposals; reliance on specialists in a variety of areas to evaluate existing arrangements and to provide suggestions for different policies; development of facilities for collecting and analyzing information on the operations of social structures; accessibility of the government to organized groups with varying needs and policy preferences; agencies of mass communication that regularly offer intelligent evaluation of official policies; and a two-party system that represents the broad range of interests found in the social organization of the community. A high level of efficiency and legitimacy of institutions seems to require the organization and encouragement of restrained conflict among major interests and points of view, with each having the opportunity to gain power and determine policy. Inflexible decision-making patterns in a changing world can hasten the decline of a society or a community.

1. Leader Interview Schedule

NAME:

General questions:

1. In your opinion, what are the principal problems facing Woodruff today?
2. What is being done to solve these problems?
3. Do you feel that the attempted consolidation would have (would not have) helped solve some of the problems of the area?
4. Were you active in Woodruff during the attempted annexation of Shady Lea Village and the Pacific Motors plant by the city in 1950?
5. Who were the men who took an active part in this issue in both the city and township?
6. Why did the proposed annexation of 1950 fail?

Questions on community leadership:

7. In your opinion, who are the top leaders in the city? (The men who get things done, who make decisions)

299

8. Who are the top leaders in the township of Woodruff?
9. Are there any leaders in the city who also are leaders in the township?
10. Are there any leaders in the township who also are leaders in the city?
11. If an important project was in the works, what leaders would have to be involved to give the project a good chance of success?

Questions about past events:

12. Which leaders were largely responsible for the revision and acceptance of the city charter in 1947?
13. Which leaders were largely responsible for the annexation of the 610 acres and the paper factory last year?
14. Which leaders are working for the redevelopment of the downtown business district?
15. What interest groups are influential in the community?
16. Who are the leaders of these groups?
17. Why do these groups have such influence?
18. Did these groups give their full support to consolidation?
19. Why?

Background questions:

20. What is your age?
21. What is your marital status?
22. If married, how many children do you have?
23. How many married children do you have?
24. If (23) yes, do they live in Woodruff?
25. How many years of formal education have you had?
26. When did you first come to Woodruff?
27. From what town did you come?
28. What is your occupation?
29. What church do you belong to, if any?
30. What organizations do you belong to? (Woodruff, County Seat, State, National)
31. Do you hold an office in any of these at present?

32. What offices, if any, did you hold in the past?
33. Do you hold any board positions? In what organizations or agencies?
34. What board positions, if any, have you held in the past? In what organizations or agencies?
35. Where do you usually eat lunch? (breakfast?)
36. With whom do you usually eat?
37. How often do you eat with————?

2. Methodology

History of the Study

The researchers lived in the Woodruff area from the fall of 1956 until August, 1963. During the first year of residency, the authors rented an apartment in the city. A few months before the initiation of the study, because of the lack of new homes in the city, the authors purchased a home in the eastern section of the township, a short drive from the downtown area. For most of the residency period in the Woodruff area, the authors were citizens of the township, privileged to vote in township elections and to attend meetings of the township board.

The study was initiated by accident rather than by design. A few months after moving into their new township home in August, 1957, they received a call from a Jaycee leader under the guise of soliciting business for his dry cleaning firm. He soon came to the point of his visit, an invitation to attend a meeting of the Jaycee leaders concerned with unifying city and township and a request to provide assistance. After attending the first meeting, the authors decided that an organized effort to reorganize the political structure of the area was worthy of serious investigation. We requested and received permission from the Jaycee leaders to attend their meetings for the purpose of making a study. Subsequently the authors also gained entree to the closed meetings of the city leaders who were assisting the Jaycees.

During the consolidation movement that was the first phase of this study, when the researchers were busily trying to attend all of the meetings connected with the campaign, they recognized the existence and importance of activity that there was no time to observe. A considerable amount of planning and discussion went on necessarily in social settings removed from the interested eyes of the researchers. Efforts to understand the decisions of the various participants in the campaign, both for and against merger, required additional data. There were many questions raised during the first seven months of consolidation observation which only a longer study could answer. There were questions of history, leadership, community institutions and organizations. Answering one question seemed to produce new "holes" in the data that led to another lengthy search and another phase in the effort to know Woodruff.

The second phase of the research consisted of formal interviews with seventy-seven leaders, mostly from the city and the township and a few from County Seat City. In addition to providing data on persons reputed to be leaders, the interviews introduced the researchers to a wider circle of influentials than those involved in the consolidation campaign. Of equal importance, several respondents provided leads on where to look for the data that would help unravel and understand the tangle of intermunicipal relationships. These "leads" included the development of the sanitary facilities of both municipalities, the history of Shady Lea Village, the reorganization of the banks in the thirties and the role of the banks in the community, the change in the form of city government in 1946, and the 1950 merger attempt. During this phase, which lasted roughly two years, the researchers also participated as actively in township affairs as time permitted. They sought in this way to develop the contacts with township leaders which had been established with many leaders of the city.

The third phase consisted of efforts to "run down" the above mentioned "leads." This lasted for at least three years, until the authors moved away from Woodruff. During this time the records in the basement of city hall were carefully examined; the proceedings of the city council and the township board were read; *The Woodruff*

Press was read from the 1900's to the present period, concentrating on actions of governmental bodies, the Chamber, the banks, sanitary facilities, annexations and mergers, and various local controversies. Additional information was sought from persons believed to be knowledgeable in these specialized areas. They included, for example, the sanitary engineers and the managers of the utilities department for both municipalities, bank officers, the executive secretary of the Chamber, etc. The authors also participated in various community organizations discussed below.

The fourth phase of the study began in the spring of 1963, when the authors again were asked to assist the effort to merge city and township. They had not planned to add a second campaign to their monograph, but the opportunity to compare two attempts could not be overlooked. This phase lasted until August, 1963, when the researchers left the community.

The fifth and final phase consisted of efforts to organize and analyze the data and to prepare a manuscript. This phase, lasted, off and on, for over five years. During this period information on the Woodruff area was obtained primarily from *The Woodruff Press* and public and private documents. Additional information on the 1963 merger campaign was obtained from correspondence with several city and township residents and from the files that were kept on the election controversy. A few additional interviews were held with Woodruff residents.

The First Years

During the first years of study, observations were made of the way in which city and township leaders went about solving or failing to solve community problems. In the first year of the research project the attempt, referred to above, was made to consolidate the city and township governments. The heated controversy it aroused created an excellent vantage point from which to view the decision-making process. Throughout the struggle, after the first Jaycee hurdle, the researchers observed the closed meetings of several city groups as they operated behind the scenes.

Gaining entree to meetings of promerger leaders necessarily limited the nature of the contacts that could be established with opponents of merger during the campaign. As township citizens, however, the researchers were free to attend the public meetings of the antimerger group and the sessions of the township board. They identified themselves to various township leaders and informed them of the research activities. During the consolidation campaign cordial but somewhat superficial relations were established with these township influentials. By playing a waiting game, the groundwork was laid for better rapport once the campaign had ended.

Subsequently, much energy was devoted to establishing communication linkages with knowledgeable and influential township residents through formal and informal interviews. For six years the researchers attended most meetings of the township board, the township Democratic party, and many sessions of other governmental bodies. They also became active in a local civic association and joined with a number of leaders in an abortive effort to organize a township civic association from the remains of the Save the Township Committee. In this manner contact was made with leaders from all parts of the township and with most political influentials.

Throughout the period of field work two problems had to be faced. First, integrity, trust, and confidence had to be maintained with persons who thought their views on government unification differed from those of the researchers. Pains had to be taken to inform the opponents of consolidation of the nature of the researchers affiliation with the Jaycees. At the same time, the frequent contacts and association with persons who had fought unification could have made us suspect in the eyes of some of its supporters. Leaders on both sides had to be educated concerning the imperatives of social research, the necessity for freedom in selecting respondents.

The terms stated in the original study request to the Jaycees indicated that it would be necessary to observe the township residents and any group that developed to fight or assist consolidation. Therefore, the researchers were seen and had been seen during the first years of this study with such a variety of city and township leaders, the least and the most prestigious, that each group assumed the association was part of the research program. On a number of occasions over the years, the writers were confidants of individuals who were in direct, personal, political, or economic conflict with each other. To maintain a high level of rapport with these acquaintances it was necessary to minimize the discussion of one antagonist to another and to restate our position from time to time. These were difficult but necessary roles to play; ones that paid high dividends in data collection. These positions seemed precarious when, at public meetings, leaders of one side or another sat next to the researchers or attempted to confer with them. Perhaps the impression was the authors' own stimulated by the pressure of feeling that they were playing both ends against the middle. On such occasions, the urgency of the matters under consideration led most participants, after a brief look at the researchers, to give most of their attention to the business of the community. In retrospect, candor in discussing the purposes of activities and commitment to the goal of research seemed to allay whatever suspicions respondents may have had. In any event, only two persons refused to be interviewed.

Numerous sources of data were used for the study of the Woodruff area. Seventy-seven formal interviews with community leaders were held with the assistance of an interview schedule. More than 150 informal interviews were conducted with representatives of civic, fraternal, social, and political organizations, occupational and status groups that gave the community structure and helped it to perform. Many of the informal interviews were held in the homes and offices of respondents, at the hotel or other gathering places, or on the street. No schedule was used for these informal meetings and no notes were taken during the interview. The procedure resembled a friendly conversation between persons who were equally knowledgeable of and interested in local problems. Notes were made later, then classified and filed.

A mail questionnaire was submitted to all directors and top officers of the two banks and the locally owned savings and loan association. For additional detailed information on the local banking situation, interviews were held with the board chairmen, president, several vice-presidents, and approximately half of the directors of each bank. To gain a balanced view of the local fiscal institutions, bankers were interviewed in three neighboring cities. Statistical data on the banks were obtained from Moody's guide to financial institutions. Banker action and inaction was observed and recorded during the course of community project development, e.g., the merger campaigns, the shopping centers, the mall.

In pertinent areas of community life, the interviews were followed by exploration of public records and information in the files of organizations, and back again. One source of information tended to illuminate data obtained from the other. Often minutes of meetings or particular items of correspondence raised questions that had to be answered by a particular person. On other occasions information in the minutes of an organization or a newspaper column illuminated events that had been recounted by respondents. The files of the Chamber of Commerce and of the city manager of Woodruff, the proceedings of city and township governments, and the property assessment rolls were examined. Every available issue of *The Woodruff Press* was read with particular reference to banking, utilities, annexation, community organizations, and action and inaction in areas of interest. This provided a seventy-eight year record of local events. Census publications provided demographic data and indicators of ecological and social structure.

Role Playing

It was obvious from the beginning of this project that the writers would not fill a strictly traditional field-work role. Most community researchers live for a year or two in their study communities and are classified as "outsiders." No one presumably believes they plan to make the research unit their home. In this sense and in all of its ramifications the position of the researchers differed. Woodruff was their home. They owned the house in which they lived, earned their daily bread within the confines of Woodruff's legal boundaries, joined as permanent, working members many of its organizations, and their child was born there.

These circumstances created both opportunities and perils. As local residents, they had the right to attend the meetings of certain public agencies. At the same time, it was no less legitimate for various persons to seek to involve them in enterprises and capacities that went beyond the participant-observer role deemed essential for completion of the research task. Occasionally efforts were made to use their status as professors and researchers to advance the special interests of a particular person or group. The boundary line had to be carefully drawn since this desire provided the basis for gaining entree to the groups that required study.

Participation in the community as permanent members also enabled many persons to observe the researchers in more general roles, such as members of a family, customer, patient, friend or casual acquaintance, as host and hostess, and as guests. The information gathered on these occasions seemed to have made the actors appear less threatening when playing the role of researcher. At the same time, extended involvement in local affairs and frequent association with certain of the residents increased the danger of losing the objective, analytical perspective.

After the first four months of study it became apparent that the "role-playing" would be mainly confined to three principle overlapping role areas: institutional-academic, organizational, and social. The first, institutional-academic, was used more than might ordinarily have been the case. Throughout the study the researchers' connection with the local university and their professional interest as academicians in the problems of the community were emphasized. This offered a certain sanction to the inquiry. The second area was organizational. By the end of the first year of Woodruff residency the writers became members of several organizations and continued to join others. One member of the team became a board member of the Woodruff Family Service Society in 1957 and served as its president from May, 1961, to May, 1963. Through this agency contacts were maintained with the Community Fund housed in the Chamber of Commerce offices. As a result of early experiences with the city leader group during consolidation, he was asked to serve as a member of the Civic Affairs Committee of the Chamber of Commerce, although he was not a member of that organization. When the chairman of the committee resigned, he was asked to accept the office; he refused. Along with the secretary of the Chamber of Commerce and the chairman of the City Planning Commission, one of the writers was appointed to a County Research Committee. Speeches were made on community development to Kiwanis, Rotary, and Lions. Although refused, the Jaycees and later Kiwanis offered membership opportunities during the consolidation controversy. Both writers joined the township Democratic party and occasionally attended city party meetings. Together they attended meetings of the local civic association, and one served as a director from 1957–58.

The other team member became a board member of the Iroquois County Planned Parenthood League, a board member and a study-group chairman of the Woodruff American Association of University Women, a member of the University Faculty Wives Organization, and a member and later board member and vice-president of the Woodruff League of Women Voters.

As participants in these organizations they played roles that members were expected to play. Membership offered opportunities to meet men and women from the various levels of Woodruff society and political parties, those with different social and economic interests, from blue-collar to industrial executive to professional, and both city and township residents.

Township opportunities for participation were limited to the political parties, civic organizations, and government committees. In general, township leaders, particularly in the Democratic party, were more interested in the status they believed the researchers' presence offered, e.g., being able to introduce them as doctor or professor to friends and outsiders. City leaders, too, used this academic affiliation. Leslie attempted to establish the level of competency of his consolidation campaign plan by requesting permission for the researchers to attend city leader meetings and indirectly allowing some of the leaders to assume their total commitment.

Under the guise of membership, it was possible to freely ask questions, observe problems and crises that these organizations encountered, and listen to the reaction of members to community problems. The informality of the setting, combined in time with a knowledge of the participants and their interrelation with others, gave a depth of understanding that a more formal approach lacks.

As League of Women Voter Constitutional Convention chairman, one team member developed a close working relationship with Lockwood, local ConCon delegate, which resulted in the inclusion of both researchers in the 1963 merger planning meetings. Community service in such areas as state constitutional revision, which did not affect the research project, offered opportunities to work with and observe community leaders acting in other areas. In turn

it allowed the latter to observe, get to know, and accept the researchers in a different context when service to the community was possible. It provided an additional basis for information exchange and
rapport development, construction, and maintenance, which was a
necessary support for this long-term project.

Pseudo-leadership Role
As the researchers moved from organization to organization, meeting to meeting, met more and more people, they began to note an
enhancement of their position which facilitated the research. Many
people in the city and township seemed to feel that the researchers
were leaders. Some candidates for township office came to call before initiating political campaigns to determine their chances and
the possibility of support. They "knew" the researchers could influence a bloc of township voters in several areas. Disputing this
supposition only strengthened their original beliefs. The writers became part of the clearing process that certain individuals and groups
carry on with some levels of leadership.

Placement on the boards of several area and county organizations,
the performance of administrative roles in several other groups,
and appointment to several governmental committees added to the
semblance of this preassumed leadership. In the seven-year period
of residency, the researchers had worked their way from the outer
periphery of community participation to a more central arena from
which to view the actors who interested them. This phenomenon in
itself offered many opportunities to gain insight into the unit of
study; it also made the evaluatory process more complex.

During the course of the investigation, a variety of field-work
roles were utilized for collecting data, from observer to participant-
observer. At times it was not possible to determine when the boundary had been crossed between the status of observer to that of
"observer as participant" and "participant as observer." It was not
uncommon to make these role changes frequently during the working day.

The length of time required for data collection tended to blur the
distinction in the eyes of some residents, which the authors persis-
tently drew, between the role of citizen and that of the researcher.
Resisting the forces that pushed in the direction of the participant

role and maintaining objectivity, especially when controversial issues absorbed the interest of the citizenry, required discipline and self-restraint.

Purposeful Involvement

As participant members in some Woodruff organizations, neutrality on some community issues was not always maintained. During the consolidation campaign one team member decided to run for the charter commission that would have been operative had the proposal been approved. The researchers wished in this manner to maintain their vantage point for observing the action process. It is extremely difficult to remain neutral on such an issue while running for office. The candidate publicly favored the proposal on the basis of professional experiences in dealing with urban problems. This explanation was accepted to the point that several leaders on both sides of the question urged the candidate's election.

The researchers felt their research position would be seriously weakened if opinions were not expressed in areas that would not jeopardize the project or upon occasions when it was important for its implementation. An opinionless participant in every area of human activity would have been excluded from the levels most interesting to the researchers. Strict neutrality would also have been defined by many leaders as an indication of ignorance. Many Woodruff meetings would have been closed had the researchers been unwilling to express some professional opinions. A professional is expected to embrace and to support, in some scientific manner, opinions in his area of competency. Failure to have fulfilled this expectation in Woodruff would have relegated the authors' activity to the lowest levels of leadership observation, if that. As long as the statement of fact or analysis is nonaggressive, its failure to agree in every respect with leader opinion does not alter the researcher's inclusion. His role is often that of sounding board for new ideas and plans. In addition, as residents of the township and as professionals connected with a city-located institution, the authors were occasionally included in some leader groups because they hoped to involve them in a more active participant role.

A researcher who ventures into a community for a brief time

period and does not take up permanent residence may experience little pressure to participate in community activities or to take positions on controversial issues. These team members were, however, "permanent," tax-paying, homeowning residents and professors who were expected to be concerned and informed about local problems.

Interviewing

In a community study a researcher need not always be bound by a uniformity of approach to those he is observing and interviewing. Three interviewing techniques were found to be effective: (1) information exchange, (2) the telephone interview, and (3) the two-man interview team.

Information Exchange

Past experience indicated that if an interviewer is able to introduce into an interview some of the elements that are present in conversations between two or more people the results are more satisfying to the participants. The attempts we made at simulation took two major forms. First, in a freely flowing conversation, the participants usually know enough about each other so that they may gauge and temper their remarks accordingly. The writers tried, whenever there was a suitable opening early in an interview, to tell enough about themselves personally or professionally so that the respondent had the impression that he knew and, perhaps, could classify them. Allowing people to share the researchers' lives may eventually develop a higher level of rapport and data.

Second, it was recognized that much of the data that was important to acquire was the type of information about activities in a community that various leaders discuss on street corners, at service club luncheons, and during informal coffee hours at the hotel or other eating establishments. And, it is the type of information that is vied for, a "you tell me what you know and I'll tell you what I know" exchange. By the end of the first month of study, we found ourselves in a position of being able to use information we possessed to appear knowledgeable and as an inducement to gain new information.

At the end of several years of field work and as a consequence of a wide variety of contact with Woodruff residents and perusal of public and private records, we possessed a wealth of information that had to be used or guarded judiciously. The trick that the researcher must learn is how to do this without giving away a trust or passing on facts or interpretation of facts he had already gotten from someone else. This was not too difficult during consolidation since meetings attended by the researchers also were attended by at least one Jaycee. Frequently the authors phoned Leslie or a Jaycee officer after a meeting to convey information or drew upon it at a following meeting. This is a technique that must be used carefully in order to maintain the independent action of the actors—that is, independent from the unplanned and undesirable manipulations of the researcher. As a change in focus to banking, environmental sanitation, etc., occurred, facts would be disseminated concerning these areas with statements such as: "It is our understanding . . . ." "Didn't such and such occur?" "It seems to us that . . . ." Many, many times the answers were phrased in such a manner that it was evident the respondent assumed the researchers knew most of the facts and were just checking them out with him. Often the answers were ones not heard before, opening new areas of investigation. On a few occasions new information was given to respondents, several times accidently and several times intentionally for the purpose of securing information. The latter involved the questioning of two of the most important leaders of the 1950 attempt by Shady Lea residents to be annexed by Woodruff. After raising the question time and time again as to why they felt the attempt had failed and always receiving the court tie-up as an answer, we asked whether they knew that Pacific Motors had been principally responsible. This direct approach offered them an explanation for a variety of hitherto unexplained actions during the campaign which they had not recalled previously and which we had not known.

The Telephone

After several years of study, the countless interviews, the meetings observed for months on end, the researchers institutional-academic position and association, and their organizational affiliations, the project was well known to most of the people in Woodruff who provided information. Their interest and willingness to assist resulted in the use of the telephone for interviewing. Basically, telephone interviewing results in poor-quality data. It is difficult to establish rapport. Without visual contact one cannot determine some of the physical aspects that assist in rapport maintenance: Are there other people present? Is the person in a hurry? Are others pounding on his door demanding his time? Does he have a half-eaten sandwich and a fast-cooling cup of coffee in front of him? Are there relevant gestures or nuances of expression that should be considered?

The people contacted by phone usually had been interviewed personally. The information was needed to clarify a point or to obtain factual answers to technical questions. For example, the file figures on the amount of water the city water works could handle per day were unclear. The answer required only a few words.

Most of the telephoning was done by persons who wished to talk to the researchers. After the consolidation movement several calls a month were received from community residents wishing to discuss an event or possible events or wishing to solicit assistance in an action program. The calls were informal, gossiping sessions. After the pattern of information exchange had been evolved we would, on occasion, call a person to ask what was happening or what a certain person was doing. The exchange, which has the same pitfalls as those discussed above in the use of knowledge, enabled us to keep abreast of changes in those aspects of the study which had been concluded or in which new developments were afoot.

The Two-man Interview Team

In 1958, the research team met an industrial sociologist who was thesis adviser of the evening industrial-management program of a local business college. He was a full-time employee conducting sociological and psychological research for the Midstate Motor Company. Over coffee one evening he mentioned the technique he was using for a company study of certain plant executives. Briefly, he used a two-man interview team, one posed the questions and the other recorded. The two-man interview team was of considerable interest. During the only interview held up to that time, both researchers had asked questions and both recorded answers. The researchers' plans were to cut this overlapping by dividing the lists and each interviewing half—much as had been done in their other studies. It had earlier been found that the observational division of labor of Woodruff groups and organizations made during the consolidation movement brought each of them to the interview with a different perspective and with different questions. The researchers decided to test the technique the industrial sociologist was using. From that day forth all of the interviews were conducted together; one acted as recorder and the other as interviewer. The former would add and ask questions when desired. The reason this technique was adopted, although it lengthened the interviewing procedure, was that the respondent, while undoubtedly conscious of the recording process, tended to forget the recorder almost completely and answered and "talked to" the interviewer. Familiarity with the schedule further freed the interviewer to concentrate and give undivided attention to the respondent. The technique was found to encourage an informal conversational tone. On many occasions the respondent would turn to the interviewer to answer a question from the recorder. In addition it was found that the pseudo-informality of this technique facilitated the holding of longer, more detailed interviews during which valuable qualitative data was obtained.

Objectivity

As the years went by and participation in the community deepened, maintaining objectivity became more and more of a problem, but the researchers were aided by a number of factors. First, they did not plan to live permanently in Woodruff. The realization that sooner or later the personal ties would have to be cut helped, at least in moments of reflection, to restore the necessary psychological distance between them and the events under observation. Second, when one member of the research team showed signs of "going native," the other member generally reacted by moving in the opposite direction. Critical comments on inappropriate behavior or attitudes helped restore the needed perspective. Third, the authors came to know many persons whose actions, at one time or another, annoyed and irritated them. At some of the dramatic township meetings observed during the consolidation efforts, when shouting, name calling, and even fisticuffs occurred, it was all but impossible not to deprecate the persons responsible. This was especially the case when the targets were persons whom the researchers held in some regard. In subsequent months, as they participated in meetings of township organizations, the authors came to know these persons better and the attending struggles and hardships. The researchers also saw how hard many of these persons worked for their municipality, tirelessly and with gusto. Some visited the researchers and their infant daughter, and expressed genuine interest. These experiences changed the authors' attitudes and feelings. Fourth, the researchers' initial opinion of merger changed as more and more information about the Woodruff area was obtained. At the outset they had accepted many of the writings on the advantages of metropolitan government. Later they came to recognize that some of the prerequisites for unification had been lacking in the Woodruff area. They also observed some of the advantages of the township's partisan politics and its role in stabilizing the Woodruff area during an era of extensive social change. Recognition of mistaken judgment led them to take greater precautions against hasty judgments and evaluations.

Fifth, the researchers recognized that certain offers to participate in the community threatened the study and had to be refused. These roles would have involved one or both researchers in highly partisan activities, as leaders of the movement for governmental reform. The offer to serve as chairman of the Chamber's Civic Affairs Committee, which just a few months earlier had helped plan the consolidation campaign, was refused. In 1963, the nomination to the position of chairman of the Citizens' Committee for studying merger also was declined. Refusal under these circumstances requires care to avoid damaging established relationships and injuring feelings.

The final problem related to objectivity is one for which the researchers have no "pat" answer. How faithfully do they report the behavior of a friend? Are there factors interjected by the friendship which will limit the ability to report or even to observe? And what will be the effect of critical and analytical reporting of the friend's actions on the friendship? There are two ethical questions involved: what does one owe his profession and what does one owe his friend? There is no felicitous answer. The commitment that was made in terms of time, energy, feeling, and money prevented compromise on the first. The researchers were mesmerized into acceptance of this decision by the belief that their friends had been interested in and, with a legion of other Woodruff residents, had known from the beginning what they were doing. It was through the co-operation of these very people that the researchers were able to perceive Woodruff's decision-making patterns.

Index

319

H

Hady, Thomas F., 9
Harding, Gerald, 67, 191, 198–99, 201, 203, 209, 213, 215, 219, 268, 276
Harding, Norman, 219
Hawkins, Brett W., 267n
Health hazards, 83, 89
Hein, Clarence J., 9n
Hempel, Carl G., 6n
Hensil, Matthew, 244, 254
Herring, E. Pendleton, 50
"Hillbillies," 86, 123, 276
Hollingshead, August B., 17n
Home-rule city, statutes on, 23
Hunter, Floyd, 17n, 48, 52, 54n, 107–8, 145n, 216n

I

Ignorance, 276
Inaction, 21–22, 49, 55, 89–90, 109
Incorporation, township, 9, 14, 19
Incrementalism, 11n
Industrialization, 7, 9, 35, 41, 76–82, 191, 279, 281–82; adaptive needs of, 8; wartime, 8
Industry, absentee-owned, 13, 30, 109, 125, 160; automotive, 29, 31
Inertia, 191
Influence, 108
Institutions, 25
Interest groups, 16, 20, 51
Intermunicipal relations, 71, 266, 287, 294–95
Iroquois River, 34; pollution of, 78
Irwin, P. Lee, 181n

J

Jacob, Philip E., 12n
James, Bill, 172–73, 180
Janes, Robert W., 168n
Janowitz, Morris, 19n, 50n, 121n
Jennings, M. Kent, 17n
Jews, 33
Jones, Gary, 68–69, 187, 190, 224–25, 230, 245, 278
Jones, Victor, 19n
Junior Chamber of Commerce, Woodruff, 70, 148, 153, 182, 198, 201, 236, 243, 271, 276, 302–3,

305; Area Improvement Committee, 172–83, 199–217, 219–20

K

Kammerer, Gladys M., 19n, 101n, 108, 109, 145n
Kaufman, Herbert, 19n
Kent Newspaper Group, 170, 185, 188, 191, 241, 288
Kiwanis, 308
Kornhauser, Arthur, 19n

L

Latham, Earl, 50
Leaders, Woodruff, 48–72, 56–64, 77, 107, 268; city, 56–64; education, 61; goals of, 19, 279; mobility of, 63; occupation of, 60–61; organizational participation, 59–60; positional, 53–54; religion, 61–62; socioeconomic characteristics, 18, 57–62; township, 56–64, 245
Leadership, 16–17, 26, 72; elitist, 52; pluralist, 52; structure, 48–49, 51, 111. See also Chamber of Commerce, Banking
League of Women Voters, Woodruff, 40–41n, 309; annexation and, 242, 259
Leites, Nathan, 12n
Lenski, Gerhard, 285n
Leslie, R. C. 206–17, 228, 313
Lindblom, Charles E., 11n
Lions Club, 67, 308
Lockwood, R. Jason, 66–67, 103, 115, 133, 135, 142, 244–45, 248–55, 263, 269, 271, 273, 276–77, 282, 309
Long, Norton, 23, 51–52, 265n, 267n, 274n
Low, J. O. 17n, 26n, 108n, 145n
Lynd, Helen M., 17n, 108, 120, 144
Lynd, Robert S., 17n, 108, 120, 144
Lyons, Schley, 190

M

Maass, Arthur, 75n
McConnell, Grant, 50
McDowell, Thomas, 66, 114, 155, 283
Mall, downtown, 128, 131

DATE DUE